ETHICAL PROGRAMS

DIGITAL HUMANITIES

The Digital Humanities series provides a forum for ground-breaking and benchmark work in digital humanities, lying at the intersections of computers and the disciplines of arts and humanities, library and information science, media and communications studies, and cultural studies.

Series Editors:
Julie Thompson Klein, Wayne State University
Tara McPherson, University of Southern California
Paul Conway, University of Michigan

Teaching History in the Digital Age
T. Mills Kelly

Hacking the Academy: New Approaches to Scholarship and Teaching from Digital Humanities
Daniel J. Cohen and Tom Scheinfeldt, Editors

Writing History in the Digital Age
Jack Dougherty and Kristen Nawrotzki, Editors

Pastplay: Teaching and Learning History with Technology
Kevin Kee, Editor

Interdisciplining Digital Humanities: Boundary Work in an Emerging Field
Julie Thompson Klein

Digital Rhetoric: Theory, Method, Practice
Douglas Eyman

Ethical Programs: Hospitality and the Rhetorics of Software
James J. Brown Jr.

DIGITALCULTUREBOOKS, an imprint of the University of Michigan Press, is dedicated to publishing work in new media studies and the emerging field of digital humanities.

Ethical Programs

HOSPITALITY AND THE
RHETORICS OF SOFTWARE

James J. Brown Jr.

University of Michigan Press

ANN ARBOR

Published in the United States of America by the
University of Michigan Press
Manufactured in the United States of America
⊛ Printed on acid-free paper

2018   2017   2016   2015   4   3   2   1

A CIP catalog record for this book is available from the British Library.

DOI: http://dx.doi.org/10.3998/dh.13474172.0001.001
ISBN 978-0-472-07273-6 (hardcover : alk. paper)
ISBN 978-0-472-05273-8 (cloth : alk. paper)
ISBN 978-0-472-12123-6 (e-book)

For Jillian and Linus and our illuminated vacancy signs

Acknowledgments

In a book that addresses hospitality, an acknowledgments section is an interesting thing to write. Acknowledging all of those who had a hand in this project points directly to the impossibility of a pure, absolute hospitality. While I will do my best to welcome all of the guests who reside in these pages, I know I will have inadvertently overlooked someone. I apologize for this, knowing that there is no way to fully thank all of those who helped in the writing and revision of *Ethical Programs*.

The biggest turning point in this project happened when Jillian Sayre pointed me to Jacques Derrida's *Of Hospitality*, a text that became the foundation for the arguments that unfold in the following chapters. I did not know at the time that Jillian would become so much more than a collaborator, colleague, and reader of sloppy drafts. As important as Derrida's work on hospitality has been for my thinking of software and networked life, Jillian's impression on this book and on me is not traceable to any single moment or text. She is everywhere in these pages and in everything else that I have written or will write.

Diane Davis has been both mentor and friend, and from the moment I first attended her seminar on rhetorical agency in the fall of 2004, she has transformed the way I read, write, and think. She is the most hospitable of readers, and this was especially true while she read early drafts of this project. In many ways, Diane has rescued the readers of this book, ensuring that they don't have to endure some of the raw thinking that she helped to cook.

The early stages of this project happened at the University of Texas at Austin, and I want to think my friends and colleagues from the UT PhD program for discussing these ideas in seminars and at backyard cookouts, especially Molly Hardy, Matt King, Anthony Matteo, Nate Kreuter, Tony Fassi, John Jones, Aaron Zacks, Jeremy Dean, Jim Warren, Doug Freeman, Kathryn Hamilton, Andrew Busch, Renee Searfoss, Patty Burns, Stephanie Odom, Sean McCarthy, Rachel Schneider, Jan Fernheimer, Bill Wolff, Brooke Hunter, Rodney Herring, Jodi Relyea, Justin Tremel, Chris Chung, Will Burdette, Tim Turner, Erin Hurt, Anthony Arroyo, Jill Anderson, and Catherine Bacon. I am also indebted to the faculty at the University of Texas in the English Department, the

Department of Rhetoric and Writing, and the Communications Studies Department, especially Trish Roberts-Miller, Clay Spinuzzi, Jeff Walker, Mark Longaker, Peg Syverson, Linda Ferreira-Buckley, Davida Charney, Jackie Henkel, Josh Gunn, Barry Brummett, and Martin Kevorkian.

I would also like to thank the faculty and graduate students in the Carnegie Mellon University English Department, where I began to first see that I did not need to leave behind my previous life as a circuit designer at MCI as I entered the world of English studies. In particular, I want to thank Alison Dwyer, Katy June-Friesen, John Newton, Jennifer Pellecchia, Sharmila Venkatasubban, and Mandy Hearne.

This book would not have been possible without the valuable insights of students at Wayne State University and the University of Wisconsin-Madison. In particular, the students in "New Media Interfaces and Infrastructures" at both universities helped me map the terrain of software studies and its links to research in rhetorical theory. I am especially grateful to those students with whom I authored an article in *Pedagogy* regarding software studies and writing pedagogy: Andrew Engel, Whitney Hardin, Donora Hillard, Jason Kahler, Michael McGinnis, Derek Risse, and Conor Shaw-Draves. I would also like to thank a number of other students: Becca Tarsa, whose work has continually helped me see the links between traditional writing pedagogy and emerging digital tools; Anna Muenchrath, who helped with copy editing and references and also helped to clarify some of the more opaque moments in the manuscript; Stephanie Larson, whose work with me on the "Making Machines" project was important in helping me refine arguments in chapter 5; Deidre Stuffer, whose efforts as a teaching assistant in my "Composition and Computation" course pushed me and my students to think differently about the relationship between computer programming and writing; Eric Alexander, who provided the insights and expertise of a computer scientist and always kept me honest.

Katherine Hayles pointed me toward work in software studies at an early stage, which completely transformed the method and trajectory of the project. Richard Grusin read early drafts of the manuscript and was instrumental in helping me develop the concept of ethical programs. Annette Vee not only read and responded to the manuscript but has also collaborated with me on a number of projects that would never have emerged without her insights on the relationships between writing, rhetoric, and procedural literacy. Byron Hawk also read drafts of this project and helped compose the title to this book. Collin Brooke had a profound impact on this manuscript, especially chapter 5. Christa Olson and Kate Vieira were especially helpful as I wrote the conclusion, and their comments in our writing group never failed to help clarify and flesh out arguments. Both Jeff Pruchnic and Richard Marback challenged me to clarify my thinking at the very early stages of the project (while also introducing me to the best beer Michigan has to offer). Cynthia Haynes taught me early on in my graduate career how to weave together theory and analysis, and I hope I've carried those lessons into this project. Robert Emmons worked his magic to ensure that the figures in this book look fantastic, but more importantly he has been the inspiration behind so many amazing projects at the Rutgers-Camden Digital Studies Center.

Many others also either read drafts or helped me work through ideas and concepts, especially Jeff Rice, Casey Boyle, Nathaniel Rivers, Jenny Rice, Kevin Brock, Derek Mueller, Thomas Rickert, Debra Hawhee, David Rieder, Liz Losh, Mark Sample, Mark Marino, Stephanie Boluk, Steven LeMieux, Patrick LeMieux, Scott Richmond, Patrick Jagoda, Matthew K. Gold, Dale Smith, Matthew Kirschenbaum, Ron Brooks, Rosa Eberly, Morris Young, Mike Bernard-Donals, Brad Hughes, Matthew Berland, Krista Kennedy, Quinn Warnick, Tim Lockridge, Jentery Sayers, Zach Whalen, Anne Wysocki, Chris Lindgren, and Kyle Jensen.

I'm also thankful to the attendees of the University of South Carolina Conference on Rhetorical Theory, an event that has often allowed me to experiment with some of the theoretical ideas that appear in this book.

An early version of chapter 4 was published in *College Composition and Communication* as "Essjay's Ethos: Rethinking Textual Origins and Intellectual Property." Both the Wayne State Graduate School and the University of Wisconsin-Madison Graduate School provided financial support for this project. I am thankful to the English departments at both of these schools for their support. While this book was written before I began my position at Rutgers University– Camden, I also want to thank my colleagues in the English Department and at the Digital Studies Center for their support.

I'd like to thank the friends and family who have often wondered what I've been working on all these years. My parents, Jim and Janet Brown, have supported me through career changes, always offering encouragement at every step. Mike Brown was always available to distract me with a conversation about the Pirates (chapter 5 is for you!) or, more recently, about Everton. Thanks also to Gina, Connor, Owen, Debra, Micaela, Clarity, Kiah, Alexis, Matt, Blaine, and Judi for their love and support. Many ideas that appear in these pages either emerged or were revised during trail runs with T. J. Thompson, and repeated trips alongside him up the Hill of Life provided me with plenty of time to ponder counter arguments. Thanks also to Kara Thompson for many years of support and encouragement. Afto, I tried to get Chili Davis to co-author this book, but he was not available.

Linus, this book is dedicated to you and your mom, but I should also note that it might have been completed a year or two earlier had I not been forced to listen to Raffi records for hours on end.

Contents

Introduction: The Swarm

Networked life forces us to interact with others, even when we haven't extended an invitation and even when we haven't been invited. Life in a network society—one in which information and bodies constantly move and collide—means never getting to be alone and never getting to be offline. It means never really getting to decide in any thoroughgoing way who or what enters your "home" (your apartment, your laptop, your iPhone, your thermostat). This situation is one defined by hospitality, but not a hospitality that involves a clearly defined host or guest. We certainly extend invitations all the time: an invite to a shared folder in the cloud or a Facebook friend request. But this is but one type of what I call an ethical program, a procedure enacted in the face of networked arrivals. As Wendy Chun demonstrates in *Control and Freedom*, these programs are often put forth on our behalf, without our knowledge: "the moment you 'jack in' . . . your Ethernet card participates in an incessant 'dialogue' with other networked machines."[1]

Chun shows us that packet sniffing technology reveals how often "your computer constantly wanders without you."[2] Our computational machines are constantly engaging in conversations, extending and accepting invitations, deciding who or what gets to enter or not. While these programmed decisions may turn away some packets or people, they never fully shut off the network connection.

We like to think that we have some control over how our digital abodes function, that we know who we are inviting or shunning. But Facebook privacy functions shift and Dropbox usernames are hacked, meaning that the concept of the invitation is mostly a pleasant fiction. The other arrives, over and beyond our choices to filter or turn away. This is not just a problem confined to digital networks. The line between online and offline, never very clear to begin with, is now difficult to trace at all. In the mid-1990s, the screech of a modem served as an aural marker. Dial tone, touch-tone dialing, screech, crackle, connect: "Okay, now I'm online" (at least until my dumb brother picks up the phone and breaks the connection). Today, such a procedure for "going online," a phrase that we still hear but that seems quaint and dated, is foreign. Mobile devices and game consoles are online as soon as they're powered up. In fact, initial plans for the Xbox One game console called for the unit to be always online, and Microsoft initially designed it so that key features would be disabled if an Internet connection was not reestablished every 24 hours. [3] After a great deal of backlash, this design was scrapped, though the Xbox Kinect camera has a default setting of "always on" that must be disabled by users.[4] These blurry lines seemed slightly less blurry in the tone-dial-screech-crackle-connect scenario, but even the bad old days of dial-up Internet access put forth the fiction that there was an offline and an online, a moment when others were arriving and a moment when we were alone. Modems could always be hacked, and one could even use "sneakernet" (the slang term for " physically moving removable media") to arrive at a computer terminal uninvited.[5]

This book suggests not that networked computing creates the predicament of hospitality but rather that it takes up this very old problem—the problem of others arriving whether we invited them or not—over and over again. Existence, even prior to what we now call the "network society," always meant taking up the question of the other. In 1967, life was perhaps not quite as explicitly networked as today, but that year brought the publication of Emmanuel Levinas's essay "Substitution," which seems to theorize the very set of relations I have begun tracing here. For Levinas, the proximity of one to another suggests a presymbolic relation, one that happens prior to any attempt to thematize the other. When one is approached by another, this comes as

> a relationship with a singularity, without the mediation of any principle or ideality. In the concrete, it describes my relationship with the neighbor, a relationship whose signifyingness is prior to the celebrated "sense bestowing."[6]

Prior to any attempt to make sense of our guest, that guest has already arrived, forcing a relation whether or not we have requested it. For Levinas, this means existents are exposed to one another and held hostage to one another, not knowing where a visitor is coming from. Avital Ronell demonstrates how this logic is programmed directly into the beginnings of networked life, by way of the telephone. When I answer my phone, I have already said "yes":

> And yet, you're saying yes, almost automatically, suddenly, sometimes irreversibly. Your picking it up means the call has come through. It means more: you're its beneficiary, rising to meet its demand, to pay a debt. You don't know who is calling or what you are going to be called

upon to do, and still, you are lending your ear, giving something up, receiving an order. It is a question of answerability. Who answers the call of the telephone, the call of duty, and accounts for the taxes it appears to impose?[7]

Again, the ring of the phone offers a demarcation point that seems to slip away when we begin to consider WiFi connections, but Ronell's analysis demonstrates that the call precedes any particular technological arrangement. Any encounter comes after an initial "Yes," which marks an exposedness to an other. Ronell's analysis of the telephone is the precursor to my own argument. *Ethical Programs* extends her question about answerability and ethics from circuit switching to packet switching, from Bell to Berners-Lee.

As Levinas argues, when I am put in relation with another, I am radically open and exposed: "Concretely, this means to be accused of what others do and to be responsible for what others do."[8] This predicament, which is entirely unavoidable, refigures ethics as something beyond individual choice. Yes, I make decisions about who or what might enter my home, who or what has access to my Twitter feed, but this only happens in the face of an ever-present exposedness to others. Prior to the large-scale availability of networked computational devices, Levinas described the relation that defines networked life. Levinas likens this predicament to that of the hostage, and he suggests that if "we" as humans share anything at all, it is this experience of being held hostage by another that resists representation, that arrives over and beyond our attempts to make sense of that other. Who can deny that this phenomenological description of existence maps directly onto networked life, which is utterly defined by the arrival of others? From social networks to online gaming communities, I am forever exposed to such arrivals. I might put in place filters, blocking the troll or unfriending a former high school classmate, but each of these filters happens only after I have entered a space of exposedness and response-ability, a space of *hospitality*.

Political theorist Carl Schmitt describes this problem in a very different register and with somewhat different terms. For Schmitt, the question of the other is a political one (one can address the question ethically, but Schmitt would insist that the political is a singular realm in which collectives make decisions), and the arrival of another engages the political decision par excellence: "The specific political distinction to which political actions can be reduced is that between friend and enemy" (870). For Schmitt, any political entity is defined by this decision about friends and enemies. The enemy need not be a villain, but that enemy is different from "us" and is identifiably other. The state, for Schmitt, is defined by a collective's willingness to die to defend itself against this other:

The political enemy need not be morally evil or aesthetically ugly; he need not appear as an economic competitor, and it may even be advantageous to engage with him in business transactions. But he is, nevertheless, the other, the stranger; and it is sufficient for his nature that he is, in a specially intense way, existentially something different and alien so that in the extreme case conflicts with him are possible. These can neither be decided by a previously determined general norm nor by the judgment of a disinterested and therefore neutral third party.[9]

Whereas Levinas's concern is with a primordial ethical relation, one that happens over and beyond any ethical decision, Schmitt's primary concern is with the distinction between friend and enemy, a distinction that he views as the launching point for the political.[10]

My own discussion of software and networked life is concerned with both of these sets of questions, both Levinas's concern for an alterity that arrives without mediation and Schmitt's concern for deciding who is "friend" and who is "foe." *Ethical Programs* takes up the procedures enacted—these may be computational procedures, but they do not have to be—when others arrive. In *The Exploit*, Alexander Galloway and Eugene Thacker pose this question in the terms laid out by Levinas and Schmitt, asking how ethics might operate in networked spaces that are defined by the constant arrival of a "faceless foe":

A swarm attacks from all directions, and intermittently but consistently—it has no "front," no battle line, no central point of vulnerability. It is dispersed, distributed, and yet in constant communication. In short, it is a faceless foe, or a foe stripped of "faciality" as such. So a new problematic emerges. If the Schmittian notion of enmity (friend-foe) presupposes a more fundamental relation of what Levinas refers to as "facing" the other, and if this is, for Levinas, a key element to thinking the ethical relation, what sort of ethics is possible when the other has no "face" and yet is construed as other (as friend or foe)? What is the shape of the ethical encounter when one "faces" the swarm?[11]

Galloway and Thacker push us to ask a number of difficult questions: How does one think an ethics of the network, which thrusts us into a space that welcomes the swarm? What does ethical decision look like in networked life, and what rhetorical actions are possible? *Ethical Programs* takes up these questions by examining software in networked spaces. How does software navigate between the unconditional welcome granted by a network connection, an invitation extended to a faceless foe, and the measured, conditional gestures that inevitably emerge in response, the gestures that begin to determine who or what is friend and foe?

The other will have to be dealt with—even if that other is shunned. The question of ethics, of how the other is to be dealt with, sifted, sorted, welcomed, turned away, is not only a question of human decision but also one of machines. In this book, these ethical problems are addressed by way of software and by examining how computational machines move between two poles: an unconditional hospitality that defines ethics and relationality as such and a conditional hospitality that is cultivated in our attempts to deal with "the swarm." Studying how software moves between these two poles—the conditional and unconditional—is crucial as we design and live within our networked dwellings.

I use the term *ethical program* to evoke both the computational procedures of software (a computer program) and the procedures we develop in order to deal with ethical predicaments (a program of action). An ethical program, computational or otherwise, is a set of steps taken to address an ethical predicament. These steps are not necessarily arrived at rationally, and they are not always the result of deliberation. In fact, we often enact ethical programs in moments when we do not have the luxury of considering all possible options. Francisco Varela describes how we "immediately cope" in moments of ethical decision, but he argues that this coping is always coupled with ethical deliberation. For Varela, ethical decisions happen in moments of breakdown when we are no longer experts of what he calls our "microworld," a lived situation in which we develop a microidentity, a "readiness for action."[12] Varela's focus on lived situations and situated ethical actions is an attempt to theorize ethics without reducing it to abstractions. He is interested in both "immediate coping" and "deliberation and analysis" as cognitive modes: "It is at the moments of breakdown, that is, when we are not experts of our microworld anymore, that we deliberate and analyze, that we become like beginners seeking to feel at ease with the task at hand."[13] In the terms laid out in this book, Varela is describing the ethical programs we might enact as we address the predicaments of hospitality.

Ethical programs are enacted constantly, by both humans and computational machines, and software studies presents a set of terms and concepts for making sense of those programs. Like Lev Manovich, my aim is to apply those terms and concepts to the software that is often considered more tool than expressive artifact. In *Software Takes Command*, Manovich carries out analyses of media editing software in order to understand how that software has actively shaped design concepts. Manovich aims to unearth the seemingly more mundane computational machines of our digital media ecologies, extending the work of those focusing on electronic literature, critical code studies, and platform studies.[14] Along these same lines, *Ethical Programs* focuses on how tools such as MediaWiki and Twitter enact ethical programs and express arguments about how best to contend with hospitality. Such work is crucial if we are to understand how computation is shaping networked life. For instance, let's consider what happens when I try to log in to my university's NetID system, and I've forgotten my password. Three failed log-in attempts results in the software locking me out of the system. This is the system coping, enacting an ethical program in the face of a breakdown in its microworld. If the software does not receive the correct credential information, it determines that someone is trying to hack the account by guessing passwords, and it locks everything down. This is a coping mechanism, one that is enacted in the interest of the safety and security of both the user and the system. This particular program may require me to make a phone call, talking to a network administrator to get the account unlocked. That person will have to enact her own ethical programs to determine identity, asking for a pin number or my mother's maiden name. Whether a gatekeeping mechanism is a computational machine or a human, and whether that mechanism is enacted as a way of immediately coping (locking me out of the system) or analyzing (verifying identity by asking security questions), an ethical program has been triggered.

In networked life, ethical programs enact rules, procedures, and heuristics about how (or whether) interactions should happen. Blogs and other websites employ systems to filter comments and to allow users to promote or demote contributions from other users. These sites often lay out detailed policies about what can or cannot be posted and how inappropriate material, from spam to trolling, will be dealt with in digital spaces. Some sites allow users to flag material, and others have human conversation moderators. These are all ways of dealing with the predicaments of a hospitable network that welcomes writing and writers from all angles. The ethical programs I focus on in this book come in the form of software platforms that shape, enable, and constrain networked life. Software on the network cannot avoid questions of ethics and hospitality, and this is because the network is based upon the assumption that others will arrive. Even firewall software that takes the shutting out of the other as its basic strategy fits this definition of an ethical program since it must address the question of the other over and over again. Readers, writers, and programmers in the network are continually confronted with the swarm, which incessantly invites faceless others. While they may never arrive at the answer to this ethical predicament, ethical programs continually address such questions. We might say that they iterate through solutions, testing out possibilities.

As I explain in more detail in chapter 1, the network serves as a constant reminder of what Jacques Derrida calls the *Law of hospitality*. This Law defines life in the network in that others are welcomed, regardless of identity or credentials. Networked technology would not exist without the Law of hospitality, since connectivity is necessary for such technology to function. On the other hand, this Law of hospitality is perverted and undermined at every turn as we filter, sift, and sort arrivals. These filters are the *laws of hospitality*, which we enact in response to the Law. I use the term ethical programs to describe our efforts to write the laws of hospitality, which are always in tension with the Law. Neither the laws nor the Law exhaust one another—they require one another. The Law provokes laws, and laws can never remain absolutely faithful to the Law. While we could examine many types of ethical programs enacted to navigate networked life—programs that cut across all kinds of human-machine assemblages—I have chosen to examine software since it stands as a particularly useful example of our attempts to author contingent responses to the universal and unending difficulties of hospitality. Software is an interesting place to trace out ethical programs since it enacts rules and procedures, shaping and constraining what can or can't happen in a given space. Just as commenting procedures lay out the rules of engagement in an online community like Reddit, this same community employs computational procedures that limit how often new users can post comments.[15] In both cases, an ethical program enforces rules, creating (or preventing) certain kinds of relations between users and systems.

The ethical decisions coded into software must continually address the problem of hospitality. This means that ethical programs are iterative, contingent responses to the Law of hospitality. As a scholar of rhetoric and writing, I am particularly interested in how the ethical programs I examine in this book confront specific situations and exigencies. Software enacts ethical programs, but such programs are only ever temporary solutions, and software can be rewritten to enact different kinds of ethical programs in different situations. Software does not simply describe procedures, it enacts them, meaning that it shapes networked life in fundamental ways. Understanding how software's ethical programs are written and rewritten and how they engage the Law of hospitality is central to understanding, in Galloway and Thacker's words, "the shape of the ethical encounter when one 'faces' the swarm." But each of these ethical programs is rhetorical. It makes an argument, marshals persuasive resources, and addresses the particulars of a situation. The university server in the lost password example above examines the situation and determines that the best course of action is to lock me out. This action implies an argument about the best way to keep the network (and my account) secure, and that argument enacts an ethical program that responds to a contingency. It makes assumptions about the shape of the ethical encounter, and it helps to determine how relations can or cannot happen in a given space. While the danger of any ethical program is that it becomes codified and calcified, that it becomes too focused on immediate ethical concerns at the expense of broader questions, networked life means that the Law of hospitality will continue to present itself. Life in the network means never being able to turn off the other (a problem that, as I've already argued, is not even actually *new*), and ethical programs have to be continually reinterpreted, rewritten, and reimagined to deal with this unending call.

In the interest of understanding how ethical programs continually engage the difficulties of hospitality in networked life, this book is made up of a number of stories about how software helps determine the shapes of our ethical encounters. My focus on particular stories means that this book takes on a "case study" tone. I address the value and limits of this approach in more detail in the conclusion, but for now I'll say that my theoretical frame for the study of software in networked environments is rhetorical theory, which is concerned with tracing the particulars of a given attempt to persuade. In each chapter, this focus on particulars is coupled with broader arguments about how that software takes part in complex activities, encouraging certain kinds of action and constraining others, welcoming some writers and bits of information while shunning or filtering others. I examine the software itself, how it is used (or abused), and how it is part of controversies and complications. This focus on particular moments allows me to look carefully at a series of rhetorical situations, teasing out how the complexities of hospitality are being negotiated and determining what this situation can tell us about software, rhetoric, and ethics in networked life.

As a rhetorician, I am drawn to this type of analysis, situating rhetorical action in terms of strategies, exigencies, purposes, and audiences. However, my hope is that these case studies are also able to move beyond the particular, enabling us to zoom out and discuss some more far-reaching problems. This balancing act between the particular and the general mirrors Derrida's concerns with the Law of hospitality and the laws of hospitality. In fact, it mirrors the tensions inherent in any ethical program: How does one move between specific ethical predicaments that call for immediate action and the universal principles that are inevitably undercut by that action? Every universal principle, taken to its logical end point, results in unethical activities. This is most clearly demonstrated by the biblical story of Lot, a troubling tale about how hospitality by no means implies kindness. When Lot (one of Derrida's more instructive examples of hospitality) turns over his daughters to be raped by a mob rather than surrendering his houseguests, he is abiding by the Law of hospitality, the insistence that the master of the house protect his visitors. The mob demands that Lot hand over his guests, but the host's ethical program forbids it, and he offers his daughters instead. Lot enacts his procedure based on the Law of hospitality, a rigid and unwavering precept stating that a host is responsible for his guests. Immanuel Kant's famous insistence, in the *Groundwork for the Metaphysic of Morals*, that lying or deception is wrong, regardless of circumstance, operates by way of a similar logic. On its own, the Law of hospitality is often far from what we might consider ethical—this is why we enact laws.

To use an example closer to the subject matter of this book, consider RFC 761, the document that establishes the Transmission Control Protocol (TCP) and determines how packets of information move through the Internet. RFC 761 lays out the philosophy of information transfer in terms of the Robustness Principle: "TCP implementations should follow a general principle of robustness: be conservative in what you do, be liberal in what you accept from others."[16] This principle (also known as Postel's Law since it is attributed to Jon Postel, one of the authors of the TCP documentation), insists that when transmitting information, a server should conform to the rules and protocols for transmission as closely as possible, but that this same server should be flexible when determining whether incoming packets conform to that same protocol. This design principle is meant to make it easier for systems to speak with one another. Eric Allman puts it this way:

> If every implementation of some service that generates some piece of protocol did so using the most conservative interpretation of the specification and every implementation that accepted that piece of protocol interpreted it using the most generous interpretation, then the chance that the two services would be able to talk with each other would be maximized.[17]

While the Robustness Principle means greater interoperability, taken to its logical end we would have an Internet that is entirely inoperable. If all systems were to be "liberal in what [they] expect from others," then the protocols that determine how packets of information move would quickly become irrelevant. Put differently, at some point we must both follow the rules and ask others to do the same.

Allman makes such an argument in his call for a "middle way" when applying the Robustness Principle. He argues that Postel's Law has come under fire and has often been ignored. Allman's explanation for why this happens hints at the predicament of hospitality in networked life: "This isn't because implementers have gotten more stupid, but rather because the world has become more hostile."[18] That hostility can be linked to nefarious activity on the part of hackers, but it can also be explained in terms of the increasing complexity of network activity: "The Robustness Principle was formulated in an

Internet of cooperators. The world has changed a lot since then. Everything, even services that you may think you control, is suspect."[19] That is, the hostility described here isn't necessarily about bad people but is instead about a distributed group of technologies and people that may or may not be cooperating toward some shared goal. Allman suggests that such a complex network requires a rethinking of the Robustness Principle:

> The atmosphere of the Internet has changed so much that the Robustness Principle has to be severely reinterpreted. Being liberal in what you accept can contribute to security problems. Sometimes interoperability and security are at odds with each other. In today's climate they are both essential. Some balance must be drawn.[20]

What Allman is advocating for here is a revisiting of the laws of hospitality in the face of the Law of hospitality. The Law will always invite packets of information, in whatever form, whether they follow procedure or not. The laws of hospitality must draw lines and sort through what should or should not be allowed to pass. Computational machines, as ethical programs, must continually navigate this tension. While broad ethical principles are imperfect, without them we would have no way of comparing specific actions in particular rhetorical situations to those enacted in other situations. This, of course, is not a problem unique to new media or to software. However, my discussion of how software shapes, enables, and constrains rhetorical action continually oscillates between these two poles, between the Law and the laws.

This discussion of the Law and the laws is traced out in more detail in chapter 1, as I explain the terms and concepts that guide my analysis. I provide a detailed explanation of Derrida's theory of hospitality, showing that he saw the problem of hospitality as one that was exposed, in a particularly radical way, by networked technologies. From wiretapping to e-mail, Derrida's work attempts to understand what happens when we confront the fiction that "the home" is somehow sealed off from the outside. Connected to networks, the home (which can stand in for our house but can just as easily be used to describe the smartphone) is defined by an exposedness to others. Networked life reminds us, over and over again, that there is no home without connections to the outside, no house without windows and doors. This is the Law of hospitality that defines networked life, and it demands that we author ethical programs that take up the questions of the other's arrival. Software is one way to author such ethical programs, and it allows us to enact rules that help shape our rhetorical dwellings.

Engaging the hospitable network means developing contingent ethical programs that somehow leave open the possibility that we have gone astray, allowing for the possibility that we might decide to revise our program. As I have already suggested, ethical programs will always have to negotiate between the immediate difficulties of a particular situation (the arrival of some specific other) and the ethical demand of the Law of hospitality. If this Law is forgotten or if an ethical program attempts to solve the problem of the other in any final way, we are confronted with both ethical problems and questions of technological feasibility. The extermination of the other is not only ethically wrong; it is also a technological impossibility. Unplugging from the network—which would seem to be the only way to answer the Law of hospitality in any complete or final way—not only makes networked technology useless but also fools us into thinking that networked life is confined to our digital interactions. From financial transactions to surveillance technology to the magnetic strip on a subway ticket, we have daily reminders that it is impossible to fully disconnect from the network. This means we will always require ways of engaging the difficulties and predicaments of the hospitable network, which welcomes everyone, from the troll to the Good Samaritan. Ethical programs are arguments, rhetorical engagements with networked life that determine how to be connected. They establish, break, and manage relations.

After establishing the relationship between ethical programs, hospitality, and rhetoric, the following four chapters move through rhetorical analyses that examine the complications of hospitality and networked life. These four chapters are divided into two sections, with each pair taking up a key question of new media studies. Chapters 2 and 3 focus on the power dynamics of networks. The case studies in these chapters examine how exploits, software that exposes security vulnerabilities, and procedural rhetoric, the use of processes to mount arguments, can open up space for rhetorical engagement in networks. Galloway defines networks in terms of protocols, "the set of technical procedures for defining, managing, modulating, and distributing information throughout a flexible yet robust delivery infrastructure."[21] For Galloway, understanding the movement and distribution of power in networks requires both that we understand the material technologies that determine how those networks work and the way power is distributed through them. Most important, such analyses must resist the temptation to theorize networks as open, free, rhizomatic, or flat. Networks are not free of hierarchies, and they feature top-down assertions of power by way of protocols. Chapters 2 and 3 attempt to map out the dynamics of two particular arrangements of networked power and to describe what rhetorical action in those networks looks like.

Through an analysis of the 2008 Obama presidential campaign's use of social networking software, chapter 2 presents one example of how protocological power operates. The Obama campaign's mybarackobama.com (which many referenced by way of an unfortunate acronym: MyBO) operated by way of protocol's bidirectional power structure, exerting influence with hierarchical structures while also allowing volunteers to operate in peer-to-peer, horizontal networks. The campaign was not the first to use social networking to expand get out the vote (GOTV) efforts, but it did pioneer certain strategies and software packages to distribute campaigning activities. Volunteers used MyBO to call potential voters, gather data about those voters, organize campaign activities, and earn points that reflected their level of commitment to the campaign. While campaign leaders guided volunteers in these activities, it also allowed those volunteers a certain amount of leeway as they, for instance, determined how best to conduct phone conversations with potential voters. Thus, the campaign made use of the hospitality extended by networked life, extending invitations to volunteers, but it did so while carefully crafting its own laws of hospitality that controlled how these "guests" of the campaign operated. In my own analysis of these activities, I describe the campaign's protocological infrastructure and how it used software to shape volunteer activities. However, the chapter also explains how Obama campaign volunteers used what Ian Bogost calls "procedural rhetoric" to navigate this complex protocological network. Procedural rhetoric is the use of processes, computational or otherwise, to persuade. Bogost uses videogames to demonstrate procedural rhetoric in action, showing how computational procedures can be used to model worlds and make arguments. But Bogost also argues that procedural rhetoric is not just useful for understanding videogames and that it can also help us understand how all procedures express arguments. This chapter puts that argument to the test, examining the procedural rhetoric of the Obama campaign and also the procedural arguments crafted by its volunteers. What we find in that analysis is that procedural rhetoric offers one possibility for taking on the complex and conflicting power relations of protocol, which extend an invitation while also providing hierarchical structures that shape and constrain activity.

Chapter 3 also takes up the question of how rhetors might resist or act within networks, but it does so by focusing on a rhetorical tactic put forth by Galloway and Thacker: the exploit. While their book, The Exploit, never uses the term "rhetoric," their understanding of how software exploits can reshape protocological structures is profoundly rhetorical. A software exploit exposes a gap in the security or functionality of a computational environment. Exploits do not necessarily step through rational arguments about how a given digital space is designed or about the ethics of that space. Instead, exploits perform their argument by hacking a networked space and, in some cases, transforming it. In the interest of understanding the exploit as a rhetorical maneuver, I examine two exploits of the leaky boundaries of the Twitter microblogging platform. The first is a cross-site scripting (XSS) attack that resulted in Twitter users unknowingly retweeting links to, among other things, pornography. The second primary example in this chapter involves a hole in a security protocol, OAuth, implemented for the Twitter Application Programming Interface (API). While the first exploit played out in plain view, affecting web users in real time, the hack of OAuth never saw the light of day. Addressed by corporations and programmers behind closed doors at a professional conference and in private meetings, the OAuth exploit was fixed before it could cause too many problems for implementations of the protocol (which extended to other companies as well, including Google and Facebook). Telling the stories of these two hacks is important as we try to understand the rhetorical possibilities of the exploit and how it presses against the vulnerabilities of hospitality. Beyond showing how the exploit is rhetorical and how it exposes some of the available means of persuasion, the two exploits examined in this chapter also stand as case studies of how particular digital spaces contend with the predicament of hospitality differently. A software exploit exposes the hospitality of networked environments, demonstrating how those spaces work (or how they don't). As Galloway explains, "protocol outlines the playing field for what can happen, and where."[22] Exploits trace the contours of that playing field, showing us what is and is not possible, and this is the exploit's connection to rhetoric. By demonstrating the possible, it exposes the available means of persuasion and foists a new rhetorical arrangement upon users and software designers. The implication of such computational arguments is that the space can (or should) work differently.

Chapters 4 and 5 move from the ethical difficulties of protocological spaces to questions of database and narrative, which Lev Manovich first theorized in *The Language of New Media*. Manovich describes database and narrative as two worldviews that compete in the age of new media. While narrative presents a sequence of events told in a particular order, database presents a number of possibilities at once, making fewer determinations and allowing competing narratives to coexist. It might be tempting to argue that the database is *more* hospitable, but such a claim would ignore the determinations that database designers must make as they decide what data and categories are reflected in a given database. Rather than determining which of these worldviews is more or less hospitable or more or less ethical, chapters 4 and 5 examine the predicaments of a world in which databases are increasingly hospitable to every keystroke. If, as Manovich suggests, narratives present particular ways of traversing databases and making sense of information, then the growth of contemporary databases has welcomed a staggering number of competing and conflicting narratives. The hospitable network extends an invitation to data, tracking every click, calling for writers and programmers to determine which ethical programs are best suited for parsing a world in which the relationship between narrative and database is shifting.

Chapter 4 addresses the question of hospitable databases by examining one of the largest writing spaces in the world, Wikipedia, and its software platform. That software platform, MediaWiki, engages the difficulties of hospitality in particularly interesting ways. Welcoming writers from all angles, Wikipedia has had its share of controversies and has forced us to confront the problem of how to present a coherent narrative (in this case, an encyclopedia article) in the face of a massive amount of data. But Wikipedia's controversies have not been confined to its content, and this chapter focuses on one of the more famous dustups regarding Wikipedians themselves. Essjay, a prominent Wikipedian who presented himself as a professor of theology, is the primary focus of this chapter, since his story demonstrates how *ethos* is one of the primary rhetorical resources in a massive database such as Wikipedia. Essjay claimed to be something he was not, but his attempts to use this constructed *ethos* to steer conversations about certain Wikipedia articles were often resisted by other Wikipedians. Most important, for our purposes, the chapter addresses how MediaWiki software creates a digital space in which a user such as Essjay can construct that *ethos* and in which other users can critique it by referencing a user's deep archive of activity. MediaWiki tracks nearly all user activity. It is a hospitable archive that files away keystrokes, building a database that is deep and wide. In such a space, *ethos* becomes the Wikipedian's primary strategy for influencing conversations about articles. In addition to examining the Essjay controversy, this chapter also analyzes a project called Citizendium, which attempts to build a wiki-based encyclopedia that avoids the trappings of anonymity. Started by one of Wikipedia's cofounders, Larry Sanger, Citizendium also uses MediaWiki software, but Sanger's encyclopedia institutes a set of procedures and protocols for determining the identity of writers. Citizendium's use of such procedures demonstrates that the use of MediaWiki does not perfectly determine how identity and *ethos* operate in a textual space. Still, while Citizendium shows how MediaWiki does not offer a single possibility space for how writers interact, this chapter does demonstrate that MediaWiki's proclivities for a deep textual archive are, in many ways, difficult to avoid in any implementation of the software. As we see in this chapter, software plays a crucial part in our networked rhetorical situations, and users can move through the hospitable database by leveraging (or suffering at the hands of) its deep archive.

Chapter 5 deals with this same problem of the hospitable database by examining how we might move between the worldviews of narrative and database. The chapter takes up this question by focusing on the world of professional baseball and examining robot writers that compose game recap stories. I examine robots developed by a company called Narrative Science, algorithms that are authored by teams of what the company calls "meta-writers" (comprised of both journalists and computer scientists). These meta-writers author software that generates stories, from game recaps to quarterly earnings reports. The company sees these algorithms as a way to transform the data of spreadsheets into narrative forms that are more useful to humans. Kristian Hammond, chief scientist at Narrative Science, argues that these computational systems take a "cognitive burden" off the reader of spreadsheets and databases, transforming data into narrative.[23] In the interest of removing this cognitive burden, robot writers make ethical decisions about what should or should not be included in a narrative. These computational machines are ethical programs that determine how to move between data and story, determining what a reader does or does not see. While many take the existence of such bots as a threat to the supposedly human realm of writing, the very fact that these machines are part of the ethical terrain of networked life suggests that any engagement with database and narrative is machinic. Thus, robot and human writers are more similar than we might like to admit. In this chapter, I suggest that rhetoric's 2,500-year history has presented us with a number of "machines" for understanding the shifting relationship between database and narrative. Rhetoric, as a set of machines for generating and interpreting arguments, provides ethical programs for moving back and forth between the worldviews of narrative and database, navigating the challenges of hospitable databases. As ethical programs, Narrative Science's software sits uneasily between narrative and database, making judgments, and its procedures share a great deal with the tools of the rhetorician, which involve attempts to see the world from the perspective of both database and narrative. Machinic understandings of narratives and arguments allow us to gain insight into the robot writers that have joined our networked conversations and also present us with strategies for mediating the worldviews of narrative and database.

In the concluding chapter, I provide a framework for understanding the *rhetorics* (plural) of software that emerge in the hospitable network. I find persuasive Ian Bogost's arguments in *Persuasive Games* that digital rhetoricians must attend to computation and that the field of digital rhetoric has too often focused on "the text and image content a machine might host and the communities of practice in which that content is created."[24] Recently, much current work in digital rhetoric is working to remedy this problem, and *Ethical Programs* counts itself among this group. For instance, Annettee Vee's detailed rhetorical analysis of how computer code has been defined at various times as text, speech, and machine is evidence that rhetoricians are no longer neglecting the realm of computation. Vee tracks arguments in law and among programmers about the legal status of code, demonstrating how those who write code attempt to influence such discussions (and how they sometimes aim to find workarounds for outdated laws by crafting their own laws that are better suited to the complexities of computation).[25] Vee is not content only to study arguments about code—she links these arguments to specificities of code and software. Kevin Brock's dissertation "Engaging the Action-Oriented Nature of Computation: Towards a Rhetorical Code Studies" takes a similar approach, offering extensive reviews of the computational gap in rhetorical scholarship and the rhetorical gaps in software studies scholarship. However, Brock also offers a way forward for rhetoricians seeking out ways to link rhetorical studies to software studies and critical code studies. He notes that work in rhetoric and writing has only begun to attend to this level of rhetorical activity, often focusing on interface at the expense of a detailed account of code and computation. He suggests a multifaceted rhetoric of code studies, one that would account both for how code itself expresses meaning and how programmers' comments are used to argue and persuade.[26] His study of the FizzBuzz test, a common test offered to those applying for computer programming jobs, is particularly enlightening, in that it explores how rhetorical style (and arguments about that style) circulate in programs and programming communities. Also important is David Rieder's work on the Oulipo conceptual writing collective and how its procedural focus is of use to those attempting to link literacy with numeracy, as is his forthcoming book on physical computing, *Suasive Iterations: Rhetoric, Writing, and Physical Computing*.[27]

Bogost's concept of "procedural rhetoric"—the use of processes, computational or otherwise, to persuade—is the clearest contribution toward this more focused and rigorous effort to account for the rhetoric of software.[28] However, an expanded understanding of the rhetorics of software—including, but not limited to, procedural rhetoric—can benefit both rhetoricians and scholars in software studies. The concluding chapter of *Ethical Programs* follows the scholars cited above as it lays out multiple levels of rhetorical activity that emerge in computational, networked environments. While the four case studies presented in the book take an inductive approach, tracing how software navigates the difficulties of hospitality in specific instances, this concluding chapter zooms out, drawing broader conclusions about how to build theoretical tools for the rhetorical analysis of software. This chapter serves to tie together the book's case studies, and it makes explicit the different levels of rhetorical activity present in each case. These levels intersect and blend with one another, as each of the case studies demonstrates. From discussions about computer programs to the actual bits of code that shape our networked environments, we find multiple rhetorics of software.

Understanding how software cuts across argument, persuasion, and communication in the hospitable network requires that we account for a range of rhetorical activity. To this end, I describe three different rhetorics of software: arguing *about* software, arguing *with* software, and arguing *in* software. Each of these realms of rhetorical activity is shaped by the ethical predicament of hospitality that defines networked life. Networked technologies invite people from diverse backgrounds to discussions about technology. This means that arguments about software are now conducted among a broad swath of people, from experts to novices. Rhetoricians have long analyzed how we attempt to argue and persuade, so arguing *about* software is most in line with the long history of work in rhetorical studies. How are discussions about software conducted? What strategies are used? What counts as evidence? What power relations are at work, and who is seen as credible in such discussions? These are the kinds of questions one would ask when addressing this first level of rhetorical activity.

Arguing *with* software, on the other hand, insists on understanding how computation itself can be used to persuade. When arguing with software, one uses software as a tool, much like the orator uses language. Computational procedures become the claims and evidence, tropes and figures, gestures and intonations. In short, they become a persuasive medium. My use of the word "with" here introduces some productive ambiguity, since "arguing with" can evoke not only tool use but also an argument between two people or positions. The concept of arguing with software accounts for both of these meanings, since any attempt to use software as a tool for persuasion will also mean confronting the constraints of software, the ways that it shapes and constrains expression. While I use software to make arguments through the deployment of procedural rhetoric (discussed in chapter 2) as well as the exploits (covered in chapter 3), these attempts will always mean that I enter into rhetorical negotiations with the software itself. Software is both tool and interlocutor. These complexities of arguing with software are evident as programmers use computation to expand the available means of persuasion and to demonstrate what is possible in a given environment. The hospitable network invites such hacking (to varying degrees) and determines how far these explorations can go.

While the idea of software as interlocutor falls within the realm of "arguing with," it also bleeds into the next category, arguing *in* software, which is a layer of rhetorical activity that accounts for how software shapes our networked rhetorical situations. Software helps to establish and institute the spaces in which we communicate and argue, and it often welcomes a deep archive of information. In this sense, we are always "in" software; we are in spaces that are shaped by computational artifacts and platforms that welcome and track data. Understanding the rhetorical strategies that emerge in these spaces is yet another of the rhetorics of software. This discussion of software as environment might lead us to think of software as "backdrop" for communication and persuasion, but the very idea that I have to lock horns with a piece of software as I attempt to communicate demonstrates that arguing in software means more than understanding software as a kind of container for arguments and persuasion. When I am arguing in software, I am negotiating a complex rhetorical ecology of audiences, from parsers and APIs (which I take up in more detail in chapter 3) to the companies tracking my keystrokes.

While rhetoricians are accustomed to theorizing what happens at the level of "arguing about," the other two levels of activity described here are just as relevant to the study of rhetoric and to determining how ethical programs shape our lives. In this concluding chapter, I explain these different rhetorics of software and make the case for allowing them to bleed into one another as we conduct rhetorical analyses of networked software environments. I argue that zeroing in on the computational artifacts at play in a given rhetorical ecology can help build a robust framework for understanding how rhetorical action is shaped, enabled, and constrained by ethical programs.

In the pages that follow, I examine controversies and flash points, moments when software exposes (and participates in) difficult ethical questions, without necessarily answering them in any final way. But these situations lay out questions and problems to which we are called to respond, and those responses can be understood as rhetorical engagements with complex exigencies. The ethical programs I analyze in this book take up the unending call of hospitality. They are arguments about how networked life can or should happen. Whereas an ethical program might conjure images of a set of rules by which we determine what behavior is more or less ethical, the programs I present here do not always lay out a plan or a series of criteria for judging what is or is not ethical. Instead, these ethical programs are incomplete, temporary attempts to address the difficult questions of hospitality. Those predicaments do in fact call for judgments and answers, for determinations about how we should act, but the answers are infinitely complex; even after we construct such answers, the questions remain.

Each of my rhetorical analyses follows roughly the same pattern by laying out one of the predicaments of hospitality exposed by software and then offering some of the rhetorical tactics available to those responding to that predicament. Rhetors (here understood as writers, speakers, programmers, and sometimes software itself) can use procedural rhetoric and exploits to navigate the complexities of protocological power. They can use *ethos* to navigate databases that track every keystroke and build a deep archive of information. They can use rhetorical theory's long history of machinic thinking to navigate the competing worldviews of database and narrative. Each of these rhetorical strategies is necessary because of the hospitable network, which sets the stage for protocological power and for the shifting relationship between databases and narratives. In *Lingua Fracta: Toward a Rhetoric of New Media*, Collin Brooke argues that a rhetoric of new media should be "actionary rather than re-actionary," that it should not be content with describing how new media spaces operate but should also develop ways of understanding how to create, code, and write (in) digital spaces: "as actionary, a rhetoric of new media should prepare us for sorting through the strategies, practices, and tactics available to us and even for inventing new ones."[29] This book operates with this same understanding of rhetoric and digital media, seeking out not only how software shapes interactions but also how rhetors continue to develop new practices for answering the Law of hospitality. Networked life calls for new ways of engaging ever-shifting ethical questions, and *Ethical Programs* traces out how digital rhetors have already begun the search for ways to argue and communicate in complex, networked spaces.

ONE

Web Hosting: Hospitality and Ethical Programs

The suicide bomber stands as perhaps the most disturbing symptom of hospitality in networked life. Entering through porous boundaries (no matter how well policed these boundaries might be), the suicide bomber reminds us that the other will arrive by way of doors and interfaces. While the openness of nation-states varies, the ease with which bodies can move through transportation infrastructures ensures that no space can be completely sealed off from the threat of a suicide bomb. But the uncertainty and complexity of networked life can affect the suicide bomber herself too.

On December 31, 2010, a suicide bomb attack was thwarted not by police or intelligence officials but by an unlikely hero—spam. A suicide bomber was killed in a safe house as she prepared for an attack on Moscow's Red Square during a New Year's Eve celebration. The bomber in this case was a "black widow," a term used in Russia to describe female suicide bombers who have lost a relative in battles between Russian and Chechen forces. The woman, believed to have been named Animat and the wife of a jailed extremist, was killed when her suicide belt was set off by "a message from her mobile phone operator wishing her a happy new year."[1] Suicide bombers often use "handlers," who send text messages to the bomber to detonate explosive devices. In this case, a spam message arrived unexpectedly, while the bomber was preparing for her attack on Manezh Square, an area near Red Square.[2] The mishap was thought to be linked to bombings at Moscow's Domodedovo Airport, which had occurred just two days prior.[3] Russia, a country not generally known as a "free" or "open" society, is continually struggling with the complications of hospitality. The question of the other, even in Vladimir Putin's Russia, which puts extreme restrictions on any form of dissent, is still constantly being negotiated and addressed.

Arriving in the Domodedovo Airport or Red Square or other public spaces, the suicide bomber takes advantage of the hospitable infrastructures of networked life. But this "black widow" perished due to this same structure of hospitality. This bombing is particularly instructive given this book's discussion of hospitality and software. The bomber's payload was detonated by a spam message from a cell phone provider. That text message, arriving on her phone through a hospitable network, arrived *because* she had connected herself to that network and, therefore, had welcomed the message. Though she believed herself to be sheltered in a "safe house," this message arrived nonetheless. The plan was for the bomber to enter central Moscow, taking advantage of the hospitality afforded to all those celebrating the New Year. Instead, her phone extended a welcome, one that led to her death. Animat fell victim to the hospitality of which she was planning to take advantage, largely because a telecommunications provider employed a computational machine to spam its customers with a holiday greeting.

But in addition to this deadly spam text message, the way that I learned of this news story opens up further questions about hospitality and networked life, questions that *Ethical Programs* will address by examining pieces of software and the controversies that arise in their wake. Those questions involve how information moves in networks that simultaneously welcome and filter. This news story arrived on my virtual doorstep via TweetDeck, an application that allows me to both read and write 140-character "tweets" via the popular microblogging service Twitter. A colleague, Clay Spinuzzi, tweeted a link to Slashdot, a website that aggregates technology-related news stories (see figure 1).

If a hospitable network means that information can flow relatively easily between nodes (though chapters 2 and 3 will complicate the argument that information flows unfettered from node to node), we require filters to sift and sort that information. As others arrive, we employ ways of determining who or what can or cannot enter. My decision of which Twitter client to use was the first one in a chain of ethical programs, a chain that also includes which Twitter users I follow, Spinuzzi's curatorial efforts, Slashdot, ZDNet, and *The Telegraph*. At each stage, software, hardware, and wetware made decisions about the information traversing a hospitable network. At each stage, information is moving through checkpoints and is offered up to human and nonhuman decision-making machines. Each of these machines makes an ethical determination. Each choice implies exclusion and that exclusion is necessary.

Information moves through distributed networks, and *Ethical Programs* will describe this situation in terms of hospitality. That hospitality is not always about a single host standing at the threshold, welcoming a guest. Further, in case the example of the suicide bomber has not yet made this clear, my characterization of the Internet as hospitable should not be understood in terms of the kindness or generosity that we typically associate with hospitality. Instead, the term describes the ethical difficulties of a network society, one in

Fig. 1. Clay Spinuzzi's tweet about the black widow suicide bomber.
(Clay Spinuzzi, "This Spam Problem Is Really Getting out of Hand http://goo.gl/Dic3n,"
microblog, @spinuzzi, [Fri, 28 Jan. 2011 16:16:00 GMT], https://twitter.com/spinuzzi/
status/31022730555949057.)

Spam Text Prematurely Blows Up Suicide Bomber

Posted by **samzenpus** on Friday January 28, 2011 @10:55AM
from the spam-redeems-itself dept.

Hugh Pickens writes

> "A suicide bomber's plan to detonate explosives in Central Moscow on
> New Year's Eve was foiled when she received an unexpected spam text
> message that <u>caused her deadly payload to blow up too early</u>. A
> message wishing her a happy new year came hours before the
> unnamed woman was to set off her suicide belt near Red Square, an
> act of terrorism that could have killed hundreds of people. Islamist
> terrorists in Russia often use mobile phones as detonators. The
> bomber's handler, who is usually watching his charge, <u>sends the</u>
> <u>bomber a text message to set off the explosive belt</u> at the moment when
> it is thought they can inflict maximum casualties."

Fig. 2. Slashdot's post about the black widow suicide bomber.
(samzenpus, "Spam Text Prematurely Blows Up Suicide Bomber—Slashdot," 28 Jan. 2011,
accessed March 17, 2014, http://beta.slashdot.org/story/146936.)

which we are forced to face up to the others that arrive in spaces, digital or otherwise. *Ethical Programs* examines the spaces established by software, the ethical questions raised by those spaces, and the rhetorical practices that emerge as a response. In this chapter, I explain the key terms that guide my analysis of software in a network society: hospitality and ethical programs. The first comes from the work of Jacques Derrida while the second is my own. Because these two concepts will serve as touchstones throughout this book, I will step through their complications while also explaining how they intersect with concerns of ethics, rhetoric, and software.

Hospitality

Derrida offers a complex and useful account of hospitality, and it is his analysis of the term to which this book responds. For Derrida, hospitality is not only about the choice to extend a welcome. He does discuss this "traditional" notion of hospitality, but he does so in the context of broader ethical questions. For Derrida, the decision to welcome the other is only part of the larger and more complicated realm of hospitality. Explaining that realm will be my task here as I attempt to both lay out the stakes and concerns of Derrida's meditations on hospitality and connect his philosophical account to software and networked life. As we will see, connecting these two discussions is not much of a leap. Derrida himself saw the Internet (and telecommunications more broadly) as profoundly engaged with the question of hospitality.

For Derrida, any theorization of hospitality begins from a "non-dialectizable antinomy" between what he calls the Law of hospitality and the laws of hospitality.[4] This distinction can perhaps be best understood by considering one's connection to the Internet. For Derrida, the Law of hospitality—which he also sometimes calls "absolute hospitality"—is that which is offered to an anonymous other, regardless of identity or name. In terms of digital networks, we can consider any network connection to be suggestive of this absolute Law of hospitality. I connect to the Internet, and I invite a multitude of others. I have, in connecting to the network, entered a hospitable space that welcomes many others. And yet, at the very moment that I extend this welcome, I immediately begin to filter arrivals. From firewall software to the users that I block from viewing my Twitter feed, I find ways to sift and sort those that arrive at "my doorstep." These filters are the *laws of hospitality* that respond to the Law. These laws are particular responses to particular others, and from the very start they are dependent upon exclusion. The laws of hospitality must always be both hospitable and inhospitable, simultaneously welcoming and excluding.

As the New Year's Eve suicide bomber learned, attempts to filter are always imperfect. She had hoped to receive a message from her handler upon arrival at her target, but a spam message leaked through a porous border. Of course, seen from another angle, from the angle of the Russian authorities, this failed filtering system was fortuitous. In any case, the Law of hospitality in a networked society is connectivity, and the laws of hospitality are written in response to this unrelenting fact of connectivity. These laws are rhetorical. They are particular, contingent responses to situations, and they are attempts to make ethical determinations. The laws of hospitality that interest me in this book are those that I call *ethical programs*, which often come in the form of pieces of software or bits of code that stand at the threshold, raising difficult ethical questions: Who or what gets access to code? How does one ethically address flaws or gaps in software? How are the complex power dynamics of networks coded by software, and how can such code be rewritten? What role does software play in a growing thicket of arguments and narratives? Each of these questions is addressed to the user (or *rhetor*) in digital environments, meaning that ethical programs can be enacted computationally or by human beings. But the human user of software is not merely making decisions on her own. Rather, each networked rhetorical situation is informed, shaped, enabled, and constrained by, among other things, software.

Regardless of how an ethical program answers the predicament of hospitality, the Law of hospitality, which is absolute and unconditional, remains in place. These "two regimes of law"—the Law and the laws—are forever linked and indebted to one another. There are no laws without the Law, for without the continuous demand of hospitality—in our example, the connection to the network—there would be no need for the laws of hospitality that determine who or what can enter my abode (my computer, my database, my Facebook profile). Conversely, there is no Law without the laws: "[the Law of hospitality] wouldn't be effectively unconditional . . . if it didn't *have to become* effective, concrete, determined."[5] Without particular instantiations of hospitality (the laws of hospitality), the Law of hospitality would "risk being abstract, utopian, illusory, and so turning over into its opposite."[6] We write the laws in order to make specific ethical determinations and in order to avoid the irresponsible piety of a pure hospitality, but each of those laws—composed in response to a particular rhetorical situation—is a betrayal. It is a filtering that excludes. Every instantiation of hospitality misses the mark and falls short of the Law, but without these misfires we would lose sight of the ethical demand of the Law of hospitality.

We might be tempted to situate ethics on the side of the Law and rhetoric on the side of the laws. Given traditional understandings of rhetoric, this formulation makes sense. Most traditional understandings of rhetoric, from Aristotle's ("the faculty of observing in any given case the available means of persuasion") to I. A. Richards ("the study of misunderstandings and their remedies") situate rhetoric on the side of discursive practice.[7] But Diane Davis has convincingly argued that the Law of hospitality also marks a rhetorical imperative. If life in a network society means that the other continues to arrive, this points directly to an exposure that "issues a rhetorical imperative, an obligation to respond that is the condition for symbolic exchange."[8] The minute "I" am called to respond to some other, to communicate, we are in the realm of rhetoric, and Davis argues that this call is not confined to linguistic representation: "If rhetorical practices work by managing to have an effect on others, then an always prior openness to the other's affection is its first requirement: the 'art' of rhetoric can be effective only among affectable existents, who are by definition something other than distinct individuals or self-determining agents, and whose relations necessarily precede and exceed symbolic intervention."[9] The Law of hospitality is Davis's rhetorical imperative, and it calls for laws of hospitality, for "rhetorical reasoning and responsible advocacy." Rhetoric includes such reasoning and advocacy, but it also extends beyond these practices—the Law of hospitality is rhetorical in that it is addressed and makes demands. This rhetorical imperative makes itself known as soon as we find ourselves enmeshed in networked life, and our answers to it can never completely face up to the Law of hospitality. They can only continue to address that Law regardless of the inevitable misfires.

Before we go any further, we should note that describing networks as hospitable runs the risk of suggesting that everyone has equal access to that network. I am not suggesting this. The digital divide remains with us, in its various forms. Whether that divide is defined in terms of access or skills, its very existence suggests that the network does not welcome all equally. We might also point to debates regarding net neutrality to question the absolute hospitality of the Internet. As network providers and legislators consider the possibilities of tiered network service (service that determines which traffic is more or less important), we are forced to pause when we think of the network in terms of unconditional hospitality. As providers begin to filter traffic, holding some packets at the border while allowing others to pass, the Internet may in fact become less hospitable. However, these attempts to filter are not a refutation of the Internet's hospitality. They are merely further examples of how organizations and individuals are attempting to write ethical programs, and the fact that computation shapes the lives of those who consciously "connect" to the Internet and those who don't suggests that the implications of these ethical programs are far reaching. The Internet, in its very structure and in its potential, embodies the two poles of hospitality: absolute, unconditional hospitality and calculating, conditional hospitality. There is no Internet without an extended invitation, without the Law, but guests must always meet certain conditions in order to traverse the network.

We can return to the case of the black widow suicide bomber to understand this tension between the Law and the laws of hospitality. In the face of the suicide bomber, we could seal off the square, but we would be establishing an ethical program that addresses immediate security concerns at the expense of the unending demand of absolute hospitality. We could eliminate all public space, but this would introduce two problems. First, it would privilege immediate concerns over broader ethical questions, closing down a space that is meant to allow for public gatherings. Second, it would put forth the fiction that the Law of hospitality can be dealt with completely, swept away and ignored. But eliminating public spaces would never completely guard against the arrival of a suicide bomber, a peaceful protester, or a wanderer passing through town. Most important, what ethical collateral damage would be created by sealing off public spaces?

But in the case of the black widow, we can extend this line of questioning even further, for the hospitality of digital networks was at play as well. The black widow would certainly have preferred to have a say in how and when messages could arrive on her cell phone. She would have liked to institute her own laws of hospitality to determine which messages could arrive. However, the very structure of SMS (short message service) protocol allowed the bomber's cell provider to send a holiday greeting to a large number of customers. In this case, the flexibility and standardization of SMS resulted in an unexpected arrival, which is interesting given how many groups have relied on this same hospitality for political action. As Matthew Fuller demonstrates in *Media Ecologies*, SMS has been used for political ends because of its affordances. Initially seen as little more than a gimmick, it eventually emerged as a cheap and effective tool for political action.[10] The uptake of SMS is a direct result of the technology's flexible affordances. The reliance on a standard mobile-phone keyboard (which is constrained by fingertip size) and the use of character constraints are just two such affordances, and though they seem obvious to us now such simple affordances make way for users to remake and repurpose technologies:

> These clear but at the same time rather awkward affordances have been taken up in unexpectedly massive quantity and variety because the technology affords further connection to other modalities of life and mediality, which it then also becomes folded into and continues to mesh with and compose.[11]

Similarly, Okoth Fred Mudhai cites a number of instances of activists using SMS to multiple political ends, from the ousting of President Joseph Estrada in the Philippines to a "Smoke Belchers" campaign by a Philippine NGO called Bantay Kalikasan (BK), which asked cell phone users to report any vehicle that was emitting black smoke to BK via text message.[12] Mudhai argues that the ability to send messages over mobile networks aids civil society organizations attempting to work with people in areas with little or no access to reliable Internet connections.

These kinds of political actions are indebted to a mobile service that invites innovation by passing simple messages across the network with few filters and with little concern for the identity of senders and receivers. SMS enacts a particular kind of ethical program, and the black widow's demise was a direct result of this. The predictability of SMS as a service means a certain amount of unpredictability regarding the messages that arrive on a cellular phone. SMS is based on standardized and "stateless" protocols. The standardization of protocols allows digital networks (regardless of provider) to "talk" to one another, and the use of stateless protocols for SMS means that each message is treated as an independent entity. Wikipedia describes a stateless protocol as one that "treats each request as an independent transaction that is unrelated to any previous request so that the communication consists of independent pairs of *request and response.*"[13] By treating each message as a brand-new relation between two nodes in a network (as a kind of singular conversation between these entities), SMS enacts an ethical program. SMS does not "care" where the message is coming from, how it is related to the sender or receiver, or how it is related to previous messages. SMS welcomes the spam message in the exact same way that it welcomes the order to detonate.

At the behest of the Federal Communications Commission, some telecommunications providers have established filters that prevent spam text messages.[14] While this benefits users pestered by spam, it also enacts a new ethical program for SMS, adding filters to a system that has thrived without them. What effect do such filters have on a technology that has emerged as an effective (if unexpected) tool for social and political engagement? Attempts to filter SMS will undoubtedly result in unforeseen complications (and perhaps even new opportunities for user innovation), but they will, more to our point, make ethical determinations about which packets of information can and cannot move through a network. Putting limits on a protocol or service is necessary and inevitable. Again, the Law of hospitality will always require the laws of hospitality, but those laws will never arrive at a complete solution to the arrival of others. Such a solution would result in cutting off the network, an eradication of the other. This eradication raises functional questions (How could a network be a network if it did not contain this hospitable gesture?) and, perhaps more important, ethical questions about how to design and delineate demarcation points.

Hospitality is the defining ethical predicament of networked life, as it describes the difficulties surrounding "what it is that turns up, what comes our way by e-mail or the Internet."[15] Life in a networked society means that terms such as place, home, host, and guest are thrown into question. We are confronted with the problems and questions of hospitality by "all those machines that introduce ubiquitous disruption, and the rootlessness of place, the dislocation of the house, the infraction into the home."[16] The boundary between home and outside is drawn both by the "master of the house" and the other that arrives. Nothing about this situation is simple, for there can be no hospitality without a guest:

> And the guest, the invited hostage, becomes the one who invites the one who invites, the master of the host. The guest becomes the host's host. The guest (hôte) becomes the host (hôte) of the host (hôte) . . . These substitutions make everyone into everyone else's hostage. Such are the laws of hospitality.[17]

The black widow, as a guest in Red Square, intended to become a host, to transform this public space into her own home if only for an instant, and to kill her guests/hostages. The square is a delimited public space, but it is defined by borders that are porous, as guests arrive on New Year's Eve. Each guest in this space becomes "the host's host," or perhaps even the host of each and every other attendee of this New Year's celebration. All of these hosts and guests (the same French term, hôte, can be used to describe both) are beholden to one another, vulnerable and exposed, enacting ethical programs in order to navigate the messiness invited by the Law. That exposure extends beyond the space of the square and into digital networks, as demonstrated by the black widow's spam text message, which arrived as an unexpected guest. The terrorist was terrorized and held hostage by a spammer, who was invited by the Law of hospitality that defines networked life.

The most disorienting aspect of the network's hospitality is the relationship between inside and outside, a point that Derrida makes by describing state intrusions into "the home." From wiretapping to censorship of pornography, governmental entities infringe upon the private or, at the very least, draw and redraw the line between the public and the private. While these attempts to censor and track introduce threats to democracy and to public space, they also reveal how the "home" is not only perverted by a network connection but also *constituted by it*. As soon as a state "gives itself or is recognized as having the right to control, monitor, ban exchanges that those doing the exchanging deem private, but that the State can intercept since these private exchanges cross public space," then the very terms of the situation of hospitality are scrambled and "every element of hospitality gets disrupted."[18] These disruptions of hospitality are, for Derrida, more than just violations of the boundaries of the home. In societies that value a separation between the public and private and that value limitations placed upon state interventions, the home would ideally be sealed off from these penetrations and wiretaps. It would be a private space. But Derrida shows that we must now recognize that the home (and here "home" stands in for any number of things and existents, from one's identity to one's personal computer or the numerous appliances that are networked) has always been constituted by connectability, by the Law of hospitality, by connections with an outside: "There is no house or interior without a door or windows. The monad of home has to be hospitable in order to be *ipse*, itself at home, habitable at-home in the relation of the self to itself."[19] The black widow's mobile device was her "home" on the mobile network, but it was only useful insofar as messages and calls could arrive. Even the detonation of her device required such arrivals. Her *mobile home* was what she hoped would allow her to enter the public square and perform her protest, but that same home, constituted by the network, was vulnerable to the guests that might turn up at any moment.

This vulnerability means that everything and everyone in a digital network is always hiding in plain sight: "This absolute porosity, this limitless accessibility of technical devices meant for keeping secrets, for encoding and ensuring secrecy, is the law, the law of the law: the more you encode and record in figures, the more you produce of this operational iterability which makes accessible the secret to be protected."[20] While protocols, software, statutes, and norms may attempt to protect these bits of information, the technologies themselves always provide the possibility of cracking the code and tracing information to its source. They always remain exposed to the Law of hospitality, the connectivity of digital networks. In the next two chapters, we will see how this possibility is explored through procedural rhetoric and exploits, both of which rely on the "open secrets" of networked life. Similarly, chapters 4 and 5 extend this question to databases, which continually welcome more data. That data is accessible to the person or machine that has the resources to access it—it is always exposed, vulnerable to the Law of hospitality. The pieces of software that determine who or what can access that information and the software written in order to access it are ethical programs, attempts to write (or, more accurately, rewrite) the laws of hospitality. These attempts to engage the hospitable space of the network are always provisional, and the rhetorical situations examined in this book show that ethical programs often raise more questions than they answer. Software does not solve the predicaments of hospitality, nor does it perfectly determine rhetorical action. Instead, it merely brings difficulties to the surface, asking us to confront morphing ethical questions. We write and institute laws to deal with "absolute porosity," but those laws never completely answer the persistent call of a hospitable network, which makes infinite demands.

Ethical Programs

The laws of hospitality are situated in the contingencies of particular situations, and I use the term "ethical programs" to describe these efforts to answer the challenges of hospitality. Ethical programs are processes (sometimes enacted in the form of software, but sometimes not) that determine the shape of networked infrastructures. These programs answer complex and conflicting exigencies, making rhetoric an ideal frame for understanding how they are written and maintained. Given that they are infrastructural—they shape and constrain how or whether writing and communication happen in networked life—it is imperative that we understand how they are constructed and what assumptions are built into them.

These twinned concerns of infrastructure and ethics have shaped a great deal of work in my home field of rhetorical studies, and *Ethical Programs* emerges from that work. For instance, John Trimbur frames questions of infrastructure in terms of the rhetorical canon of delivery in an influential essay entitled "Composition and the Circulation of Writing." Arguing that theorists of rhetoric and writing have neglected delivery (which perhaps gets more attention in studies of oratory than it does in studies of writing), Trimbur turns the field's attention to how the materiality of systems shapes writing. Through a Marxist lens, Trimbur wants to shed light on how "the process of production determines—and distributes—a hierarchy of knowledge and information that is tied to the cultural authorization of expertise, professionalism, and respectability."[21] He argues that teachers and theorists have lost sight of infrastructural concerns, causing them "to miss altogether the complex delivery systems through which writing circulates."[22] Many have responded to this challenge. Rebecca Dingo's *Networking Arguments* examines how "global gender policies and initiatives . . . travel, their meanings shift and change depending upon the contexts in which policy makers and development experts use them."[23] Jeff Rice's *Digital Detroit*, a text I address in more detail below, takes a similar approach, examining the networks of meaning surrounding the city of Detroit. In each of these cases, the attention to circulation and the delivery of meaning insists upon the complex, discursive relationships one must trace in order to understand contemporary rhetorical ecologies. While my own project might be seen as part of this same citational chain, I'm turning my attention not only to how discourse moves through networks—Rice is focused on how "ideas are spatialized . . .

put into proximity to one another" and Dingo addresses "how meanings shift and change due to context, history, and even intention"—but also to the networks themselves, the computational infrastructures that enable or disable argument, communication, and interaction.[24] In the terms that I use in the concluding chapter, I am interested both in discursive rhetoric (arguing *about* software) and what we might call computational rhetoric (arguing *in* and *with* software). The former accounts for how discourse works, and the latter extends those concerns to the computational infrastructures that prop up or impede that discourse.

These infrastructural concerns are ethical ones, since they actively shape the relational spaces of networked life. If ethics is about relations, as the previous discussion of hospitality suggests, then rhetoric becomes a significant tool for managing those relations. Jim Porter examines such tools in terms of a "rhetorical ethics." For Porter, ethics is woven through any act of writing in networked life: "Every act of internetworked writing requires ethical questioning. Given this view, ethics is not just a matter of the occasional problematic episode; rather, ethics, like audience, is a factor of every rhetorical act."[25] Porter argues that the key words of a rhetorical ethics are "maybe" and "it depends," and his focus is on how network technologies force us to question previous pedagogical commonplaces.[26] But his approach is still useful for my own discussion of networked software platforms, ethics, and rhetoric:

> As we open the borders to the writing classroom, our formerly well-established conventions for classroom ethics are disturbed. Now we are in the realm where "our" classroom practices have to be negotiated with campus computing policy, Internet policy, and the diverse contentions of different electronic communities and technologies.[27]

Here, we might take issue with Porter's assertion that the classroom was ever sealed off from such concerns. As I have argued in the introduction, these questions are not new but are rather heightened by networked environments. Still, Porter's discussion of borders and ethics is useful for my own discussion of hospitality and computation, and his notion of "rhetorical ethics" is a precursor to what I call ethical programs.

But *Ethical Programs* enters territory that only gets brief attention in Porter's *Rhetorical Ethics*. Like Porter, my interest in ethics is not in definite answers but rather in contingencies and mess. A rhetorical ethics does not offer an answer as to whether a particular practice or technology is unethical, but it does "suggest some strategies to help us decide how to decide."[28] In addition, my notion of ethical programs is similar in that it's meant to account for how we author responses to ethical problems in the moment and in response to forces, pressures, and exigencies. However, Porter is primarily focused on language and writing, and my own approach is an attempt to bring digital rhetorical studies into a discussion of computation as a rhetorical and expressive medium. This is not a massive leap from Porter's approach. While *Rhetorical Ethics and Internetworked Writing* does not directly address computation, it does remind us that a rhetorical ethics is, like software, procedural.[29] So, while Porter's concern is primarily with the procedures enacted by writers in response to ethical problems, we can quite easily extend his discussion into the realm of software, which operates by way of computational procedures.

In fact, extending Porter's discussion in order to account for software allows the rhetorician to approach rhetorical and ethical problems that might otherwise remain obscured. For instance, if we shift our frame to software and computation, an episode that Porter describes as "less interesting ethically" than other episodes, gains depth and texture. He argues that his book is primarily concerned with complex ethical problems and that certain ethical questions are simply answered and "uninteresting." Porter presents one example of a simple and obviously unethical episode early in the book:

> For instance, in 1994, a student at Texas A&M University broke into a professor's computer account and used it to send racist electronic messages to perhaps 25,000 people (The Chronicle of Higher Education, October 26, 1994, p. A24). Although this case might be interesting for its initial novelty, I contend that it is less interesting ethically. First, the break-in itself is unethical (constituting a computer crime, a clear misuse of computer facilities). Second, the "spamming" of a racist message (i.e., its indiscriminate mass distribution on the networks) is also unethical—although its legal status is less clear.[30]

However, as I will argue in chapter 3, this episode is not so easily dismissed as "unethical." If we begin to consider software platforms as part of the ethical conversation, rather than as the mere tools that we use to write or communicate, then we can ask different questions about this e-mail hack: What is revealed about the technologies involved (e-mail, in this instance) when we begin to see this hack in terms of the ethics of networked life? Who or what is responsible for this break-in? The hacker? The e-mail system's security gap? The professor who was sloppy with a password? The author of the password encryption program? Of course, we cannot shift blame completely away from the person who hacked this account, given that he or she broke into a system illegally.[31] However, in a hospitable network that will always welcome such hacks—by welcoming others, by connecting, by opening up a space of relation—these actions are both interesting and within the realm of Porter's notion of rhetorical ethics. Responsibility is not so easily assigned in such instances, if we consider that the security of a network is perhaps best understood in moments of breakdown. It is for this reason that many companies invite hacks of their systems and offer rewards for those willing to share the result of these hacks. For instance, a company called HackerOne helps companies better their security systems by facilitating bounty payments to white hat hackers and helping companies to patch the gap.

But even as I am extending Porter's notion of rhetorical ethics into the realm of computation and bringing it to new rhetorical ecologies (Porter's text was published in 1998), his discussion of ethics and networked life prefigures my own focus on hospitality, even if only very briefly. During a discussion of LISTSERV technology, Porter discusses the responsibilities of the host:

> The "guest-friend" relationship is an important ethic, perhaps the most important, in Greek tragedy: The principle says that as host or hostess you have a sacred duty to protect and care for the Other, the visiting alien. In Greek tragedy, violating this ethic leads to war, death, destruction, and chaos. (Usually only the intervention of the gods, *deus ex machina*, can restore order.) If we think about such a principle as applied to the management of LISTSERV groups, we can see that it would call the listowner to take on some responsibility, as host or hostess, for those "guests" participating in any particular electronic community.[32]

Here we see the early intimations of my own project, which is concerned with this guest-friend relationship and responsibility. However, my own concerns with hospitality, guests, and hosts would call into question whether the host (the listowner) is the clear locus of responsibility in such a situation. For while the person managing the list clearly serves as the host in some sense, enacting ethical programs to determine who can join the list or e-mail to it, this is but one factor in determining the ethical terrain of a LISTSERV that includes not only list members but also the mailing list software, mail servers, Simple Mail Transfer Protocol (SMTP), Multipurpose Internet Mail Extensions (MIME) protocols, and a host of other computational artifacts that participate in a complex rhetorical ecology. The list manager may be host to those sending e-mails, but she is the guest of protocols and software platforms.

Like Porter, Jeff Rice is concerned with a rhetorical ethics that raises difficult questions and that addresses the complexity of the network with a method that is sufficiently messy. Rice's *Digital Detroit* asks how we might build a digital rhetoric for connecting information and constructing new narratives with those connections. In his analysis of Jean-François Lyotard's discussion of databases in *The Postmodern Condition*, Rice suggests that "informational proximity should not be used to keep ideas apart, but rather, to allow their connectivity even when those connections come from different bodies (disciplinary, ideological, compositional), often in unanticipated ways."[33] For Lyotard and for Rice, the procedures by which we make these connections are paramount, and while Lyotard would not necessarily associate these procedures with rhetoric, Rice (and I) would. An ethical program is just this kind of procedure—it is a rhetorico-ethical tool for connecting information and for making ethical determinations. Further, Rice's book is not only interested in the procedures used for connecting bits of information—he is also concerned with the ethical question of how we decide which connections to make. While critics such as Paul Virilio argue that networks collapse space and time, leading to "incalculable economic and political consequences," Rice insists that networked life does not necessarily lead to the incalculable. [34] He argues instead that calculation remains in any moment of decision, even if that decision results in the combination of previously separate domains of knowledge: "Boundaries that may have previously kept such categories distinct now merge with one another in complementary and antagonistic ways. In this merger, agency does not vanish. Decisions are made; in the crossing of borders categories break down or expand."[35] Rice doesn't mention hospitality explicitly, but the concept is never far away as he discusses border crossings, and it is hovering right around the edges when he cites Marshall McLuhan:

> Following McLuhan, one might argue, then, that the age of new media affects the age of decision making. In what McLuhan identifies as a preelectronic state, decisions mostly are made by others; in the electronic age, one plays a more active role in informational decision making so that one works among supposed "others." "We have," McLuhan and Fiore note, "become irrevocably involved with, and responsible for each other."[36]

This responsibility makes decision difficult, since it is never clear with whom or what I am involved at any given moment in a given network. This difficult responsibility leads Rice to theorize the ethics of networked life in terms of the "good-enough," a mode of decision making that, like Porter's rhetorical ethics, never aims at being the final answer to the question. One draws lines and makes decisions, but such choices are only ever contingent and temporary:

> Good enough may feel like an odd trait of network thinking or even a contradiction given the hype often attributed to new media and networks. Good-enough's importance, however, results from the complexity of network borderlines, fuzzy areas of connectivity that are not clearly demarcated.[37]

We should not read the "good enough" as a flippant gesture but rather as one that is profoundly rhetorical and contingent. The gesture of good-enough does not aim at resolution, and it does not necessarily follow a "rational" path. In Rice's words, it is not a "revolutionary" gesture but is rather inventive and contradictory: "Connections may, indeed, contradict one another while also providing me with further information to explore and build from."[38] The good-enough is an ethical metaprogram (perhaps akin to what some programmers might call a "design pattern") for life in the network. We will see the contradictory nature of ethical programs throughout the coming chapters, from an exploit of Twitter that simultaneously revealed a flaw in the software (something we might deem "ethical") and caused users to distribute links to pornography (something we might deem "unethical") to the Obama campaign's use of software to both centralize and distribute decision making during the 2008 campaign. The ethical program could be thought of in terms of Rice's good-enough. It is never clearly right or wrong; it merely addresses a given rhetorical ecology in the moment, and it is sometimes (though, not always) rewritten.

Digital Dwellings

If the infrastructural ethics of networked life have been of concern to scholars of digital rhetoric, this is likely because rhetoric has long been tasked, at least since Quintilian, with addressing what it means to act and speak "well." *Ethical Programs* turns our attention to software's rhetoric since it plays such a massive role in our decisions about how (or whether) to relate to one another. If Quintilian was concerned with the good "man" speaking well, then this book urges us to situate any attempt to speak well in terms of the computational infrastructures that shape and constrain speech, writing, and code.[39] In order to understand the relationship between ethical decision and software environments, it's helpful to see *ethos* as a hinge point. Any attempt to account for ethical action in networked life must account not only for individual choice but also for the digital environments that determine how those choices take shape. For the rhetorician, questions of ethics are always tied directly to these questions of *ethos*, a concept typically associated with the character of a speaker or writer. The ethical programs enacted by a rhetor are part of *ethos*, part of how an audience makes sense of a speaker or writer's character and credibility. One cultivates an *ethos* by using particular kinds of language, claims, or arguments, and this is what Aristotle would call *artistic* proofs (sometimes called constructed *ethos*), since they are crafted with the tools of rhetoric. But a rhetor arrives upon the rhetorical scene with an *ethos* that is tied to her identity or self, and Aristotle would assign this type of *ethos* to the inartistic realm (others would call this the rhetor's situated *ethos*), since it is not constructed or crafted by the rhetor.

We will see in chapter 4 how this distinction can fall apart in networked life and how one might construct a situated *ethos*. However, for the time being I want to draw attention to the idea that *ethos* can actually have yet another meaning; it need not be confined to the realm of a speaker or writer's character, the realm of constructed and situated *ethos*. The term's roots evoke a certain kind of space or dwelling. Michael Hyde's anthology *The Ethos of Rhetoric* returns to what he calls this more "primordial" notion of *ethos*, one that accounts for dwelling places as well as the rhetorical tactics one uses to cultivate credibility. Whereas much rhetorical criticism focuses on *ethos* as the moral or ethical character of a speaker or writer, Hyde's collection examines *ethos* as

> the way discourse is used to transform space and time into "dwelling places" (*ethos*; pl. *ethea*) where people can deliberate about and "know together" (*con-scientia*) some matter of interest. Such dwelling places define the grounds, the abodes or habitats, where a person's ethics and moral character take form and develop.[40]

Hyde draws upon Aristotle and Martin Heidegger to rethink *ethos* in terms of how a rhetorical situation "transforms the spatial and temporal orientation of an audience, its way of *being situated or placed* in relationship to things and to others."[41] Whereas notions of *ethos* that focus on a rhetor's character are mostly concerned with one's reputation or one's effort to identify with an audience, this recognition of *ethos* as dwelling is concerned with how a rhetor "clears a place in time and space for people to acknowledge and 'know-together' (*con-scientia*) what is arguably the truth of some matter of importance."[42] This work of clearing does not originate in the rhetor, for while a rhetor might enact an ethical program, that program is always linked to the programs that establish a space or the communities in which they are situated. This dual meaning of *ethos* demonstrates how ethical programs are always the result of the interplay between rhetor and space, and in computational environments this means that the ethical programs of writers and speakers are always in conversation with those of the software that shapes (and sometimes establishes) that space. This understanding of ethos is very much tied to what Kitchen and Dodge call "coded infrastructures," which they define as "both networks that link coded objects together and infrastructures that are monitored and regulated, fully or in part, by software."[43] While they never use the term ethos, their term for computational infrastructures that regulate and shape activity fits well with Hyde's return to ethos as dwelling, even if Hyde's discussion ascribes much of the power to discourse itself. In addition, Kitchen and Dodge's discussion of wearable computing suggests that the line between ethos as character and ethos as dwelling is often difficult to locate:

> The fibers and fabrics of clothes and accessories gain digital functionality, some awareness, and become programmable to a certain degree; they can identify and sense the person wearing them and something of the environment around them; they can potentially communicate with other wearable devices and coded infrastructures; and they can act as interfaces to other devices.[44]

As ubiquitous computing begins to code more and more space, our ethos—how we sense others and how others sense us—becomes more and more inextricably linked to the digital dwellings in which we move, work, and play. That these devices can sense and identify us is further evidence that ethical programs cut across the boundary of human/nonhuman.

In her contribution to Hyde's volume, Carolyn Miller further clarifies this notion of *ethos* and makes clear that this dwelling is constructed collaboratively by a community:

> Those who dwell within a rhetorical community acquire their character as rhetorical participants from it, as it educates and socializes them. The community does this at least in part by supplying the Aristotelian components of *ethos*—the judgment (*phronesis*), values (*arête*), and feelings (*eunoia*) that make a rhetor persuasive to other members of the community.[45]

Thus, a rhetorical community can construct a dwelling, an *ethos*—writers can be what Hyde calls "rhetorical architects"—in which participants learn how to cultivate their credibility, their *ethos*. In networked, computational environments, these architects are designers, users, and the computational devices themselves, and this realization forces us to ask: What kinds of dwellings are being built and coded? And how do those dwellings deal with the persistent, nagging Law of hospitality?

In networked life, rhetorical responses to the Law of hospitality happen by way of ethical programs, procedures that expose and address an ethical predicament by addressing arrivals. Software addresses the ethical challenges of the network. But does it offer the flexibility required for the ethical predicaments of hospitality? The laws of hospitality will need to be continually rewritten in order to adequately address the demands of the Law of hospitality, which is unconditional. Can software, with its desire for the discrete and the binary, effectively address this demand? In their preface to Derrida's *On Cosmo-*

politanism and Forgiveness, Simon Kritchley and Richard Kearney express a distrust of computation, suggesting that a mechanized ethics would no longer adequately address ethical questions:

> On the one hand, pragmatic political action or legal action has to be related to a moment of unconditionality or infinite responsibility if it is not going to be reduced to the prudential demands of the moment. Political action has to be based on a moment of universality that exceeds the pragmatic demands of the specific context. But, on the other hand, such unconditionality cannot, must not, Derrida insists, be permitted to programme political action, where decisions would be algorithmically deduced from incontestable ethical precepts.[46]

While I take up this skepticism regarding algorithms and computation in more detail in chapter 5, I want to emphasize here that this argument is not uncommon among theorists of ethics and hospitality. Emmanuel Levinas also expressed similar concerns about a programmatic approach to ethics, or the "simple subsumption of cases under a general rule, of which a computer is capable."[47] That these critics discuss ethics using terms such as programs, algorithms, and computation is of the utmost importance for the present discussion. If software helps to code our rhetorical and ethical engagements, then do we run the risk of putting in place an ethical structure that is immovable, that loses sight of the unconditional, that focuses too much on a specific context, and that treats ethical questions as settled? While this is a concern with any kind of ethical infrastructure, a general distrust of computing makes us especially aware that software may code our ethical dwellings in final, inflexible ways. However, this book attempts to demonstrate how computational artifacts are not necessarily as rigid as these theorists suggest. Software is rather one more example of the contingent, mutable laws of hospitality, and it is crucial that scholars from across disciplines examine it if we are to gain a deep and complex understanding of our digital dwellings.

The laws of hospitality will always be enacted differently in different dwellings, and we can return to the discussion that opened this chapter for just one example of this. My own discovery of the "black widow" story came via a Twitter post by Spinuzzi and was thus circumscribed by how Twitter addresses the Law of hospitality. Twitter is an "asymmetric follow" social network. This means that Spinuzzi has a certain number of followers who read and sometimes redistribute his tweets (by way of a "retweet") but who he does not necessarily follow. In fact, as of October 2014, he had more than 2,000 Twitter followers but was only following 535 people. This asymmetry is different from a social network like Facebook, which typically requires that users are "friends" before they are able to share information with one another. Facebook has begun to incorporate asymmetric functions into its software, allowing users to "subscribe" to other users. However, the symmetry of "friending" on Facebook remains an important feature of the software and of the social graph that the company continues to build. Different software platforms and different social networks are shaped by how the software imagines relations between users—that is, by different ethical programs.

My choice to follow Spinuzzi on Twitter emerges out of a complex negotiation between the Law and laws of hospitality. I am able to follow nearly any user on Twitter, save those who have decided to "protect" their tweets (these users "approve" followers before sharing with them). Thus, Twitter's network taps the power of the Law of hospitality, relying on a vast network of users who broadcast 140-character tweets to anyone who cares to listen. In fact, Spinuzzi's more than 23,000 tweets serve as a reminder of the textual overload welcomed by networked life. And if that sounds like a large number, consider that writer Neil Gaiman had tweeted more than 70,000 times to his two million followers as of September 2014, and this number is dwarfed by many users of Twitter as well as by the vast number of "bot" accounts that computationally generate tweets. Not every tweeter is so prolific, but Twitter's asymmetrical network does require that users craft their own laws of hospitality to manage the text, image, and sound welcomed by the Law of hospitality.

As a user of Twitter, I enact my own laws as I decide how to navigate this massive network, and these laws are ethical programs. They are open-ended, contingent attempts to deal with the predicament of hospitality. These ethical programs are not necessarily rigidly "programmatic." They are moveable, changeable, and always open to revision. I choose to follow people based on criteria, including the user's tweeting patterns, my relationship to the user, or whether I share interests with them. I enact filters in order to determine what does or does not enter the stream of information that I follow each day for news and for information about research in new media studies, rhetoric and writing, and the digital humanities. I even unfollow certain users as circumstances change (too many tweets filling up the timeline, a shift in that user's tweeting patterns, and so forth). My criteria and these filters can change based on how I choose to use Twitter differently at different times or based on how much information I am capable of consuming. And my ethical programs are different from those of others who use Twitter to follow celebrities or athletes. These users enact their own ethical programs, their own "laws," in the face of the Law of hospitality.

But in addition to individual users making decisions about how they will write their own laws of hospitality, the choices these social media services make to enact certain types of policies (symmetrical or asymmetrical networks or choices they make when designing their Application Programming Interface) also rewrite laws of hospitality. Twitter and Facebook make decisions about how information can or cannot be found, and they make determinations about how a particular digital space is shaped. Twitter potentially allows me to reach a broader audience than Facebook, since my tweets are broadcast to the network. Facebook, which is defined by a network of "friends," makes for a very different audience. When posting a status update to Facebook, I have to consider the audiences that I am addressing, audiences I've constructed by choosing to "friend" family members, former high school classmates, and colleagues at other universities. One might be tempted to call Twitter "more hospitable" than Facebook, but such evaluative claims distract from the more important notion that each of these platforms enacts different ethical programs and raises different ethical questions. In addition, these claims would be immediately undercut once the ethical program of the platform shifts. In fact, in September 2014 Twitter announced plans to begin moving toward an algorithmically managed feed that resembles Facebook's, moving away from a "live stream" and toward a cultivated, crafted stream of information that attempts to make decisions for users.[48] This shift would radically change the ethical program of Twitter, shifting more of the responsibility for filtering information from individual users to the company's algorithms and no doubt making it easier for advertisers to target certain audiences. The very possibility that this change can be enacted by Twitter means the software's ethical program can never be essentialized as "open" or "hospitable." Any ethical program is reprogrammable. Of course, this feed was always procedurally generated; it was always the result of ethical programs, even if those programs were written by users as they made choices about who to follow. However, this change by the company would mean that the ethical programs that one crafts when following users (or muting them, or blocking them) would be coupled with those of Twitter's computational rules, and users would be working alongside computational machines to determine the shape of this rhetorical ecology.

In the chapters ahead, my primary goal is not to evaluate digital spaces as good or bad, open or closed. Regardless of such evaluations, each platform engages the problem of hospitality in unique ways, simultaneously opening up and foreclosing certain possibilities. In particular, this book addresses how certain software platforms can be understood as ethical programs. The ethical programs I study in subsequent chapters do not answer ethical questions in any final way. If anything, they merely continue to ask questions about the relentless Law of hospitality. Ethical programs are more likely to expose ethical problems and to provisionally answer the difficult ethical questions of life in the network. These programs come in forms—from APIs to content management systems to software that determines "regular expressions" (regex)—that can only ever provisionally address the Law of hospitality. They continually expose the difficulties of the network: Who or what gets to participate in a given network? How do the entities that collide in networked life address one another? Do they interact with one another at all, or are they separated by barriers? Who or what is writing the laws of hospitality in a particular situation? These are the questions that I address through a close examination of software and networked life.

PART 1

Hospitable Networks

TWO

Processing Power: Procedural Rhetoric and Protocol

It is now commonplace to argue that the Internet has fundamentally changed the nature of political campaigning. Presidential campaigns such as those of Howard Dean, George W. Bush, and Barack Obama have shown us how fundraising, get out the vote (GOTV) activities, and volunteer mobilization all change significantly when certain new media technologies are deployed. Rhetoricians and scholars in many disciplines continue to examine how web technologies are shifting the terrain of political campaigns by examining campaign websites, the tools that campaigns use to distribute information, and how volunteers use the Internet to organize. While this work has provided a number of detailed accounts of how text and image express arguments and how the Internet allows for various kinds of collaborative efforts, my focus in this chapter will be to explore how procedures, computational and otherwise, express arguments and how they shape and constrain writing and political action. In this discussion of what Ian Bogost calls procedural rhetoric, I discuss the ethical predicament of hospitality in terms of how power is organized in networks. The focus of this chapter is the 2008 Obama campaign's efforts during the Democratic primary and the general election. I focus on this campaign because it is credited by many as a kind of tipping point in the use of new media for campaigning. While previous campaigns certainly used networked technologies, the 2008 Obama campaign was seen as a giant leap forward. In fact, the 2012 campaign brought into focus the fact that Obama's election machinery was still far beyond some of his opponents. In postmortems of Mitt Romney's failed presidential bid, analysts noted a number of technological failures. The campaign's "Orca" software, a system designed to help the Romney campaign coordinate volunteer efforts, melted down on Election Day. Sean Gallagher of *Ars Technica* detailed the system's failures, from inadequate mobile server infrastructure to the distribution of invalid PIN codes.[1] While most would agree that these glitches were not the cause of Romney's loss, they were evidence that campaigns were still working to catch up to the mechanisms and procedures built by Obama in 2008.

This chapter will describe the infrastructure that the Obama campaign established in 2008, detailing how it was able to coordinate a network of supporters, one that they managed from the center. However, that network was distributed and offered a certain amount of autonomy to volunteers. This chapter takes up these conflicting dimensions of power by way of Galloway's theory of protocol, examining how the campaign constructed a complex and contradictory ethical program for addressing the predicament of hospitality. How did the campaign create, manage, and maintain this network? In addition, my analysis will ask how volunteers, as nodes in that network, constructed their own ethical programs in response to those of the campaign. The difficulties facing volunteers and the Obama campaign are a version of a broader ethical predicament: How does the administrating entity of a network balance freedom with control? How does a member of that network move through it, avoiding a rigid programmatic ethics handed down from above while also avoiding the fiction of pure, autonomous freedom? In short, how did both the campaign and its volunteers engage the Law of hospitality, and what ethical programs did they craft in response?

In my examination of the Obama campaign and its volunteers, I suggest that procedural rhetoric offers one way of understanding how both the campaign and volunteers navigated these problems. Obama's campaign team included paid and volunteer workers, and all involved authored sets of procedures to make arguments. These procedural arguments by no means solved the ethical predicaments of networks and power, but they did offer a novel mode of rhetorical action in such spaces. As we will see, the authoring and execution of procedures is not confined to software. One of my focuses will be the Obama campaign's social networking software, MyBarackObama. com (hereafter referred to by its popular and unfortunate moniker, MyBO). Through its software and its campaign infrastructure, the Obama campaign deployed procedural arguments, providing volunteers with scripts for the telephone calls they would make to potential voters and with procedures that expressed what kinds of activities were most important. These scripts were not necessarily followed verbatim, and volunteers authored their own procedures. By tracking the arguments embedded in the Obama campaign's software and its phone-banking scripts, we can gain a more complete picture of its complex, conflicting, and contradictory messages, and we can see how contemporary campaigns must continually engage the complexities of a hospitable network. As political campaigns continue to take advantage of digital media, procedural rhetoric offers one way to both welcome and control volunteers, but (perhaps more important) procedural rhetoric also allows the volunteers themselves to move through and write back against and, in some cases, resist networked power. I describe this as "writing back" not in order to describe the volunteers as freely acting agents—we will see that this is far from the truth—but rather to suggest that procedural rhetoric presents one strategy for attending to the complex power dynamics of networks.

In *Hamlet on the Holodeck*, Janet Murray argues that digital environments have four essential properties. They are procedural, participatory, spatial, and encyclopedic. They are procedural because software is an authored set of procedures, which can be used to "write rules . . . that are recognizable as an interpretation of the world."[2] Her focus is on storytelling, but we will see that any piece of software can be seen as an expressive, rhetorical model of a system. In addition to being procedural, digital environments also invite participation in that their rule-based behaviors are "responsive to our input" and they also "represent navigable space."[3] From navigating hyperlinks to playing first-person shooter games, we experience this spatiality in myriad ways. Finally, digital environments are encyclopedic in that they allow us to "store and retrieve quantities of information far beyond what was possible before."[4] Websites, video games, and digital fiction all take advantage of the ability to store massive amounts of information in databases.

All of these properties intersect with a discussion of new media and political campaigning. But while we might expect that a discussion of political rhetoric and software would focus on the participatory nature of digital environments, my focus here will be on procedurality. As Murray argues, authorship in electronic media is much more than constructing a narrative (or, we might add, an argument):

> Authorship in electronic media is procedural. Procedural authorship means writing the rules by which the texts appear as well as writing the texts themselves. It means writing the rules for the interactor's involvement, that is, the conditions under which things will happen in response to the participant's actions.[5]

Thus while we might continue to study "the texts themselves," a study accounting for software also requires us to understand the rules by which those texts appear—their procedurality. What is truly novel about the text of digital environments is not only its appearance on screens or even its organization via hyperlinks. To be sure, these two traits are important, but the ubiquity of software, a relatively new medium of expression as compared to text or speech, asks us to consider the role of rules and processes in digital environments.

The theorist who has done the most to connect procedurality and rhetoric is Ian Bogost. In *Persuasive Games*, Bogost develops his theory of procedural rhetoric. He explains this theory with examples from video games in order to demonstrate how games are one example of "persuading through processes."[6] Video games use procedural expression to make arguments; players interact with those arguments and, depending upon how the game is designed, are offered a conceptual space to critique them. For instance, Bogost examines the procedural rhetoric of the video game *Grand Theft Auto: San Andreas*. In particular, he analyzes one of *San Andreas*'s more innovative features—the requirement that the player-character must eat to maintain stamina and strength: "Eating moderately maintains energy, but eating high-fat-content foods increases CJ's weight, and fat gangsters can't run or fight very effectively."[7] Bogost admits that the game's features with regard to nutrition are "rudimentary," but he also insists that these features make an important argument:

> The fact that the player must feed his character to continue playing does draw attention to the limited material conditions the game provides for satisfying that need, subtly exposing the fact that problems of obesity and malnutrition in poor communities can partly be attributed to the relative ease and affordability of fast food.[8]

Through its computational processes, *San Andreas* expresses arguments about problems with inner city life. The player of *San Andreas* is placed into a world and asked to interact with that world, and the game's design invites such engagement and expresses its worldview via procedures.

Procedural rhetoric offers a useful analytic tool in at least two ways. First, it offers a range of scholarly fields (rhetoric included) a way to examine software that generates text, sound, and image. As Bogost argues, much work in digital rhetoric "tends to focus on the presentation of traditional materials—especially text and images—without accounting for the computational underpinnings of that presentation."[9] While digital rhetoricians have often attended to visual rhetorics and to the genres emerging in online spaces, procedural rhetoric offers a way to deepen this work by thinking about the authorship of procedures that generate image and text and that invite or discourage interaction. Such work can be part of a larger project of cultivating software literacies, something scholars of rhetoric, writing, and speech can and should participate in. But procedural rhetoric also offers a broader rhetorical theory, one that can be used to study "any medium—computational or not—that accomplishes its inscription via processes."[10] We interact with procedures on a daily basis, and those procedures express particular worldviews. Procedural authorship is not confined to software design, and Bogost argues that processes can have complex relationships to ideologies and cultures: "Processes like military interrogation and customer relations are cultural. We tend to think of them as flexible and porous, but they are crafted from a multitude of protracted, intersecting cultural processes."[11] In my own discussion, these two uses of procedural rhetoric—the study of software and the study of procedures more broadly—intersect. Here the double meaning of ethical programs is crucial, as the Obama campaign's use of software and its volunteers' use of procedures (specifically, the crafting of phone-banking scripts designed to persuade) mirror one another. In both cases, procedures are authored in response to the predicament of hospitality. The campaign navigates between absolute hospitality and conditional hospitality by funneling volunteers to certain kinds of activities and encouraging them to make certain kinds of arguments; volunteers accept the campaign's welcome and also attempt to write their own arguments, even though such arguments are circumscribed by the campaign's desires and directions. By examining procedures used by the campaign and those authored by volunteers, I show both how the Obama campaign operated within a protocological network, one that simultaneously exerted vertical, hierarchical power while also allowing volunteers to operate in a distributed fashion, and how volunteers used procedural arguments to navigate their way through that protocological infrastructure.

Networks do not merely distribute power horizontally, allowing nodes to freely communicate with one another. They are not rhizomatic spaces in which rhetorical agents act on their own. Rather, Alexander Galloway's work shows us how protocological power operates in networks, coupling rhizomatic distribution with hierarchical organization. The 2008 Obama campaign is a perfect example of how these two contradictory machines work in tandem. But more than this, the volunteers who helped propel Obama into office present evidence that procedural rhetoric is one way to navigate protocological networks. Galloway argues that though one cannot oppose protocol (just as one cannot oppose gravity), political action is indeed possible in spaces of protocological control, and he presents possibilities for acting within networks, such as hacking, tactical media, and Internet art. In this chapter, we will see that procedural rhetoric is yet another example of how one can move through, resist, and write in networks by examining how Obama campaign volunteers used procedures to work within the protocological network established by the campaign. Those volunteers were not necessarily looking to resist or subvert that network, unless they were John McCain or Hillary Clinton supporters looking to sabotage the campaign (something that will no doubt become more prevalent as campaigns like the 2008 Obama effort become more common). However, volunteers were looking to help shape the campaign. From within a carefully constructed protocological network, volunteers received procedural arguments from the Obama campaign, arguments that aimed to shape how volunteers encountered potential voters and how they recruited other volunteers. Those volunteers interacted with these procedures and often authored some of their own.

Digital Media and Political Campaigns

The examination of new media and political campaigns has been under way for well over a decade. During their focus group study conducted prior to the 2000 New Hampshire presidential primary, Jennifer Stromer-Galley and Kirsten Foot examined how potential voters interacted with campaign websites, and they determined that voters were well aware of the promises and challenges of new media technologies:

> Participants viewed the Internet as offering potential for political participation; at the same time, they were skeptical of whether candidates are willing or able to use the human interactive capacity of this new medium to the fullest extent. Some expressed an awareness of the limited power they have as citizen-users to engage with campaigns online.[12]

Participants in this study saw candidates offering interactive features on their websites (such as the ability to e-mail candidates, search for information on issues, or participate in forum discussions), but they also understood the challenges of inviting "genuine interaction between candidates or campaign staff and citizens."[13] From the sheer number of possible interactions to the difficulties of message control, study participants understood the delicate dance of interactive websites. This is something that nearly all of the scholars I will mention here address: How do new media technologies that invite interaction both participate in and resist the tightly controlled messages of political campaigns? The fact that study participants were aware of this problem indicates the degree to which this approach to campaigning has reached critical mass.

While many participants spoke of having "control" when it came to surfing campaign websites and seeking out their own answers, Stromer-Galley and Foot argue that interactive elements of websites allow campaigns to "give an appearance that users are in control of the experience and getting the information from the candidate that they want while masking the actual, relatively limited scope of user control."[14] Thus, campaigns still exert a great deal of control over their message, even if users are afforded ways of interacting with information. Stromer-Galley and Foot argue that this asymmetrical power relation could be reduced by "increasing the possibility of human interaction" and that "to date, most U.S. campaigns have not employed the human interactive capacity of the Internet."[15] Writing in 2000, prior to campaigns such as Howard Dean's in which the web was used to connect voters with the candidate's platform and with one another, Stromer-Galley and Foot suggest how candidates might seek out opportunities to interact with potential voters.

In a text that draws upon the volunteer mobilization efforts of the Dean and Bush campaigns, Foot and Steven Schneider argue that web campaigning expands the possibilities for political action. Foot and Schneider move beyond the study of candidate-to-voter interaction and examine how potential voters interact with one another. To account for expanded possibilities afforded by technology, they examine the rhetorical strategies of web campaigning: "The essence of campaigning is persuading. Within the general framework of persuasion, we define and examine four practices in web campaigning—informing, involving, connecting, and mobilizing—suggesting that each practice involves a distinct type of relationship between campaign organizations and other political actors."[16] By studying how campaigns employ these four practices, they hope to account for the strategies specific to web technologies. Most important, for our purposes, Foot and Schneider view the new media objects of campaigns as artifacts that express political arguments, and the authors are attuned to the expressive and rhetorical potential of web objects:

> We view Web objects—whether pages, features, texts, or links—produced by actors in electoral contexts as artifacts manifesting political strategies and actions. Many, but certainly not all, aspects of Web producing activity can be inferred through careful observation of Web objects. In our observational analyses, we engage in a kind of "Web archaeology" whereby we infer practices from artifacts, that is, Web objects. Campaign sites are surfaces on which campaigns' Web production practices are inscribed dynamically during (and beyond) an electoral cycle. They carry online structures that simultaneously evidence the communicative and political actions of the campaigns that produce them and enable the organization of sociopolitical actions on the part of site visitors—some of which may also become inscribed on the campaign site.[17]

This description of web objects as manifesting political strategies is one that software studies scholars would take for granted. Nonetheless, it is an important observation. Political platforms are not only the product of a candidate's speeches or pamphlets—they are also created, expressed, and reinforced by way of digital media. Further, Foot and Schneider also explain that campaigns fully recognize that merely having a website is not enough. Campaigns must also "manage their Web presence as it is mediated across the electoral Web sphere on sites that they do not and cannot control. . . . The dispatching of campaign site visitors to other Web sites to promote the candidate stimulates coproduction of the campaign's Web presence and of the electoral Web sphere."[18] As we will see later in this chapter, this strategy played out in interesting ways with the Obama campaign as volunteers were tasked with authoring their own arguments about Obama's political platform.

One more early study of new media and campaigning is worth mentioning here, since it documents some of the earliest attempts at using games: Gary Selnow's *Electronic Whistle-Stops*.[19] While he does not address voter-to-voter interaction, Selnow does examine some of the computational artifacts with which campaigns in the 1990s experimented. He explains how campaigns used database technologies to carve up voters by traits and how they used such technologies to present the illusion of personal contact between candidate and voter: "A closer look reveals that these warm, personal messages, in most cases, are generated by cold, compassionless computers. Truly personal or not, the candidates have been looking for a sure course around the wire, tube, or print, and computers can provide it."[20] Such concerns continue to trouble scholars. Writing in the wake of the Obama campaign, Bruce Gronbeck argues that digital campaigning's reliance on niche marketing and carefully groomed e-mail lists is one more manifestation of the "clustering of America."[21] Gronbeck argues that emerging technologies allowed candidates to "[chart] voters geodemographically" and to produce "microtargeted, audience-based systems of political messaging, as niche marketing became fully integrated into the presidential campaign communication processes."[22] But the characterization of computers as cold and compassionless is one that a great deal of work in software studies disrupts. These voter lists and "personal messages" are not generated by "computers" alone but rather by collaborations between humans and machines. The messages generated by such collaborations may in fact be artificially personal, but they are generated by software, which is authored by humans and which uses procedures to express ideas and arguments.

While Selnow's main focus is on how the Internet invites interactivity and connectivity, he does devote some space to a discussion of games. In particular, he discusses games such as The Third Millennium organization's *Balance the Budget Game*, which allowed players to "estimate the proportion of the $1.5 trillion federal budget spent in nine categories."[23] Selnow argues that such games were little more than experiments and novelties and that they were focused on collecting data about users. Further, he argues that most ran in batch mode and did not allow for true interactivity. Users entered data, and the program returned a result, making for a less than dynamic gaming experience. Even so, these games were many steps ahead of campaign websites in the late 1990s. As Selnow explains, Bob Dole's campaign page allowed for user interaction, but this was mainly focused on allowing users to print their own posters or send electronic postcards. As limited as this seems, Selnow notes that the site was somewhat revolutionary: "As far as political Websites went, it was a minor Treasure Island of amusements."[24] Still, Selnow's discussion of games and interaction seems prescient. He argued that increased interactivity and a shift away from batch mode would make for interactions that "will be a lot more interesting."[25]

While certain aspects of campaigning with new media have become more interesting and complex, the use of games has not moved as quickly as we might expect. This is not to say that political games have been completely absent. In fact, complex, procedurally expressive games about laws and policies have appeared more and more often in recent years. One example is *The Redistricting Game*, developed by researchers at the University of Southern California to educate citizens about gerrymandering.[26] The game models the process of drawing boundaries for voting districts, and it demonstrates how this process is driven by party politics. However, such procedurally rhetorical games have not emerged in the sphere of political campaigns, and Bogost argues that most political games fail to tap the affordances of procedural expression. Rather than making it possible for players to "embody political positions and engage in political actions that many will never have previously experienced," most contemporary political games are little more than gimmicks.[27] Games like *The Redistricting Game* use procedures to make arguments about corruption and party politics, allowing players to face situations they might not otherwise have the opportunity to face. According to Bogost, politicians have largely failed to create such procedural artifacts. He extends this argument in *How to Do Things with Videogames*, arguing that most political games are more interested in "politicking" and winning elections than in policy, and he once again argues that this approach misses the powerful, expressive potential of computational procedures. Procedural arguments could be used to model political policies, allowing citizens to experience other possible worlds and leading them to reflect on how policy decisions might affect their lives. But I am less interested in evaluating whether or not campaigns have successfully deployed immersive procedural rhetorics than I am in understanding how the procedural rhetorics of campaigns reveal arguments and worldviews and how they are used to exert control. Further, I am interested in how procedural arguments invite interaction and, at certain moments, invite further procedural authorship. As we have seen, both scholars and citizens are aware of the value of a campaign staying "on message," even as they invite participation from volunteers and supporters. Understanding how procedural rhetorics operate (in particular, those that invite interaction) helps us see how emerging technologies are part of the dynamics of control.

The Howard Dean campaign's videogame is an example of how procedural arguments can make complex and sometimes contradictory arguments. In an attempt to create a political videogame that made better use of procedural authorship, Bogost teamed up with Gonzalo Frasca to design a videogame for the Howard Dean campaign. That game made two arguments. One was about "the logic of grassroots outreach."[28] Players of the game were tasked with recruiting volunteers, just as they would as volunteers for the Dean campaign. The second procedural argument of the game involved the activities of volunteers: "sign-waving, door-to-door canvassing, and pamphleteering."[29] Bogost and Frasca were attempting to build a game that moved beyond some of the more hollow attempts at political games. And while Bogost and Frasca's game succeeded in making a particular argument about grassroots activism, "it inadvertently exposed the underlying ideology of the campaign."[30] That ideology was, in the words of one critic of the game, more about "handing out leaflets" than about Dean's policy positions.[31] This particular critic pointed out that the game made no explicit arguments about the Dean campaign itself and demonstrated only that the campaign was trying to expand the number of volunteers. Instead of using procedures to make arguments about health-care reform by, say, simulating the experience of what it's like to be unemployed and without insurance, the game only modeled the process of recruiting volunteers and carrying out GOTV activities. Thus, the game presented no procedural arguments about why one would want to vote for Dean or join his campaign. Further, the procedures revealed something that the campaign would not necessarily argue overtly—namely, that campaigning is primarily about recruitment, not about issues. By modeling this argument procedurally, the game actually undercut the campaign's attempts to enlist volunteers to spread Dean's policy arguments.

As we will see, this is perhaps one of the central difficulties of procedural arguments. They model systems in ways that may or may not align with the discursive arguments forwarded by political campaigns. While my own discussion here does not examine videogames, it does locate procedural arguments in a different kind of campaign software—the MyBO social networking software. Like the games analyzed by Bogost, that software mounted arguments. Much like the Howard Dean videogame, the software used by the Obama campaign "inadvertently exposed the underlying ideology of the campaign." This "undercutting" of the campaign's narrative indicates that procedural rhetorics are not necessarily the best fit for campaigns that aim to stay "on message." If procedural arguments open up a space for users/audiences to reflect on procedures, then it's possible that procedural rhetoric will necessarily undercut and contradict the dominant message of a political campaign. Procedural arguments involve explicit statements ("If X, then do Y"), but this does not mean that the arguments themselves are explicit. Like an enthymeme that omits one of its premises, a procedural argument has embedded assumptions, and this invites the audience to interact and interpret. Engaging with a procedural argument involves more than reading content—it involves reading the rules that generate that content and understanding how those rules express certain worldviews. Further, procedural arguments simultaneously insist on the execution of sets of instructions and invite interaction with those instructions. Once again, we are presented with the predicament of hospitality—procedural rhetoric both invites interaction and attempts to hold it at a distance. Without interaction, the procedures of the Obama campaign (or any other political campaign) would be useless. The phone-banking scripts, letter-writing instructions, and social media functions of contemporary political campaigns (all of which lay out procedural arguments) require a distributed network of volunteers. However, those same procedures are attempting to exert control over how volunteers interact with potential voters and with one another.

Alexander Galloway's work on protocol, a term he uses to describe contemporary organizations of power, offers a useful way of understanding these attempts by the campaign to exert control via a distributed network. In *Protocol: How Control Exists after Decentralization*, Galloway describes how power and control circulate through networks. For Galloway, the contemporary organization of power is best described by protocol, specifically computer protocols that "govern how specific *technologies* are agreed to, adopted, implemented, and ultimately used by people around the world. What was once a question of consideration and sense is now a question of logic and physics."[32] In this sense, protocol in networked life isn't a question of how one should address the queen of England. While there is a protocol for such an encounter and while that protocol is an ethical program, it is different from the protocols that Galloway theorizes, since the latter are primarily focused on how computation shapes what one can or cannot do in a given networked space. Technological protocols establish a possibility space, and on the Internet they determine how (or whether) packets of information flow between nodes. This means that protocols are central to determining political and rhetorical action in networks and that they are the primary method for regulating activity in networks.

Galloway argues that protocol is "a technique for achieving voluntary regulation within a contingent environment."[33] However, protocological power is not the simple exertion of force by way of top-down regulation. It operates in a complex fashion and is the result of what Galloway describes as "two opposing machines": "One machine radically distributes control into autonomous locales, the other machine focuses control into rigidly defined hierarchies. The tension between these two machines—a dialectical tension—creates a hospitable climate for protocological control."[34] Galloway argues that protocol is best understood by examining how Transmission Control Protocol/Internet Protocol (TCP/IP) and the Domain Name System (DNS) work together to regulate and control Internet traffic. As I discussed in the introduction's discussion of RFC 761, TCP/IP is a set of protocols that defines how packets of information move between servers. It is a set of rules that ensures that these servers know how to format and read those packets of information, and it ensures the flow of information among nodes. However, this flow is always accompanied by the vertical, top-down mechanism of DNS. DNS matches particular IP addresses with particular domain names, ensuring that the information moving through the Internet and sitting on servers can be accessed. DNS establishes a rigid hierarchy of top-level domains (TLDs), such as .com and .net, and it sorts servers into each of these categories. Google falls under the .com TLD and the University of Wisconsin's website falls under .edu. This hierarchy determines how an Internet server is discovered and accessed. But this tree-like structure is more than just a sorting mechanism, because "each branch of the tree holds absolute control over everything below it."[35] This top-down structure means that one can "turn off" a website by removing DNS support.[36] In this situation, the data may in fact still be present on servers, but the removal of DNS would mean that servers would have no way of finding that data.

This discussion of DNS and TCP/IP reminds us that the notion of a purely "rhizomatic" Internet is a fiction. The flow of information must always pass through hierarchical machines, which determine what packets can and cannot pass. Galloway's mention of how networks are hospitable spaces for protocological control is, of course, essential to my discussion of rhetoric and ethics in the network. As I have argued, networked life is instituted by the Law of hospitality, the unconditional welcome of the other. As Wendy Chun puts it, channeling Derrida, "fiber-optic networks open the home."[37] That opening of the home means that "electronic contact . . . cannot be divided into the 'safe' and the 'dangerous' based on content because the risk of exposure underlies all electronic exchanges."[38] Protocol's response to this exposure is the development of a technique for control, allowing for the flow of information (without which there would be no network) but carefully controlling how and whether that information flows. Protocol is another instance of the laws of hospitality, the rules authored in response to the unrelenting Law of hospitality.

Building upon the success of the Howard Dean and George W. Bush campaigns, Obama's campaign authored its own laws of hospitality, instituting a protocological network by way of a website that made procedural arguments. Those arguments served to organize volunteers and funnel them to certain kinds of activities, but the MyBO site was much more than a campaign brochure. Obama volunteers used the site to phone bank from home and to determine how to most efficiently "block walk" in their neighborhoods. In certain cases, the procedural arguments of the Obama campaign's software directly contradicted the campaign narrative. While Obama built an argument for engaging opponents (or enemies) and building broad coalitions, the campaign software often argued that volunteers should focus on motivating those who were already likely to support Obama. As we will see, the procedures for making phone calls to potential voters make the argument that volunteers should end the call if faced with a supporter of Hillary Clinton (during the primary) or John McCain (during the general election). And while the campaign argued that volunteers were organizing in a horizontal, distributed fashion, a closer look at its procedural rhetoric reveals that it also exercised a great deal of centralized control. We could read these contradictions as examples of how campaigning is different from governing, and this certainly explains part of the story. Politicians make promises, and those promises are often abandoned once the realities and complexities of legislation assert themselves. However, these complex and contradictory arguments also reveal something important about protocological power. The ability to argue simultaneously that the United States should engage enemies such as Iran and that volunteers should avoid any engagement with supporters of McCain or Clinton stems directly from the operations of protocological power. These tensions mirror the structural contradictions of the campaign, which was built on the tension between hierarchical power and distributed power. Making both of these arguments at once is much more than a cynical attempt to win office (although it may, in fact, be that). It is also an indication that citizens and digital rhetors should be aiming to be, in Annette Vee's terms, "procedurate," cultivating tools for composing and understanding computational procedures.[39] Becoming procedurate is part of preparing oneself to face up to the contradictions of networked life. Procedural rhetoric is one of these tools, and it is a particularly interesting one given that it was deployed by both the campaign and its volunteers. Procedural rhetoric's insistence on the modeling of a worldview and on an interaction with that worldview means that it is both a tool for control and a tool for gaining insight into control. Becoming procedurate does not lead to a citizenry free from manipulation, but it could mean that procedural rhetoric is a particularly useful tool for civic engagement in networks. Through a closer look at the Obama campaign, we can begin to see how protocol operates and how procedural rhetoric offers ways to move through and reshape networks.

Political Rhetoric, Procedurality, and MyBarackObama.com

Many have argued that the 2008 Obama campaign signaled a significant shift in campaigning, and this suggests that a close analysis of its procedural rhetoric will be a crucial part of understanding contemporary, emerging political discourse. The Obama campaign's MyBO website made procedural arguments about which kinds of volunteering activities were most important. The MyBO user's home page featured an "activity index" that tracks a volunteer's activities.[40] A Facebook page called "Students for Barack Obama" explains the tracker:

> The Activity Tracker helps Obama supporters measure the work they're doing on behalf of the campaign. Whereas before, the points system tried to measure lots of different activities down to a "point value," the new Activity Tracker simply displays up front exactly what activity users have been engaged in.[41]

The activities that went into the calculation of this index were events hosted, events attended, phone calls made, doors knocked on, number of blog posts written, number of donations made to your personal fundraising group, amount of money raised, and number of groups joined. The site's original mode of motivating volunteers involved assigning point values to certain activities. In an August 2007 blog post, Chris Hughes (a co-founder of Facebook) explained the points system:

> Just about every action you can take on My.BarackObama now will give you points to make it easier to see all the hard work you're putting in to make this campaign succeed. If you host an event, that'll show up on your profile and you'll get 20 points. Write a blog post and you'll get 15.[42]

While Hughes was insistent that "earning points isn't what this campaign is about," he did use the blog post to announce that hosts of "Barbeques for Barack" would earn 50 points and house party hosts would earn 100. By assigning higher values to particular activities and by publishing a list of those with the highest point totals, the campaign made procedural arguments about which campaign activities held the most value.

The existence of both the activity index and the point system might be seen as instances of "gamification," a term that has caused a great deal of heated debate in many circles. Bogost has argued that the term is merely a cynical attempt by corporations to cash in on the success of videogames. His argument, which is similar to his critique of political games, is that advocates of gamification care little for the affordances of games and instead are out "to capitalize on a cultural moment, through services about which they have questionable expertise, to bring about results meant to last only long enough to pad their bank accounts before the next bullshit trend comes along."[43] He suggests the term "exploitationware" is a better descriptor of such practices. Sebastian Deterding, Dan Dixon, Rilla Khaled, and Lennart Nacke have argued that such heated debates should not discredit the study of gamification but that scholars might require a new term for the phenomenon. They define gamification as "the use of game design elements in non-game contexts," but they suggest the term "gameful design" as an alternative to those hoping to avoid the baggage of the term "gamification."[44] The term "gameful design" originates with Jane McGonigal, who, despite offering a number of critiques of gamification, is often put forward as a proponent of the concept. While McGonigal's book *Reality Is Broken* does suggest that games can offer effective ways of solving social problems and motivating people, she sees gamification as a superficial attempt to dress things up as games. She hopes that gameful design can offer a more thoughtful approach: "Instead of thinking about the things that we can do to make something look like a game. 'Oh, I see badges. I see levels. I see points. It must be a game.' What can we do to make something feel like a game?"[45] If we were to plug MyBO into this debate, we could categorize it in multiple ways: as a way to exploit volunteers, as a way to make an already "hip" campaign even hipper, or as an attempt to guide volunteers toward certain types of activities. My own approach will lean toward the latter, but it would be just as valid to analyze MyBO as a piece of exploitationware.

Cynical or not, exploitative or not, the MyBO site's use of points and other metrics to measure volunteer activities was most certainly an attempt to control the efforts of its massive network. Discussions of gamification are central to any discussion of ethical programs, since the use of procedures to manipulate an audience would certainly fall within the realm of both rhetoric and ethics. However, I'm less concerned with categorizing MyBO's effort in terms of gameful design than I am with tracking how the campaign used a range of artifacts to manage a distributed network of volunteers. While critics of gamification would focus on whether MyBO used game features in meaningful ways, it seems clear that volunteers were motivated by these features and that the site *felt* like a game to those atop the leaderboard. Most interesting for our purposes are the arguments forwarded by the MyBO system itself, which were somewhat contradictory. MyBO's point system led game designer Gene Koo to proclaim it "one of the most important game titles of 2008," but he also pointed out that the game tended to (perhaps unintentionally) devalue certain kinds of activities:

For example, in January, my partner and I drove down to South Carolina and spent a week in the trenches, eventually helping to run a staging location in a bellwether precinct. For this—and for our subsequent work in MA, VT, and PA, we scored a big fat zero, because there was no way to let MyBO know what [we] were doing. Meanwhile, others were apparently gaming the system by hosting bogus events or flipping through phone numbers without actually calling anyone, perhaps hoping to win various awards. (The site did limit the number of numbers it would give you within a specific period of time to limit this kind of abuse—or, I suppose, wholesale data-mining).[46]

The point system established by the Obama campaign made procedural arguments about what volunteers should do to contribute to the effort, and it inadvertently devalued certain activities "in the trenches." On the other hand, one could argue that those operating "in the trenches" did not require a point system for motivation. Either way, the point system revealed important arguments about how the campaign hoped volunteers would allocate their time and resources.

When the point system was scrapped in favor of the "activity tracker" in August 2008, some of the point leaders were upset. But, as Koo notes, the activity tracker's 1–10 scale allowed a great number of volunteers to feel like they were contributing. The first iteration of the point system was purely cumulative, and a leaderboard showed who had earned the most points. Koo argues that this was somewhat disconcerting to volunteers who logged in and saw that "there were 266,441 other people doing more work than you."[47] The new system made it clear that sustained and regular volunteer activities were valued. A volunteer could no longer rack up a large number of points and shoot up the leaderboard. Instead, she or he had to continue to carry out certain volunteer activities to keep the activity index from dropping. Hosting one-time events or spending a day making phone calls wouldn't keep your index high forever. Competition was still part of this system, but it shifted. Rather than attempting to compete for point totals, volunteers were now encouraged to keep their activity index high. The index was published on a MyBO user's profile page, meaning that volunteers could gauge one another's commitment by visiting profiles and comparing activity index numbers. As Rahaf Harfoush, a community manager for MyBO, explains, users needed to continually contribute and to contribute in a variety of ways to keep their index up: "Even if you made 100 calls, if you didn't do anything else for a while, your score would drop, motivating people to come back and do more campaign activities."[48]

Both the activity index and the point system are perfect examples of procedural authorship. While the layout of the web page and the tools for organizing are worthy of our attention, this minor game-like feature of MyBO is an example of how procedures can express arguments. As Koo explains, the point system was probably a "curiosity" for most people, but it served an important rhetorical purpose: "the point system helped signal what kinds of activities really mattered, and it probably had something to do with the over 200,000 events hosted and 27,000 groups created on MyBO—an impressive number even after you discount some set of bogus ones put on to game the system."[49] The point system put forward important procedural arguments, specifically that certain activities are most important and that campaign volunteers best serve the cause by remaining involved.

But what might be most striking about the game-like structure of portions of the MyBO website is that it reveals how much the campaign exercised protocological control over volunteer activities. The campaign used this game to guide and funnel volunteers to particular activities at particular moments in the campaign while also encouraging individual empowerment and horizontal collaboration. Software expert Martin Fowler sees this as the true innovation of the Obama campaign: its ability to simultaneously deploy top-down and peer-to-peer structures. Fowler argues that the Dean campaign made use of peer-to-peer interaction but failed to combine this with a "mass-organization model." The latter involves "direct contact from the campaign leadership to activists on the ground."[50] The mass-organization model is not a pure "command-and-control" model in which a clear hierarchy is in place. Rather, mass-organization cuts out the middle layers of bureaucracy. With a combination of peer-to-peer and mass-organization, the Obama campaign "directed activities from the center, but also encouraged peer-to-peer collaboration."[51] Fowler explains how the MyBO software enacts both of these models simultaneously:

> Here's an example of this fusion. An important part of the software for both the Dean and Obama campaigns is event planning software to help volunteers plan meetings. In the purely peer-to-peer mode a volunteer decides to have a meeting on a pressing topic, say health-care. They go to the event planner and enter a meeting date, time, place, topic, capacity etc. They can advertise it in the various social groups that they've set up in the system. Another volunteer who uses the same political website may see the meeting advertised in the online group, or might search for upcoming local meetings. The guest volunteer can then use event planning software to RSVP to the meeting, giving the host an idea of who's coming. Weaving in the mass-organization model, the key difference is that the process can be kicked off by the campaign leadership. They can decide that they would like to see a coordinated push to discuss health care over the next couple

of weeks. So they suggest to volunteers that they may like to try and organize meetings around this. They may provide catalysts such as articles to read or DVDs to watch. This creates a buzz around the topic that makes it more likely that meetings get set up. This buzz reaches out to potential attendees as well who are now more likely to try and find local meetings on the topic.[52]

The MyBO site suggested a list of event types, and volunteers would choose their theme. A party might have been focused on making phone calls to neighbors, or it might have been a potluck in which volunteers gathered to discuss health-care policy. One example of the campaign's use of themed parties was the organization of the "Unite for Change" events held around the country on June 28, 2008. These events were organized just weeks after Obama had clinched the Democratic Party's nomination and one month before the Democratic National Convention. After a hard-fought primary, the Obama campaign was looking to unite the party and prepare for the general election. MyBO provided a "Host Guide" for the event that suggested procedures that hosts could carry out before, during, and after the event, a document that is striking given this book's concerns with hospitality.[53] Each organizer served as host, and the Obama campaign's guide served as a kind of Emily Post–like document for those hosts. The hospitality of the campaign, which aimed to welcome more volunteers to the fold, was distributed to all of these nodes (individual homes, in this case) and was controlled by way of a protocol. The campaign suggested ways to promote the event and what the actual event might entail (literally, a *protocol* for the event), and it laid out a possible agenda for volunteer hosts. For instance, the guide suggested that hosts could show the campaign's "Unite for Change" video and open up a discussion about the next stages of the campaign. The guide also provided links to customizable flyers and to sign-in sheets for guests. Sign-in sheets asked guests to provide phone numbers and addresses, and hosts were encouraged to gather these sheets and enter the information into the campaign's database via a web interface on MyBO.

While the campaign suggested an agenda for these events—such as encouraging guests to stay involved in the campaign and asking guests to share what had inspired them to be active in the campaign—it insisted that this agenda was only a suggestion: "This agenda is meant only to be a suggestion to guide you in your activities. Feel free to organize your Unite for Change event according to your preferences."[54] Just as the activity index and point systems made procedural arguments that funneled volunteers to certain tasks, the Unite for Change host guide included procedures for gathering data about those in attendance and guiding discussion in certain directions. These procedures reveal that the events were less about explicit discussions to unite supporters of Clinton and Obama and much more about one more effort to gather information about volunteers. While the title of the event and the video—Unite for Change—suggested that these events might offer former Clinton supporters (or perhaps even Republicans and independents) a "way in" to the campaign, the main goal of these events seemed to be to continue efforts to build a database of potential supporters. The seven-minute "Unite for Change" video was primarily about the value of community organizing and not about "uniting." The procedural arguments of the campaign suggested that these events were about gathering data and recruiting volunteers, and this was the theme of most Obama volunteer events. The Unite for Change title was primarily just a new banner for hosts to hang up in front of the house.

MyBO didn't only distribute talking points. It also laid out procedural arguments via its social networking site—suggesting themes, tasks, and sample agendas for meetings and parties. Procedural arguments allow for a kind of finessing between explicit instructions or directions (which would ostensibly offer little flexibility) and rhetorical engagement. The Obama campaign planted seeds for themed get-togethers and it used procedural arguments via documents such as the "host guide" and the activity index "game" in order to persuade supporters and volunteers to carry out particular kinds of activities. This does not make the campaign any less interesting, important, or (for some) inspiring. But a closer look at the procedural arguments forwarded by the MyBO campaign website allows us a full picture of the campaign's arguments and motives. The arguments made by the activity index, the point system, and the "host guide" are examples of procedural expression. The campaign could have provided a ranked list of volunteer activities rather than a point system, but the choice to make these arguments procedurally meant that volunteers responded by interacting with the procedures. As we have seen, the Obama campaign was not averse to controlling activities from the center, and a ranked list would have been in line with the campaign's hybrid strategy (fusing what Fowler calls "mass-organization" and "peer-to-peer"). By making such arguments procedurally, the Obama campaign took advantage of the massive network it had built, inviting volunteers to contribute while also carefully orchestrating activities via hierarchical structures. However, this was only half of the story when it comes to the procedural rhetorics of the Obama campaign.

Phone Banking: The Procedural Rhetoric of a Script

```
<?php
boolean $supportObama;
boolean $volunteer;
```

```
string $name;
string $phone;
string $email;

if ($supportObama==TRUE) {
    print ("Great! Would you be willing to Volunteer for the campaign?");
        if ($volunteer==true){
        $name = $_GET('name');
        $phone = $_GET('phoneNumber');
        $email = $_GET('email');
        }
            else
            {
            print ("Okay, no problem. Please remember to vote on
                November 2!");
            }
    }
else {
    print ("Thanks for your time. Have a great day.");
    }
?>
```

If we were to convert an Obama campaign phone banking script to PHP programming code, it might look something like this. But this code is fictional in a number of ways. For one, it's not operational. There are some statements missing, and we would need to create some additional files in order to make it run. Further, the phone-banking script (the *procedure*) authored by the Obama campaign is sometimes more involved than this short piece of code. The campaign's scripts involved more questions, and they sometimes accounted for the undecided voter.[55] If the potential voter was undecided, certain phone-banking scripts offered procedures for persuading that person to vote for Obama. These kinds of procedural arguments were used in swing states and during moments in the campaign when the Obama campaign thought that persuading undecided voters was a reasonable use of resources. However, much of the phone banking operation was about GOTV activities and about educating Obama supporters about how and when to vote.

In order to extend this program further and to truly depict the phone script as a program, we would have to include a number of instructions after the first "print" statement. In fact, the program might have included a number of nested if-then statements, and the caller would query the potential voter (much like querying a database) for information. But my main purpose in including this bit of fictional PHP code is to make the point that the scripts given to Obama volunteers were procedural arguments and that they could have been written as computational artifacts. Understanding procedural arguments provides a window into a deeper understanding of software and how it is used to build arguments. We can write the phone-banking script in PHP code, and we can write MyBO software's procedures in plain English. This translation work is important for understanding the arguments being made by the Obama campaign, and it is also important if we want citizens to cultivate a deeper, procedurate understanding of how software is used to make arguments.

Further, I want to make the point that the answer to the question that opens most of these phone calls—"Who do you plan on supporting in the upcoming election?"—will instantly determine how long the call will last and how involved the conversation will be. If the potential voter indicates that she or he is a McCain or Clinton supporter, the call may very well be over. The campaign volunteer is instructed to thank the person for his or her time and hang up the phone. Such a phone call is not a failure, from the perspective of the campaign, because it is now able to update its database to ensure that this particular person is not called again, resulting in the conservation of time and resources. If the potential voter is a strong Obama supporter (or, many cases, undecided), the procedure continues through a series of if-then statements. The caller asks questions, provides information about absentee ballots or polling locations, and sometimes even recruits a new volunteer. What is most interesting for our purposes is that many of the scripts provided by the campaign offer few instructions for how one might persuade a McCain or Clinton supporter to change his or her mind. The campaign's procedural arguments often guided volunteers to politely bow out of rhetorical engagement with Clinton or McCain supporters. This was not always the case. Depending on the location of the potential voter, the circumstances of the election at the time of the call, or the target audience of the call, certain phone-banking procedures provided instructions for persuading those who were not already Obama supporters.

However, in many cases the procedures for attempting to persuade supporters of McCain or Clinton were authored not by the campaign but rather by the volunteers themselves. For instance, a *Daily Kos* blogger named Elise details a possible procedure for convincing Iowans to caucus for Obama:

An example:

JOE: Oh, I'm planning on voting for Edwards because he's against the war.

ME: I completely understand your frustration (if that's how they sound—or maybe anger? Depends on the call) with the war. Actually, this is one of the reasons I chose Obama over Edwards. I really like Senator Edwards, but did you know that he actually co-sponsored the resolution that gave President Bush the blank check to take us into war? Senator Edwards had a lapse in judgment here, and for me, it was an awfully large mistake. Senator Obama has been against the war since back in 2002 when he was running for Senate in Illinois.[56]

Note that the procedure is contingent on the rhetorical situation. Elise's parenthetical statement about how the caller "sounds" is a kind of "if-then" statement, a fork-in-the-road moment in the discussion where the caller decides which path might work best. Procedural arguments in the form of phone-banking scripts were distributed by the campaign, but Obama volunteers were not rigid, unwavering machines. They did not always execute the campaign's code, or at least not in the way that we normally imagine the process of execution.[57] They interpreted it, changed it, and made it their own. For instance, a volunteer by the name of "Renata Hussein Hussein" posted her thoughts about what does and doesn't work when calling voters on her MyBO blog.[58] That post not only details Renata's thoughts about how to best approach the phone call script but also cites the recommendations of a volunteer named "Barath" who, in turn, had borrowed some ideas from "Dave C." Dave explains that he has developed his own script that allows him to "just kind of vamp," and he recounts his own attempt at procedural authorship. In order to combat the Clinton campaign's arguments about Obama's lack of experience, Dave experimented with a change to his script:

On Sunday I had thrown in a line saying that "Obama has the right kind of experience to address the challenges we have at home and abroad. Challenges like our economy, our health care system . . . etc." I wanted to get at the heart of Clinton's argument. Out of six or seven women, five that I spoke with were polite and were totally with me until I said that bit about experience, and then interrupted me and said they didn't want to talk with me and hung up. It wasn't happening with the guys.

I wondered if it was the new line? So I tried calls without it. I replaced it by saying that "I'm spending my time reaching out to my neighbors on Obama's behalf because I believe that he's the only candidate running in either party who can genuinely bring us together to get things done at home and abroad. I'm calling because I believe in him[.]"

It was a total 180. Suddenly, the women I [talked to] weren't hanging up on me, and some were asking "why do you say that?" Boom. I was in.[59]

Dave's script tinkering is not evidence of a scientific study, and his assumptions may have been a bit hasty. Seven phone calls is not exactly a large sample size, and it is difficult to know whether the change in the script was truly more persuasive for women. Further, we have no real way of knowing whether the language of "experience" is what caused these potential callers to end the conversation. But what is most important, for our purposes, is Dave's attempt at procedural argument. Yes, he changed the content of the script, and this would seem to fit within the realm of existing rhetorical theories about how language can be crafted to persuade particular audiences. But he also authored a new procedure. Crafting his own if-then statements, Dave worked through a new procedure. He shifted his script based on the audience, and engaged in procedural expression. In addition, he shared his script with other volunteers, and at least two others posted this story on their own blogs. The lesson of Dave C's script may have persuaded others to adopt his language, and it may have convinced them to avoid the "experience" argument that he attempted to use (and which he decided was the reason for his failure). But Dave's story also provided other volunteers with an example of procedural authorship, and it is evidence that the Obama campaign's scripts served as loose templates for volunteers.

While the Obama phone-banking script is in fact an ethical program that manages relations between callers and potential voters, it is not an example of the campaign *programming* its volunteers. Instead, it is evidence that the campaign was authoring procedural arguments and that volunteers *engaged* with those procedural arguments by editing, revising, and extending the procedures provided by the campaign. We can read the Obama campaign's scripts as expressions of certain arguments. The nested if-then statements of these scripts lay out an ethical program, they present arguments to volunteers about the best way to address a potential voter, they indicate who is worthy of attempts at persuasion, and they provide some instructions about how and when to distribute information (about polling locations, absentee ballots, and so forth). This is not quite the same as the "talking points" that campaigns and political parties often distribute. Talking points were provided, and they offered a kind of campaign brochure. Procedures manipulate the brochure content, rearrange it, or decide which content should be presented in particular rhetorical situations. In addition to editing or "remaking" the content of the Obama campaign's arguments (this was happening as well), volunteers in phone banks were changing procedures based on the rhetorical situation.

And phone-banking scripts weren't the only procedural arguments at work. The campaign also deployed a "letter to the editor" function on the website. While there was evidence that volunteers on the phone were adjusting the scripts to fit their rhetorical needs, the "letter to the editor" function on MyBO resulted in rhetorically ineffective form letters. Fowler explains how this played out:

> The "letter to the editor" feature helped supporters write letters to newspapers advocating a particular position. In use a supporter would search to find local newspapers for her area, and then get assistance to compose a letter to that newspaper. Early implementations of this feature included sample text to help [with] composing the letter, but this fell out of favor as it led to too many letters which obviously came from the same source. So later advice [came in the form of a] list of arguments to cover in the letter, to encourage writers to make a more individual expression.[60]

The new letter to the editor function offered volunteers the ability to write letters to the editor in support of health-care reform or other Obama administration policies. Users could choose an issue such as health-care reform and then were presented with an explanation of how their letter could help:

> By writing a letter to the editor, you can help educate decision-makers and the public about the urgent need for reform. Remember, you don't need to be an expert. We'll provide information to get you started, but the most powerful message is your personal story about why health insurance reform is so urgent in your life and the lives of those you know.[61]

Rather than offering a form that users would complete, the software now explains that a "personal story" is more persuasive. After entering a zip code, the user is presented with a list of local and national newspapers along with each newspaper's estimated circulation. This latter detail is important. The software could present other bits of information here, but it chooses to present circulation numbers. It persuades users to consider the size of the audience they would like to reach. After choosing a newspaper (users can choose more than one), the website offers a text box in which the writer can compose the letter. That text box is accompanied by a list of suggested talking points, but it is also accompanied by a link to "writing tips." It is more than a little disconcerting that clicking on this link generates only two words of advice: "Be concise."[62] The procedural argument of the "letter to the editor" function makes it clear that the campaign wants volunteers to write to their local newspapers and that it wants them to make use of talking points while also including personal anecdotes. Again, centralized control (talking points) is accompanied by a volunteer's freedom to express herself (personal stories).

The Ethical Programs of Networked Life

During the 2008 U.S. presidential campaign, candidate Obama was criticized for saying that he would meet with certain enemies of the United States "without precondition." During a debate sponsored by CNN and YouTube, Obama said that he would be willing to meet with leaders of Iran, Syria, Venezuela, Cuba, and North Korea:

> The notion that somehow not talking to countries is punishment to them—which has been the guiding diplomatic principle of this administration—is ridiculous. Ronald Reagan constantly spoke to the Soviet Union at a time when he called them an evil empire. He understood that we may not trust them, and they may pose an extraordinary danger to this country, but we had the obligation to find areas where we can potentially move forward. And I think that it is a disgrace that we have not spoken to them.[63]

In addition to these arguments about engaging foreign enemies, Obama has often expressed admiration for Doris Kearns Goodwin's book *Team of Rivals*, which details how President Abraham Lincoln was willing to fill his cabinet with people who had run against him.[64] Indeed, as we know, Obama nominated one of his fiercest rivals, Hillary Clinton, to the post of secretary of state. During debates about health-care reform and financial reform, President Obama continually insisted upon this ethical program—that he was willing to listen to his opposition's arguments. In addition, the Obama campaign also continually repeated the mantra of "Yes, we can." Both volunteers and those outside the campaign understood this slogan as an expression of the campaign's networked, grassroots structure. The Obama campaign presented itself as a peer-to-peer network, and candidate Obama often referred to volunteer organization efforts. He compared those efforts to his own previous experience as a community organizer, and these peer-to-peer activities were indeed happening. Neighbors were holding meetings and barbeques; volunteers were knocking on doors.

Whether or not these arguments are evidence of mere political posturing, the point I want to make is this: Obama continually positioned himself as someone willing to engage his opposition and positioned his campaign's volunteer operation as a peer-to-peer network. However, a closer look at some of the procedural arguments made during the Democratic primary and the general election reveals a more complex and sometimes contradictory stance. From the MyBO website to the phone scripts provided to volunteers, the Obama campaign's position with regard to engaging with or attempting to persuade the opposition was not so clear cut. Obama's speeches may have argued for a "big tent," but the ethical programs of MyBO and the phone-banking scripts suggested something quite different—that volunteers bow out of rhetorical exchanges with the opposition.

In addition, we have seen that the campaign's procedural arguments reveal a delicate dance between hierarchical control and peer-to-peer interaction. I offer this not as a way of debunking the campaign. Rather, I want to suggest that these conflicting arguments indicate that a deeper understanding of procedural rhetoric offers us new ways to understand all types of arguments, political and otherwise. But what is perhaps most interesting about the range of procedural arguments made by the campaign is that only a small number of them relied on computation. While the activity index and the point system used computational procedures to lay out a kind of "game space" for volunteers, many of the procedures discussed in this chapter did not rely on the computational power of a computer for expression. The campaign certainly used the encyclopedic and interactive affordances of computational technology to organize volunteers, but their use of procedures did not always make use of computational machines. In many ways, the campaign used digital technologies to distribute, rather than author, procedural arguments. A videogame uses the power of computation to create a procedural world that uses rules to expresses arguments; a phone-banking script, though it does deploy rules persuasively, does not necessarily require computer processors.

While these different noncomputational ethical programs might mean that the 2008 Obama campaign still doesn't address Bogost's concern that politicians have yet to truly tap the affordances of procedural rhetoric, a close examination of the campaign in terms of procedural arguments across media and situations is still useful. It presents a different lens through which to examine the campaign, and it links the concerns of software and computation to extradigital spaces. Further, it provides an ideal way to understand how the campaign organized itself, how it established and leveraged a protocological network, and how volunteers navigated that network. Procedural rhetoric was both a way to control volunteers and a way for volunteers to write back. Not all of these attempts by volunteers should be understood as resistance, and it is not my aim to present procedural rhetoric as the "magic bullet" for the manipulations of networked life. Instead, I am arguing that procedural authorship is both a method of controlling and reining in the complexities of the hospitable network and also a method by which we might act, argue, persuade, identify, and communicate in such networks.

As software becomes more and more prevalent, the cultivation of a procedural literacy becomes necessary. Close attention to the procedural rhetorics at work in political arguments can reveal complex and contradictory messages about the ethical stances of politicians. In a political climate that values staying "on message" and controlling the narrative of a campaign, paying careful attention to procedural rhetorics can offer a glimpse of the range of arguments put forth by campaigns and of the methods by which they seek to control a distributed network of volunteers. But procedural arguments also invite interaction, and this allows us to read them as much more than manipulation or the covert programming of the *polis*. Procedural arguments do not lay all their cards on the table, and this could lead us to read them as "sneaky" or as propaganda. But procedural rhetoric also calls out for audience interaction, asking others to fill in the blanks. The Obama volunteers' willingness to rewrite the campaign's phone-banking script is evidence that such arguments open up a space for rhetorical exchange. That space is an uncertain one, and it is not necessarily a space of symmetrical exchange, but it does allow for rhetorical action in networks of control. Procedural rhetoric provides rhetors with a way to understand how power moves through networks and how they can sometimes exploit that power.

While such ethical programs could lead to manipulation, they also leave political campaigns open to a morphing message as audiences interact with (and, in some cases, author) procedures. As we have seen with the activity index and with phone-banking scripts, procedural arguments call for us to engage with them and to determine assumptions embedded within them. Game play and software use, like reading or listening to an argument, asks the audience to fill in the gaps. Through this interaction, citizens, activists, and rhetors can reflect on procedural arguments and can (in some cases) challenge them, refute them, or make them their own. This kind of interaction presents an opportunity for reimagining what political action looks like in a hospitable network.

THREE

Possibility Spaces: Exploits and Persuasion

In 2010, an onMouseover exploit spread through Twitter, the popular micro-blogging service that allows users to post 140-character tweets. The exploit—a piece of code that takes advantage of a security vulnerability—was the result of a flaw that allowed users to post executable code in Tweets using the Java-Script programming language. The spread of this exploit meant that certain users could, among other things, inadvertently repost links by hovering over certain areas of their screen. The code of this exploit is relatively simple, but to those unfamiliar with programming or with JavaScript the exploit was a curiosity. Further, the average user would likely be confused as to why anyone would create such an exploit. Most instances of the onMouseover exploit were not malicious, and even those that were did little more than propagate links to pornographic sites. No data was stolen; no passwords hacked. Still, the exploit affected the Twitter feeds of celebrities and public figures, including White House press secretary Robert Gibbs and Sarah Brown, wife of former United Kingdom prime minister Gordon Brown. Due to the exploit, Brown's Twitter page displayed a large "h" and linked to a Japanese porn site. As the exploit hit more high-profile users, blogs and other technology publications worked to explain the exploit to readers, and one publication—The Guardian—even published a detailed account of how the hack worked, an account that I'll examine in more detail below.

This curious exploit seems like little more than the tinkerings of a prank-ster, but it is actually much more than this. This hack and others like it are a direct result of a hospitable network that welcomes exploration and hacking, and they can tell us a great deal about how our digital spaces operate. My aim in this chapter is to use two different examples to demonstrate how exploits serve as ethical programs. Wikipedia provides a concise and useful definition of the term "exploit":

> An exploit (from the English verb to exploit, meaning "using something to one's own advantage") is a piece of software, a chunk of data, or a se-

quence of commands that takes advantage of a bug, glitch or vulnerability in order to cause unintended or unanticipated behavior to occur on computer software, hardware, or something electronic (usually computerized). Such behavior frequently includes things like gaining control of a computer system, allowing privilege escalation, or a denial-of-service attack.[1]

Programmers find a gap and exploit it, and this once again points to the difficulties of hospitality. Short of disconnecting altogether, networked software can never remove the possibility that someone will discover a bug and exploit it. Exploits raise discussions among programmers and nonprogrammers alike about security and about ethics, and in this sense their link to rhetoric is clear. The exploit triggers conversation and has the potential to open up a space for discussions about code and software, but this is only one way of understanding the rhetoric of the exploit. While the onMouseover exploit did not articulate what we might normally call a rational, deliberative argument about web security, it did demonstrate some of the available means of persuasion. Exploits demonstrate what is possible in a given space, and they show us what is or is not available to writers and programmers. So, while the onMouseover exploit did trigger discussion about web security, Application Programming Interfaces, and third-party applications—discussions that I will cover in this chapter—its most important feature was the role it played in performing an argument about what Twitter's website allowed users to do, thus forcing a particular feature of the Twitter ecosystem into view.

The value of this performance comes into focus when we compare the onMouseover exploit to a different, less reported Twitter exploit. Unlike the onMouseover exploit, which spread in the world of the web browser, this second exploit fell primarily in the realm of "apps"—it was a security flaw discovered in the OAuth authentication protocol that was designed to protect users of third-party applications. The OAuth protocol is part of the Twitter API (and is used by other web APIs as well). It is a security protocol that is meant to protect users of social media sites such as Flickr and Twitter who want to allow third parties access to their data (pictures, tweets, and so forth). Many of the arguments and discussions that emerged because of the onMouseover exploit revolved around the security problems with the Twitter.com interface. One blogger interpreted this incident as a reason to avoid using Twitter.com and to instead access the microblogging service via a third-party application such as TweetDeck. As networked platforms proliferate, APIs offering developers and users the capacity to build third-party applications have become more and more prevalent. They provide users and programmers with ways to access certain information and functions while also allowing companies to protect proprietary resources. The onMouseover exploit did in fact only affect users of the Twitter.com website, while those who access Twitter's services via third-party applications were spared the annoyance. However, the OAuth exploit is evidence that no networked space is completely safe from exploits. OAuth was initially implemented as a way to make third-party applications more secure. Prior to the institution of OAuth, users of applications such as TweetDeck, might need to provide the developers of these third-party applications access to their user credentials. The TweetDeck application would then act on behalf of the user, making requests to the Twitter API to access content. This was an insecure solution, and OAuth offered more security through a "token" system, which is discussed in more detail below. However, early in its implementation OAuth suffered its own exploit. Just as Twitter had fallen prey to a gap in its code, OAuth left itself open to an exploit that allowed programmers to gain unauthorized access to user resources.

When dealing with networked software, exploits are inevitable. Website or app, it makes no difference. Because of the hospitality built into the network, hacks will happen, but what is most instructive for our purposes is what happened in response to the discovery of the OAuth exploit. The conversation about the OAuth exploit happened among the programmers and companies that had collaborated on the design of the protocol. In fact, the existence of the exploit was kept a secret until after the problem it exposed had already been addressed. Given that the onMouseover exploit led many commentators to argue that third-party applications were more secure than the Twitter website, the OAuth exploit offers us some insight into how an exploit might emerge (and be quashed) in the world of apps. Whereas the onMouseover exploit was released on the network and raised a public discussion about how the code operated, the exploit affecting OAuth triggered discussion among a smaller group of people who were much more experienced and who had a vested interest in avoiding a public discussion.

This chapter addresses how exploits trace the edges of a digital space, demonstrating what is or is not possible. As I will argue, rhetorical theory offers ways of theorizing such possibilities. However, this requires a complex understanding of rhetoric, one that not only moves beyond popular notions of rhetoric as lying or deceiving (what Wayne Booth calls "rhetrickery") but also beyond an Aristotelian understanding of rhetoric as a method of rational deliberation and discursive persuasion.[2] If rhetoric is only the exchange or analysis of arguments, then it may have little force in the world of protocol, which is often concerned less with deliberations about ethics and laws than with whether or not code is operational. In addition, if we hold to a narrow reading of Aristotle's definition of rhetoric as "the faculty of observing, in any given case, the available means of persuasion," we might also be at a dead end for considering rhetoric's utility for understanding the exploit. Aristotle was interested in how the speaker or writer constructed probable truths by determining what evidence or strategies were most applicable to a situation. He was interested in what was immediately available for the task at hand, and this means that an extension into the world of the possible might land us outside of the realm of rhetoric.

My argument is that rhetorical theory has a role to play in the worlds of both "hack" and "yack" (to use a set of terms popular in digital humanities circles) because it can be productively applied beyond the space of probability and into the space of possibility. This chapter's discussion of the fraught ethical terrain opened up by exploits will demonstrate how a rhetorical framework helps us both analyze and rewrite possibility spaces by taking up exploits as both opportune moments for analysis and as ethical programs that engage networked hospitality. More than justifying my own discipline's relevance to software studies and networked environments, this chapter argues that exploits offer a useful pathway for understanding the rhetorical possibilities of a hospitable network. Those possibilities are exposed in a way that raises complex ethical questions. This chapter asks two questions: How do ethical programs like the onMouseover exploit and the OAuth exploit expose ethical predicaments, and how can both conversations about code and code itself respond to those predicaments?

Rhetoric and/of the Exploit

Understanding the two exploits discussed in this chapter will require that we move beyond the notion that the web is open or free. It is not my intention to argue that the "view source" option of the web browser is free from the complications of protocological control. In fact, I am less interested in evaluating the worlds of the browser and the app than I am in examining how exploits explore possibilities and raise questions in these two types of spaces. Who gets to exploit gaps in software? Who is part of the conversation when an exploit emerges? What does the exploit tell us about the software or protocols in question? These are the questions that drive this chapter. These questions are about the rhetoric and ethics of our digital spaces, about who gets to speak, who gets to code, and who gets to explore the possibilities opened up by software platforms.

But all of this is complicated by the ethics of the exploit, a practice that is less about what one *should* do than about what one *can* do in a given digital space. This is largely due to how protocological spaces work. As we learned in chapter 2, protocol operates by way of two machines, one vertical and the other horizontal. While we might be tempted to think of digital networks in terms of the horizontal, unstructured flow of communication, a closer examination of the technologies that regulate how information moves demonstrates that this is only one half of the story. Protocological power is distributed throughout networks, exerting control by enforcing rules about how or whether information can move from node to node. These rules are enforced computationally, meaning that discussions of how they operate (or of how they should operate) will take us only so far. For Galloway, nothing is stopping us from arguing how things should happen in such networked spaces, but these arguments won't necessarily have the greatest impact: "Opposing protocol is like opposing gravity—there is nothing that says it can't be done, but such a pursuit is surely misguided and in the end hasn't hurt gravity that much."[3] That is, the exploit operates by the maxim "more hack, less yack."[4] This move toward code and away from discourse doesn't mean that we are completely given over to rigid, unforgiving machines. Networked software establishes possibilities, but it does not necessarily do so in any final or thoroughgoing way. There is a constant push and pull between the Law of hospitality and the laws of hospitality, welcoming others to explore possibilities while also provisionally defining what those others can and cannot do.

This push and pull reminds us that though our digital spaces are *programmed*, they are not necessarily rigidly *programmatic*. Indeed, regardless of the insidious nature of protocological control, Galloway does not see it as foreclosing political action or activism. His work with Eugene Thacker in *The Exploit* most clearly demonstrates this and also provides us with an understanding of how rhetorical action takes shape in networks. As Galloway and Thacker note, political action in networks does coincide with a clear shift in power: "within protocological networks, political acts generally happen not by shifting power from one place to another but by exploiting power differentials already existing in the system."[5] In a situation of networked hospitality, locating the origin point of power becomes difficult, if not impossible. Rather than clearly defining host and guest or locating power as a discrete thing that is exchanged between parties, the exploit becomes a rhetorical and political tactic for understanding and manipulating networked spaces. The exploit begins from the assumptions that thresholds are not clear and that the porousness of boundaries offer up the possibility of exploring multiple solutions or answers. In protocological networks, the exploit becomes a way of "discovering holes in existent technologies and projecting potential change through those holes."[6] These gaps serve as reminders of our constant predicament of hospitality, and acting from within this new power dynamic requires a shift in thinking, a shift that leads Galloway and Thacker to argue for thinking in terms of "possibility" rather than "probability":

Informatic spaces do not bow to political pressure or influence, as social spaces do. But informatic spaces do have bugs and holes, a by-product of high levels of technical complexity, which make them as vulnerable to penetration and change as would a social actor at the hands of more traditional political agitation.[7]

This move away from probability, political pressure, or influence could be read as a move away from rhetoric. Rhetoric is typically understood as the study or practice of "influence" (that is, persuasion), but a closer look at Aristotle's famous definition opens the door to a broader understanding of rhetoric. As translator George Kennedy explains, Aristotle's definition—"an ability in each [particular] case, to see the available means of persuasion"—is very much concerned with possibility.[8] Aristotle's phrase *endekhomethon pithanon* is typically translated as "the available means of persuasion," but Kennedy explains that "*endekhomenon* often means 'possible.'"[9] In this sense, "availability" might be understood as casting the net widely in an attempt to see all possible persuasive resources. To be sure, Aristotle's *Rhetoric* circumscribes this possibility, suggesting that rhetoric does not "theorize about each opinion . . . but about what seems true to people of a certain sort."[10] The orator does not necessarily seek "Truth" but is more concerned with what is true for a particular audience or situation. Further, the rhetor's primary persuasive tool, the enthymeme, is concerned with probability. The enthymeme, or what Aristotle calls a "rhetorical syllogism," is founded on the values of a community; when a rhetor builds a well-reasoned argument, she or he does so with premises that "are sometimes necessarily true but mostly true [only] for the most part."[11] These premises are within the realm of probability. So, while a speaker or writer may be concerned with the "possible" means of persuasion, she or he is primarily focused on what is probable, attempting to persuade an audience about what should be done given only partial information, what is best for a given community, or what is most likely to achieve a certain goal. Still, the role of "possibility" in the rhetor's toolkit should not be overlooked.

While Galloway and Thacker's account seems to suggest that persuasion would be much less useful than exploits, Aristotle's use of *endekhomenon* at least suggests that rhetoric has a role to play in the exploiting of gaps and holes in networked spaces. At first glance, the idea of forcing a situation by way of an exploit might appear to be outside the realm of rhetoric, which is concerned more with discursive attempts at persuasion by way of claims and evidence and less with brute force. Rhetoric is often positioned as what we use when we don't want to use force—a set of tools for persuading rather than exploiting. Given all of this, one might be surprised as I attempt to align the work of the exploit with rhetoric, and so I will need to step back to go forward, making clear the relationship between the exploit's interest in possibility (what is or is not possible in a given digital space) and rhetoric's interest in persuasion and influence.[12] I offer this all too brief detour to set the scene for my own argument about how rhetoric intersects with the exploit and also to deepen software studies' relationship with rhetoric. As we saw in the previous chapter, Bogost's procedural rhetoric plays a part in my own theorizations of rhetoric and software. However, the remainder of this book will demonstrate the broader usefulness of rhetorical theory for the study of software and computation.

Dilip Gaonkar offers the most succinct description of how rhetoricians have wrestled with probability, possibility, and contingency.[13] Gaonkar argues that Aristotle's focus on probability and contingency in his *Rhetoric* was an attempt to rescue rhetoric from Plato's famous critique that it was flawed in "its reliance on appearance, its entanglement with opinion, and its linguistic opportunism."[14] By placing rhetoric in the category of the contingent and thus opposing it to necessity—rhetoric deals not with what *must* be true but rather with what *could* be true—Aristotle opens up space for rhetoric outside of philosophy, and his *Rhetoric* theorizes that space by offering a method for deliberation:

> If human beings can act in more than one way (and if the outcome of their actions is uncertain, capable of unanticipated consequences), then it makes sense to deliberate and choose. Rhetoric is the discursive medium of deliberating and choosing, especially in the public sphere.[15]

For Gaonkar, Aristotle's description of rhetoric in terms of probability is a way to "domesticate" it. Aristotle is not interested in pure contingency but rather in what is *probable* within the space of the contingent. Gaonkar describes this approach aptly, suggesting that Aristotle is not interested in a "Kafkaesque world of sheer uncertainty and terror but rather a world made familiar by Emily Post—of gamesmanship and good manners displayed by those adept at ideological bricolage."[16] Thus, Aristotle finds a safe and stable home for rhetoric in contingency and probability, one that can be systematically theorized.

But the space of probability and contingency might rein things in too much, making rhetoric's purview too neat and tidy. Even if Gaonkar has little interest in expanding or "sizing up" rhetoric, he does suggest that the "unyoking of the contingent from the probable, if rendered explicit and thematized in future studies, might produce new and challenging possibilities in our understanding of rhetoric."[17] One such effort is carried out by Nancy Struever in *Rhetoric, Modality, Modernity*, and while Struever's text never touches upon software or networked life, her unyoking of the contingent from the probable offers us a way to theorize rhetoric alongside the exploit. Struever argues that rhetoric's promise lies not in a focus on probability but rather in its openness to multiple paths of thought. The details of Struever's analysis of Thomas Hobbes, Giambattista Vico, and Walter Benjamin and her concern for the relationship between rhetoric and philosophy are outside the scope of this project, but they are at least worthy of mention here. Struever convincingly argues that Hobbes, Vico, and Benjamin provide valuable resources for thinking through contemporary civic inquiry, but the value of these thinkers is more in their penchant for possibility (and their sometimes unwitting turn to rhetoric) rather than in philosophy's traditional terrain of necessity. In these thinkers, she sees "modal rhetorics" that are more attuned to the problems of modernity (and, we might argue, postmodernity) than is much of the Western philosophical tradition. But most important, for our purposes, is Struever's argument that a rhetorical approach is "non-dismissive":

> There is a deep compatibility between the very specific analytic techniques rhetoric must develop to fulfill the demands of persuasion, the core political functions, and the very general commitment to the modality of possibility as the domain of rhetorical duty. There is a beneficial interactivity of modal proclivity and analytic habits that energises; it is *profoundly non-dismissive.*[18]

For Struever, rhetoric is defined by its mode of possibility, its continuing hospitality to approaches to problems. This is an ethical stance, one that welcomes any attempt as a possible solution, even if it is initially unclear what that attempt will yield. While Gaonkar's account of the Aristotelian tradition shows a persistent link between contingency and probability among theorists of rhetoric, Struever pries these two terms apart, radically expanding rhetoric's possibilities. The focus on possibility means that Struever's rhetorician aims to explore all avenues, follow all pathways, and trace the edges of a given rhetorical space. Rhetorical tactics demonstrate these possibilities, regardless of whether or not they appear logical at first glance. This profound nondismissiveness is also what defines Galloway's notion of the exploit, which sometimes proceeds regardless of a clearly considered ethical program. Just as Galloway and Thacker's exploit seeks out "power differentials already existing in the system," Struever's understanding of rhetoric emphasizes its "remarkable capacity for renewal, for 'modernizing,' the reinvention of its civil strategies in response to novel civil affairs."[19] Struever's focus is on the challenges of modernity writ large as she demonstrates how rhetoric has been renewed from early modernity forward. This project of renewal is all the more necessary as we are faced with novel rhetorical problems in computational environments. The rhetorician of networked, computational environments must be nondismissive, seeking out the exploits that pry open gaps and demonstrate possibilities. It should be noted here that the world of the exploit is not a rosy one, and we'll see examples of this in the analysis below. I'll return to the troubling ethical terrain of the exploit at the end of this chapter.

Struever's insistence that rhetoric is "non-dismissive" suggests that rhetoric and the exploit share a radical openness to possibility. The exploit is rooted in profound nondismissal and is pure possibility. It is not always a rational or well-considered attempt to institute a political or ethical program, and it is many times not even sure of its own direction. It is about exploration. Again, the parallel between rhetoric's nondismissiveness and the exploit is striking. As Galloway and Thacker suggest, the exploit lays the groundwork for political (and, I would add, *rhetorical*) action: "look for traces of exploits, and you will find political practices."[20] While these exploits are not always so obviously pragmatic, they are also not always malicious:

> Contrary to popular opinion, not all computer viruses are destructive (the same can be said in biology, as well). Certainly computer viruses can delete data, but they can also be performative (e.g., demonstrating a security violation), exploratory (e.g., gaining access), or based on disturbance rather than destruction (e.g., rerouting network traffic, clogging network bandwidth).[21]

The exploit is profoundly rhetorical in its search for possibilities and its desire to demonstrate and perform those possibilities. Anyone who has been the victim of "clickjacking" on Facebook is aware of hacks that are more about performance and possibility than about stealing login information. In June 2010, many Facebook users following links that read "Justin Biebers [sic] Phone Number Leaked!" were taken to a page with another link that read "Click here to continue if you are 18 years of age or above." Clicking anywhere on this page "launches an invisible iframe [an HTML element that contains another HTML document] which contains a Facebook like button, thus spreading the link to more and more users."[22] If you fell for the Bieber clickjacking exploit, your friends discovered that you were at least mildly interested in Justin Bieber's address and telephone number. But this embarrassment (which may or may not be mortifying, depending on the victim) is the extent of the damage. In this particular case, the clickjacking "attack" contained no real threat and stole no personal data. This kind of hack is more about doing what is possible than about gaining access to data or resources, and it is here that the intersection between hacking and rhetoric makes the most sense. But even if such hacks are not overtly political and even if they seem to be little more than annoyances, they do, as Galloway and Thacker suggest, point the way to political practices. They also expose ethical predicaments. The exploit, in its search for endless possibilities and in its willingness to accept the welcoming gesture of the hospitable network, is a powerful (even if sometimes troubling) ethical program.

The onMouseover Exploit

In August 2010, Masato Kinugawa noticed a vulnerability that would allow a Twitter user to post JavaScript into a tweet. This security flaw left Twitter open to an XSS worm, "a malicious (or sometimes non-malicious) payload, usually written in JavaScript, that propagates among visitors of a website in the attempt to progressively infect other visitors" (Wikipedia, "XSS Worm"). A user could post lines of JavaScript code as a tweet, which would then execute on any machine used to view that tweet via the Twitter Web page. The flaw was actually rooted in Twitter's decision to allow the "@" symbol in URLs posted in tweets.[23] We can see this by looking at the Twitter text-processing library, the documentation that explains how Twitter's software converts a URL into a clickable link. A website called Stackoverflow.com, a question-and-answer site for programming issues, points us to the problem code:

```
60  # Allow @ in a url, but only in the middle. Catch things like http://
    example.com/@user
61  REGEXEN[:valid_url_path_chars] = /(?:
62  #{REGEXEN[:wikipedia_disambiguation]}|
63  @[^\/]+\/|
64  [\.\,]?#{REGEXEN[:valid_general_url_path_chars]}
65  )/ix
66  # Valid end-of-path chracters (so /foo. does not gobble the period).[24]
```

A post to Stackoverflow.com by a user named Brian McKenna explains the "offending regex": "The @[^\/]+\/ part [line 63 in the code above] allowed any character (except a forward slash) when it was prefixed by an @ sign and suffixed by a forward slash."[25] Regex stands for "regular expression," and it defines how certain strings of characters should be matched to other strings of characters. In this case, the regex is controlling how a URL entered by a user is converted into a clickable link. While investigating the regex, Kinugawa noticed that a URL ending with the character string @" would trick the Twitter parser into thinking that it had received a valid URL and would also allow someone to include JavaScript in a tweet. Another contributor to Stackover-flow.com explains the flaw this way:

> Here's an example of a link one could post in a tweet prior to this flaw be-ing patched:
> **http://**thisisatest.com/@"onMouseover="alert('test xss')"**/**
>
> Twitter's software notices the link and puts it in an href tag:
> <a href="http://thisisatest.com/@"onMouseover="alert('test xss')"rel/"
> target="_blank"="">http://thisisatest.com/@"onMouseover="alert('test xss')"/</a></span> [26]

Twitter's parser sees **http://** and a trailing slash (the "**/**" character at the very end of the tweet) and assumes that this is a valid URL. Because the above regex allows any set of characters in between the @ symbol and the trailing slash (except for a forward slash), **the text between the @ and the / ** is a virtual playground for the JavaScript hacker.

The onMouseover portion of this code is what caused problems for people such as Robert Gibbs and Sarah Brown. When users dragged their mouse over this tweet, any number of events could be triggered: users could be redirected to other web pages, pop-up windows could appear, or the user's own account could be used to "retweet" (Twitter lingo for passing along another user's tweet) links to any website. Many who used this exploit, including Kinugawa, used colored blocks to entice users to mouse over this section of the tweet (see figure 3).

Twitter eventually fixed this problem by changing the regex so that only valid URL characters were allowed. Thus, when quotation marks are included, they are now converted into the character string **"** (the HTML entity for a quotation mark). This conversion prevents quotation marks from acting as they would in JavaScript code, but it doesn't stop the user from entering the quotation marks into a tweet. Nothing stops someone from attempting this same exploit, but that attempt no longer allows the user to create executable JavaScript. One could still enter the same string of text that caused problems previously, but the Twitter parser no longer allows for executable JavaScript code. This is an important example of protocol at work. Rather than stopping users from typing the string of characters that caused the problem (policing the behavior that caused the problem), this change to the regex merely neu-tralized the power of that string of characters, preventing it from executing code (policing the effects of the behavior).

Upon noticing this problem in August, Kinugawa claimed that he noti-

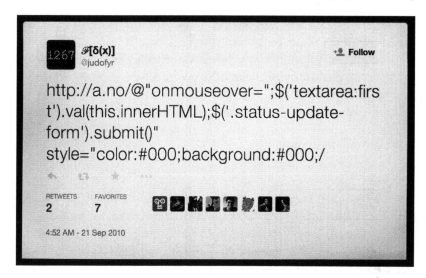

Fig. 3. Example of a tweet using the onMouseover exploit.

fied Twitter, and Twitter claims that it did in fact fix the problem with the re-gex.[27] However, Kinugawa noticed the problem again in September, and this is when he experimented with the exploit. Twitter's blog explains that the flaw was inadvertently reintroduced sometime between August and September: "We discovered and patched this issue last month. However, a recent site update (unrelated to new Twitter) unknowingly resurfaced it."[28] The mention of "new Twitter" is important here, as Twitter's damage control was not only about a technical flaw but also about marketing their newly designed web page. Around the same time the onMouseover exploit caused these problems, Twitter had rolled out a newly designed web interface. This blog post insists that the flaw had nothing to do with that new design, and there is no reason to think otherwise. But more important, Kinugawa's exchanges with Twitter demonstrate the difference between pointing out the problem and exploiting it. Notifying Twitter of the problem did in fact trigger a fix, but that fix was inadvertently undone. Kinugawa, assuming that Twitter had failed to address the problem, chose a different rhetorical tactic, demonstrating the problem by way of the onMouseover exploit. Rather than pointing to the problem (a strategy that seemed to fall short), he used code to demonstrate what could be done when such a flaw was present. Kinugawa's exploit stands as an ethical program that demonstrated what was possible in this computational space. By exposing the problem—and not necessarily solving it—the exploit trig-gered a great deal of public debate. That is, it was rhetorical twice over. It demonstrated the possible means of persuasion in this computational, networked space while also triggering a wide-ranging discussion about web security, cross-site scripting attacks, and third-party applications.

While Stackoverflow.com provided a detailed discussion of how the exploit worked and opened up discussions about the implications of the exploit, news outlets also tried their hand at explaining the incident. Gawker, better known for its snark than its technology reporting, provided a concise explanation of what happened:

> Kinugawa's techniques, now shown in the wild, were rapidly picked up by others. What he'd discovered was that Twitter failed to properly filter tweets for Javascript code. Or rather, it did filter out Javascript, unless your URL contained the "@" symbol, in which case you could trick Twitter into accepting your Javascript in a tweet, and then embedding that Javascript when it displayed your tweet to other users. This sort of attack, known as "cross-site scripting," or "XSS" for short, is a classic and well understood phenomenon that Web developers are routinely badgered to be on guard against.[29]

Reporting like this provided readers with an explanation of the code rather than merely providing a description of the exploit's fallout. This is at least some evidence of a public that is interested not only in being told that a software problem exists but also interested in understanding how that software works.

But the most comprehensive coverage seems to have come from *Guardian* reporter Charles Arthur, who teamed up with software developer Richard Gaywood to provide an explanation of how the hack worked. The *Guardian*'s coverage is worth citing as a way of understanding the onMouseover exploit, but also important is the very fact that this major news publication spent time on an explanation of the actual code. As Noah Wardrip-Fruin argues in *Expressive Processing*, such detailed and accurate journalism is crucial if the public is to gain a meaningful understanding of the cultural, ethical, and expressive implications of computation. In his discussion of Selmer Bringsjord and David Ferrucci's Brutus story-generation system, Wardrip-Fruin notes that press coverage of the system described it as "a story author." Wardrip-Fruin provides a painstaking account of the system's operations, showing us that the stories generated by Brutus are, by and large, not generated by the system's procedures and operations. Instead, the operational logic of Brutus is "that of a child's picture puzzle. Each piece can only fit in one place, in a manner determined by the authors before the system is set running."[30] Thus, Brutus wasn't authoring stories. It was arranging story content that had been authored by

Bringsjord and Ferrucci. But this didn't stop the *New York Times* from suggesting that Brutus could "spit out its story in seconds."[31] Wardrip-Fruin points to such press accounts (and corrects them) in the hopes that software studies can "become pervasive enough that, in the future, those writing for the media will be less easily fooled."[32] The detailed account of the onMouseover exploit published by *The Guardian* offers some hope in this regard.

Gaywood explains the code as "a classic piece of Javascript injection," and he provides much the same explanation as the Stackoverflow.com contributor. He includes an example of a tweet using the XSS code that had caused so much havoc and explains how Twitter's software would handle it. He correctly diagnoses the problem, explaining that the @" text string "broke their parser" and allowed people to embed JavaScript in their tweet. He also explains that Twitter did not follow the knee-jerk reactions of those who suggested blocking users from including the string "onMouseover" in tweets: "Twitter fixed this not by blocking the string onMouseover (which some dim-witted blogs were calling for) but by properly sanitising the input. The "quotation marks in these tweets are now turned into "—the HTML-escaped form."[33] Blocking the text string "onMouseover" is a "dim-witted" response because it does not get at the root of the actual problem—it treats the symptom but not the cause. This would solve the problem of this particular hack, but it does not address the actual gap opened up by the flaw in the Twitter regex. It would enact a short-sighted ethical program, without accounting for the deeper problem exposed by Kinugawa's exploit. By converting quotation marks to their HTML-escaped form, Twitter correctly solves the problem at its root, even if, as Gaywood explains, such a simplistic attack is "rather embarrassing for Twitter." This coverage by *The Guardian* is one of the more detailed accounts of what happened, although blogs and websites such as *Wired*, *PC Magazine*, and *Lifehacker* covered the story as well (I address the coverage of these publications below). This discussion of code in language that most average readers can understand provides some hope that Wardrip-Fruin's concerns are being addressed by certain publications. In fact, readers praised the coverage in the comments section and Arthur answered critiques of the coverage by joining the blog comment conversation.

But this discussion about software—a rhetorical exchange *about* code—is triggered by a rhetorical action *with* code, an exploit that demonstrated its argument instead of explaining it and used computation as a rhetorical medium. In effect, Kinugawa's little bit of code finds a small (and, as many argued, embarrassingly simple to fix) gap in Twitter's architecture and exploits it. It's not clear whether users saw Kinugawa's exploit and copied it, or whether they discovered the flaw in Twitter's regex independently (though, the latter seems unlikely given how quickly the XSS script spread throughout the day). Regardless, the XSS worm took on various forms. While Kinugawa demonstrated how to create colorful blocks of text in a tweet, Magnus Holm extended the exploit so that users would retweet and spread "infected" tweets by mousing over certain parts of the screen.[34] This hack is arguably the one that was most jarring to average users of Twitter (in particular those who had no experience with JavaScript). While the average user may in fact know that mousing over an image will trigger certain kinds of events (for instance, displaying a caption or a pop-up window), the norms of web design have meant that very few users expect the onMouseover event to lead them to a different page or to trigger a retweet from their own account. This is one more instance of the onMouseover exploit gesturing toward the *possible* and alerting users to how software works. The exploit moves beyond norms and generally accepted design principles (moving away from arguments about decorum) in order to perform the possible (moving toward the execution of ethical programs that demonstrate what can or cannot happen in a given space).

Reshaping the Possibility Space

When interviewed, Holm insisted that that he "simply wanted to exploit the hole without doing any 'real' harm."[35] Another user who explored this security flaw was Pearce Delphin, a 17-year-old Australian. As with Holm, Delphin insisted that this was about discovering a vulnerability. In their piece on the exploit, the website Mashable.com included some finger-wagging for Delphin:

> [Delphin] hopes he won't get into trouble, but he very well could—the proper course of action in situations like these is reporting such a vulnerability to Twitter. Exposing a security flaw like he did, even inadvertently, is at the very least an error in judgment.[36]

This tsk-tsk regarding the "the proper course of action" and the accompanying mention of a lapse in judgment points to the difficult ethics of the exploit. Kinugawa claims to have initially followed the "proper course of action," but after seeing that the fix had not been implemented (or that the fix had not remained in place) he chose a different course of action. But to simply blame Delphin, Kinugawa, or Holm for a lapse in judgment is to misunderstand the ethics of the network and the ethical programs that institute our digital spaces. Moralism and recommendations about what *should* have been done by these hackers is not a particularly useful response to this situation. Exploits tell us something about the software, about the network, and about what is possible in this space. Further, one would have to admit that the exploit was more rhetorically effective in ensuring that this particular gap was addressed. *Yack* did not result in a solution. *Hack* did.

But in addition to fixing this particular problem with Twitter's parser, the onMouseover exploit is a useful example of how public discussions about code can help educate programmers and nonprogrammers alike. The exploit opened up a discussion about how Twitter handles URLs and how its parser works. Thankfully, news outlets such as *The Guardian* presented us with an accurate and carefully considered description of the problem. This explanation of code provided the public with a deeper understanding of how this digital space works. Assigning responsibility is difficult when thinking through the ethics of the exploit. Who is responsible? Twitter, for not patching this hole in any thoroughgoing way? Kinugawa, who initially (by his own account) attempted to aid Twitter in patching the flaw? Delphin and Holm, who were exploring the possibilities opened up by Kinugawa? Despite the search for an origin story, the onMouseover exploit forces us to confront difficult questions of responsibility. However, it provides us with no clear answers. Given this predicament, it seems more fruitful to understand the ethical questions being negotiated by way of both code and language than it does to search for a blameworthy subject.

Responsibility in such situations is difficult, and digital spaces are not a free-for-all in which anything goes. But what can happen (the possibility space) in a given networked environment is largely defined by the ethical programs that shape it, and those programs accept the invitation extended by the hospitable network. Oftentimes this means that the possible is continually redefined by the ethics encoded into the software. Who or what can or cannot arrive in a digital space? Who writes the ethical programs of a digital environment? Who writes the code that stands as gatekeeper, simultaneously welcoming and patching up the exploit? When the actions of Holm are characterized as a lapse in judgment, the assumption is that he has breached the ethical code of this space. But the software would suggest otherwise. Twitter is essentially useless without the hacking and exploration of users like Holm. From hashtags (labels that allow users to aggregate similar tweets) to the third-party applications developed to aid victims of natural disasters, Twitter relies upon users and programmers for its very existence. This space invites hackers and developers to explore, but it does so only to a certain point, and this is what the onMouseover exploit truly exposes. The exploration of the possibilities of Twitter—in other words, the rhetorical tinkering of users in this space—reaches its limit when a hack is disruptive. This should not surprise us, and we would never expect Twitter to welcome all exploits, malicious or otherwise. But recognizing these limit cases as ethical programs allows us to carefully consider how the laws of hospitality are continually in conversation with the Law of hospitality.

One might ask: What does an exploit like this one transform? It seems to be little more than a playful attempt to hijack Twitter feeds and startle users. However, this prank became a justification for a profound shift in our software landscape that is already under way. A minor glitch, allowing an @ symbol at the end of a URL, set in motion not only an XSS worm but also a conversation about software. The onMouseover exploit was about exploring the possibilities opened up by that minor glitch, but the response to the exploit and its aftermath led many to argue that third-party applications were preferable to websites. Many publications used the onMouseover exploit as evidence that the third-party applications (or even Twitter's own mobile applications) are more secure than the Twitter.com website. In the aftermath of the onMouseover exploit, *PC Magazine* suggested that users who hadn't already moved to a non-HTML based client should consider doing so:

> One good defense is to use a third-party, non-HTML based Twitter client. Some could be vulnerable, but it's less likely. The solution for Twitter, filtering out JavaScript, should be relatively straightforward and may be applied by the time you read this.[37]

The technology blog *Lifehacker* gave the same diagnosis and advice:

> The exploit has spread to thousands of accounts now—some with hardcore porn pop-ups, other with jokey references to the exploit—so stick with a third-party Twitter client for the time being to read and send your short updates.[38]

But while *PC Magazine* and *Lifehacker* seem to suggest third-party applications as a short-term solution, *Wired* author Tim Carmody went so far as to say that this episode was evidence that the desktop browser was good for only one thing:

> [The mouseover exploit] reinforces my longstanding belief that web browsers' only legitimate use on the desktop is for viewing and watching porn (including, naturally, technology-and-gadget porn, like what you find here at Wired.com–TC); client applications, whether on a personal computer or a mobile device, are ideally suited for consuming and exchanging information.[39]

Along these same lines, Gawker also noted that people shouldn't be accessing tweets via Twitter.com, and that the exploit should be seen as a teaching moment:

One lesson, though, is clear: It's absolutely safer to have people reading tweets through a diverse array of software products than through a single website. Given that Twitter is trying hard to draw people back in to Twitter.com, where it can show them large-format ads featuring images and video, it must regret serving them up such a harsh lesson in the danger of trusting a single company to be the hub for so much information.[40]

Most agreed that the onMouseover exploit was one more reason to shift away from websites and toward third-party apps. This exploit did not *cause* the shift from the web to apps, but it was certainly used by many as justification for sliding away from the world of web pages and toward the world of apps. This conversation about the possibility space of Twitter turned into a conversation about avoiding such problems altogether. Rather than entering a space that extends an invitation to the exploit, a space that is open to these kinds of tinkerings, many recommended that the world of APIs and third-party applications was a more secure and pleasant digital space.

As we will see, the worlds of apps and APIs are not free of exploits. How those exploits are addressed points to the difference between websites and apps. But it is worth pausing to consider what this move toward apps and APIs means when considering the possibility of, to use Annette Vee's term, a procedurate public. This move would mean that a broader swath of people, should they desire to gain a deeper understanding of software, would have to learn the ins and outs of APIs. APIs provide a threshold between software companies and outside software developers—they are the filtering mechanisms that allow companies to provide those outside the company with the resources to extend the value of the company's software. Facebook, Google, Twitter, and a host of other companies have APIs, and these APIs are their primary answer to the predicament of hospitality.

The push to open up software has been answered by the API, but this response to hospitality does not merely throw open the front door. Instead, it stands as an instance of the laws of hospitality, simultaneously inviting and filtering those seeking access to software and data resources. One could easily argue that the API provides programmers with more access to software and code than ever before. The API offers a middle way between proprietary, guarded software and open source software. However, that middle way still carries with it a definitive split between those with programming know-how and those without it. We can examine the possibility space of APIs and apps by comparing the onMouseover exploit, which triggered a broad conversation, to an exploit that resulted in a conversation among a decidedly different group of people.

OAuth: A Different Conversation about Code

As the footprints of social networking sites grow, the importance of web APIs grows as well. APIs allow developers to request data from a service such as Twitter, and applications designed with APIs often make these requests on behalf of software users. These requests are API calls, and they require that the application prove that it has permission to access certain resources. This permission is regulated through the use of certain authentication protocols—rules that the software must follow in order to gain access to information. In August 2010 (around the same time that Kinugawa noticed the flaw in Twitter's URL parser), Twitter instituted a significant change and turned off basic access authentication (Basic Auth). This forced all API calls to use the Open Authorization (OAuth) authentication protocol, meaning that a user's credentials could no longer be sent along with the API request. Under Basic Auth, API requests include the username and password. So, when an application—say a third-party Twitter application—wanted access to a user's resources (their tweets) in order to display them or, in the case of one application, in order to calculate a user's "Tweet Stats," it would have to authenticate with Twitter's servers by including that user's credentials. This protocol was flawed for a number of reasons. It forced users to hand over login information, made the application useless if the user decided to change passwords at a later date, and gave users no way to easily track which applications had access to their credentials. As more and more developers began to design third-party applications (and as more and more malicious applications began to abuse access to user credentials), Twitter realized that it needed a more secure authorization protocol. Twitter was not the only company looking for a solution to this problem. Google, Facebook, and other companies with popular APIs also needed a more secure way for users to allow access to data.

Enter OAuth, which Eran Hammer-Lahav, one of the architects of the protocol and eventually one of its more vocal critics, describes as a "valet key" for the web:

Many luxury cars come with a valet key. It is a special key you give the parking attendant and unlike your regular key, will only allow the car to be driven a short distance while blocking access to the trunk and the onboard cell phone. Regardless of the restrictions the valet key imposes, the idea is very clever. You give someone limited access to your car with a special key, while using another key to unlock everything else.

As the web grows, more and more sites rely on distributed services and cloud computing: a photo lab printing your Flickr photos, a social network using your Google address book to look for friends, or a third-party application utilizing APIs from multiple services.

The problem is, in order for these applications to access user data on other sites, they ask for usernames and passwords. Not only does this require exposing user passwords to someone else—often the same passwords used for online banking and other sites—it also provides these application[s] unlimited access to do as they wish. They can do anything, including changing the passwords and lock users out.

OAuth provides a method for users to grant third-party access to their resources without sharing their passwords. It also provides a way to grant limited access (in scope, duration, etc.).[41]

Whereas Basic Auth asked developers to send user credentials along with an API request, OAuth provides users with the option of approving access to their resources. Further, it allows users to grant access to certain resources while protecting others. This is why the valet key metaphor works so well. Users are no longer required to provide access to all data. Instead, they can provide limited access.

The change from Basic Auth to OAuth is a significant one that adds a layer of complexity to the API call. For instance, under Basic Auth, a user could use his or her own credentials to access any other user's Twitter timeline. This functionality is lost with the move to OAuth. Under Basic Auth, the following command would allow developers to access a Twitter timeline:

```
%curl -u jamesjbrownjr:jimstwitterpassword http://twitter.com/statuses/
    user_timeline.rss
```

Notice that this command sends the username and password along with the request. Typing this command today triggers the following error code:

```
<error code="53">Basic authentication is not supported</error>
```

This is understandable, since sharing actual usernames and passwords is not the most secure way of dealing with user credentials. In the case of a third-party application, it means that the application making the request is "pretending to be the resource owner."[42] If the resource owner (the user who is granting an application access to his or her information) has handed over her credentials, then this transaction is aboveboard.[43] I hand over my credentials, someone/something acts on my behalf, and I do this so that I can gain the functionality of a useful third-party application. But given that my credentials can easily fall into the wrong hands, a more secure protocol would need to find a way for me to grant access to my resources without revealing my username and password. This is what OAuth allows users and developers to do. Rather than providing credentials, the user instructs Twitter to grant access to his or her resources via a token credential:

> Token credentials are used in place of the resource owner's username and password. Instead of having the resource owner [the Twitter user] share its credentials with the client, it authorizes the server [Twitter] to issue a special class of credentials to the client [the third-party application] which represent the access grant given to the client by the resource owner. The client uses the token credentials to access the protected resource without having to know the resource owner's password.[44]

OAuth allows users to grant access to their data without granting access to their credentials.

OAuth is an open protocol. No single entity owns it, and any number of people and companies had a hand in designing it. This means that OAuth is the result of a massive collaboration. However, this does not mean that all parties to that collaboration had an equal voice or an equal stake in determining how the protocol should work. One contentious moment in OAuth's development involved the requirement of "signatures" as a way of ensuring that user credentials were secure. Rather than transmitting a password over a network and relying on that network to employ secure protocols, the use of signatures would mean that a secret (a password) would be "used to calculate a value which cannot be converted back [into] the secret itself."[45] The secret value is never transmitted over the network, protecting users from situations when secure protocols such as Secure Sockets Layer (SSL) have not been implemented. Signatures ensure that secrets are not sent "on the wire," but they require some extra effort on the part of those designing APIs. The difficulty of implementing signatures led large companies to bristle, and signatures were removed in the move from OAuth 1.0 to OAuth 2.0. This meant that the token credentials were still used but that the "secret" behind that token was sent through the network without any encryption. Thus, this solution was not as secure as it could have been.

Hammar-Lahav argued for the use of signatures, suggesting that companies such as Twitter, Google, and Microsoft should create useful libraries for developers and make implementation of signatures easier. This would mean that developers would not have to code things from the ground up each time they needed to implement signatures. Instead, developers could rely on a set of prefabricated functions. However, instead of building such libraries and working through the difficulties of implementing a more secure solution, Google and Microsoft proposed their own protocol called WRAP. Instead of using signatures, WRAP relied on cookie technology for security. In response to this proposal, Hammar-Lahav asked (sarcastically): "Why bother to create something more secure if it makes it harder for developers to use, while not actually improving the overall security of the service[?]"[46] Hammar-Lahav served as the primary editor of the OAuth protocol. So, when WRAP began to siphon off interest in OAuth, he was concerned. While he did not accuse the creators of WRAP of attempting to replace OAuth, he did realize that the creation of WRAP meant that the battle over signatures was all but over: "At the end, due to internal corporate politics and product release schedule, Microsoft and Google decided to ship WRAP implementations and positioned it as a complete solution available as an OAuth replacement."[47] Ultimately, Hammar-Lahav recognized that the move to a signature-less protocol was inevitable, largely because powerful companies were leading the charge: "The bottom line is that the OAuth community who created the original specification doesn't exist anymore. Instead, we have a few individuals who carry enough recognition to make others follow them as if they represent a community."[48]

Eventually, WRAP was deprecated, but not before the functions that the WRAP creators were pushing for had been incorporated into OAuth. Thus, OAuth 2.0 was released without requiring signatures, something that Hammar-Lahav believed was a big mistake. OAuth 2.0 was, for Hammar-Lahav, a step backward. He was not alone. Mozilla software engineer Ben Adida argues that OAuth 2.0 "might actually be worse than passwords." It uses tokens, but those tokens are sent directly over the channel. If the channel is not secure—if, in Adida's words, someone "forgets to turn on SSL"—the token is left in the open for all to see. This means that users are at the mercy of web developers:

> [A]t least you can work to educate users about SSL (and after their Facebook account gets hacked, they might actually care), but it's very hard for users to gauge whether web applications are doing the right thing with respect to SSL certs when the SSL calls are all made by the backend which has trouble surfacing certificate errors.[49]

OAuth puts security in the hands of individual developers, and if those developers make a mistake there is little the user can do (short of not using the application anymore). Adida, like Hammar-Lahav, recognizes that good web security requires effort:

I understand. Security is hard. Getting those timestamps and nonces right, making sure you've got the right HMAC algorithm . . . it's non-trivial, and it slows down development. But those things are there for a reason. The timestamp and nonce prevent replay attacks. The signature prevents repurposing the request for something else entirely. That we would introduce a token-as-password web *security* protocol in 2010 is somewhat mind-boggling.[50]

Doing things the right way would have certainly been more difficult, but the WRAP compromise was an easy fix that compromised security. Despite all of this, Hammar-Lahav recognized that open protocols require compromise, and he still remained a central voice in the project.

The conversation about OAuth happened among software developers, corporations, and anyone else with the know-how and desire to get involved. In theory, anyone could be part of this conversation. In practice, those who are plugged into such issues, who attend conferences on software design and web security (many meetings concerning OAuth happened at conferences), and who wield the most power will determine how this particular ethical program is authored. This means that a piece of software that serves as a key player in determining how users and software navigate the hospitable network was designed and implemented by a small circle of people and companies and that the resulting ethical program answers to the needs and desires of that circle. Regardless of how open the conversation about this protocol was—or, perhaps *because* it was so open—certain voices and interests were able to drive the writing of the protocol. Given the clout of Google and Microsoft and the ease with which WRAP dealt with security, it did not matter that OAuth 1.0 was most likely the more secure solution. Many (including Adida and Hammar-Lahav) agreed that OAuth 1.0 was too complicated and needed to be reworked.

We can see that this conversation was conducted very differently than the conversation surrounding the onMouseover exploit. When Kinugawa's exploit emerged it resulted in a conversation among a fairly broad range of people. The conversation about OAuth was much more limited, and while a close look at how OAuth deals with signatures provides some important insight into how software and protocols are built, a more apt comparison between the world of the web and the world of apps would require looking at how a particular exploit was dealt with by the OAuth community. This is where we turn next.

OAuth Exploit

In April 2009, a security flaw was discovered in OAuth (the exploit did not have anything to do with signatures). Following how the exploit emerged and how it was addressed can help us understand the difference between the ethical programs enacted in the wild and those that emerge in the more cloistered world of software developers and corporations. The world of apps is not closed, and the world of the web is not open. However, the two are very different, and the OAuth exploit triggered a very different set of events compared to the onMouseover exploit.

Twitter had recently rolled out its OAuth authentication service, and it had announced that Basic Auth would soon be disabled. However, when they shut OAuth down in April without any explanation, many complained. Twitter provided no explanation for its decision, something that became understandable once developers (and the press) discovered what was happening behind the scenes. We now know that the shutdown happened because a hacker had discovered an exploit. Scott Loganbill of Webmonkey.com explains the exploit this way:

> Determined to find an exploit, the hacker (who prefers to remain unnamed due to the terms of his employment) targeted OAuth. The hacker found that if he started a request, then directed a victim to initiate the authorization form on his behalf from a bogus trap site, the victim would submit the login form and provide the hacker access to the victim's data.[51]

Like Kinugawa, this unnamed hacker used the exploit to perform (and not merely point out) a flaw in the protocol. Those designing and implementing the protocol now had a significant security problem on their hands.

OAuth's normal flow of events goes like this: a user visits a third-party site, that user approves access to their resources, and he or she is then redirected to an authentication page in order to enter login information. At this point, the third-party receives a token allowing that third party access to the user's resources. What this programmer discovered was that this entire process could be stopped in the middle, that the third party could take note of the token information and then direct users to a "trap site" on which the user would grant access to his or her account. A hacker taking advantage of this exploit never actually has access to the user's credentials, but that hacker now has access to the user's resources (pictures, Tweets, and so forth). This is called a "Session Fixation" attack, and Marshall Kirkpatrick of *Read Write Web* explains it succinctly: "The problem arose if an attacker could convince you to complete their request for account permission with your login. At the end of the process they would have access to your account."[52] The exploit takes advantage of the ability to pause the flow of information and credentials midstream.

As Loganbill explains, this exploit was discovered early on, and most stakeholders were present at a conference called Foo Camp when the exploit emerged:

The good news is the exploit was found before it was used on any other use case than Twitter. The bad news is that once the exploit was discovered, OAuth experts realized other OAuth partners weren't safe either. Because around 75% of OAuth adopters were gathered at Foo Camp by luck, the primary shareholders all agreed on a course of action to take to minimize damage.[53]

That course of action involved Twitter shutting off its OAuth service without explanation, since it was Twitter's implementation that had been hacked. This is why Twitter had to deal with a great deal of outcry and also why it could not explain the decision to shut down its OAuth authentication system. Hammar-Lahav explains that many of the other companies using OAuth (including Netflix, Google, Yahoo, and a host of other small companies) sent e-mails to Twitter "thanking them for taking that hit."[54] Hammar-Lahav also convinced all 30 companies involved to keep quiet for one week, and he organized an e-mail list for this group as everyone set to work to fix the problem.

Keeping the secret was difficult, and CNET actually got wind of the story early on. However, as Kirkpatrick reports, they chose not to publish the information they had "in the interest of online safety."[55] The reporter choosing not to release this information was at the Foo Camp conference along with a large number of OAuth adopters, and she may have received word of the exploit there. However, CNET did eventually force the hand of Twitter and the OAuth group. Twitter posted an announcement on its blog, acknowledging that they were attempting to fix a security gap in OAuth. The OAuth blog did the same, and it also publicly thanked Twitter for "helping to minimize premature publicity of this threat."[56] Soon after, the problem was fixed. The group developed a solution on the very last day of their one-week, self-imposed gag order. To fix the problem, the OAuth protocol was rewritten to ensure that "the redirection URI used to obtain the authorization code, is the same as the redirection URI provided when exchanging authorization code for an access token."[57] With this solution implemented, hackers could no longer stop the process in the middle, lead users to a trap site, and then make use of the token.

The emergence of this exploit and the response to it were very different from the case of the onMouseover exploit. Hammar-Lahav explains that this exploit was something that the OAuth community had missed: "This has been a solution that has been reviewed for a year and a half now, and it has been reviewed by most well-known security experts and they just missed it. Nobody ever thought of this particular security exploit."[58] As I have already argued, this is entirely unavoidable when it comes to developing software, and it is the reason I have chosen to discuss these issues in terms of hospitality. Any software or protocol must somehow deal with the predicament of hospitality, with the arrival of others. Even the best web security software in the world will have to deal with exploits, but the events leading up to the patching of this security gap are striking. Consider that many of the stakeholders were present at the same conference, allowing them to meet and discuss a solution face-to-face. Also consider that the technology press and corporations were able to control when information about the exploit leaked. Whereas the onMouseover exploit was released into the wild and dealt with on the web, the OAuth exploit was addressed before it could wreak havoc on the network. The conversation that happened in the wake of the OAuth exploit's discovery happened among a relatively tight circle of developers, companies, and security experts. Those experts implemented a solution, and the more public discussion about the exploit happened after that solution was in place.

In the case of the OAuth exploit, the conversation happened behind closed doors in order to protect the reputations and profit margins of companies. This mirrored the discussion that led to the writing of the OAuth protocol, and as we have seen when examining the controversy over signatures, that discussion was not always driven by what would make user credentials the most secure. The decision to do away with signatures in OAuth 2.0 was seen by many as a mistake, but it was a decision driven by the companies that were going to dictate whether OAuth would become a useful protocol. The only way a protocol like OAuth sees the light of day is if it is adopted by the likes of Google, Twitter, and Microsoft. This complex web of interests and programmers means that conversations about code and security take strange turns and happen outside of public view. This same type of conversation happened when the OAuth exploit emerged. The way in which this community dealt with the exploit was entirely different from the conversation about code and protocols that emerged after Kinugawa initiated his "RainbowTwtr" account and began exposing a flaw in Twitter's parser. The OAuth exploit was (potentially) much more harmful than the onMouseover exploit, but this does not change the fact that the two emerged (and were addressed) in very different ways. Understanding these conversations, how and why they happened, and the decisions made are crucial to understanding the possibility space regulated and instituted by software and protocols.

Difficult Ethics

In her meditation on Galloway and Thacker's exploit, Cynthia Haynes reminds us that "there is a thin line between *exploit* and *exploitation*."[59] Haynes focuses her attention on the deployment of IBM technology to sort people, paying special attention to a World War II era punch card's "Hole 8," which was punched to designate that a Nazi prisoner was Jewish. This use of computation must be seen alongside contemporary attempts to sort by way of metadata: "sorting machines became the search engines ranking and optimizing the fate of millions of Jews."[60] Hole 8 was an exploit, forcing us to carefully consider our consideration of the exploit as an ethical program. Haynes suggests that any theorization of the exploit must come to terms with the fact that "you cannot penetrate a system without your own version of malicious code."[61] Put in the terms laid out in this book, there is no ethical program that does not fall short of the Law of hospitality, smuggling in its own ethical problems. This is unavoidable, and a close analysis of any exploit makes this clear. This is why an ethics and rhetoric of the exploit is difficult, but this is also an entirely unavoidable problem.

The two exploits examined in this chapter demonstrate these difficulties, calling into question who is responsible and what the "correct" course of action is when one is confronted with a gap in the computational infrastructure. "Projecting change" through that gap, the strategy that Galloway and Thacker describe, will lead in multiple directions at once. It is difficult to plan for what follows the exploit, which provides yet another reason to question arguments that computation necessarily forecloses decision or operates "mechanically." Recall from the introduction that Levinas is guarding against the "simple subsumption of cases under a general rule, of which a computer is capable."[62] The fear is that computation cuts off the possibility of an authentic future (one that has not been programmed), an idea I return to in the conclusion of this book. But while that fear might be founded when any ethical program goes unquestioned, the examples traced out in this chapter demonstrate that any ethical program presents a complex ethical problem. We often end up with more questions than answers.

This is especially visible in the conversation that emerged after the onMouseover exploit. In the push to avoid malicious exploits like Kinugawa's, users were encouraged to move away from Twitter's web interface and toward third-party applications. Such recommendations help to initiate a significant shift in how the possibilities of digital spaces are determined and explored. Exploits provide a "teaching moment," but that moment could easily be smoothed over in an attempt to plug the hole and move on. How might we use such situations differently? What would change if we thought of such exploits as moments when the public can be educated about the spaces in which they interact? What happens to the possibilities of exploring the boundaries, limits, and possibilities of software when exploits are addressed behind closed doors? In an environment that moves away from the web and toward apps, we can still have conversations about code among programmers and nonprogrammers alike, and the move to APIs arguably allows for spaces that are more hackable. But that hackability is clearly defined by companies such as Twitter, Google, Microsoft, and Facebook that determine what will be available. This is exactly what I have in mind when I argue that ethical programs have to engage with the difficult questions of hospitality. APIs are an answer to the arrival of the exploit, which pushes possibility to its limit. The exploit will often explore such possibilities regardless of utility or rationality. Assuming we are willing to expand the received notion of rhetoric as the art of the probable and to move rhetoric closer to the realm of the possible, the exploit finds a home in rhetorical theory. The exploit, as ethical program, demonstrates what is possible.

There will always have to be filters for the possibilities opened up by exploits, as the Twitter response to the onMouseover exploit shows. However, the move to APIs actually provides a much higher level of control to the likes of Facebook and Twitter (and Google) under the guise of freedom. Nonetheless, the move to APIs and apps also affords us an opportunity. While we may be moving to a world in which we have fewer opportunities to click "view source," we can still gain some insight into the infrastructures of digital spaces. The API will filter that insight and will only allow us access to certain ways of manipulating the resources and databases of companies like Twitter. But understanding the API, protocols, and third-party applications as responses to the predicament of hospitality shows us that digital spaces constantly engage the difficulties and promises of hospitable networks. Understanding how such APIs work will require a procedurate public that takes advantage of the opportunity to understand and tinker with all of the possible means of persuasion. The task is not necessarily to ensure that everyone knows how to exploit, hack, transform, or reshape digital spaces. My argument is not that everyone should be a master programmer or that everyone should have complete access to code, though I do believe that more people learning to write code would be a good thing. Rather, what's most important is that we work to understand how the possibilities of our digital spaces are determined and how (or whether) they can be rewritten or reenvisioned.

Who is at the table when software and protocols are written? Who is present when an exploit is discovered and patched? How does that conversation affect users and developers alike? These are the questions we land on when we consider code and software to be part of the rhetorical situation. The possibilities of a given networked environment are shaped by code and by discussions about code. What we have seen in this chapter is that exploits are rhetorical in two senses: they demonstrate what's possible in a given space and they trigger discussion about how those spaces should operate. If the exploit is about the possible, then it is rich with ethical and rhetorical questions: What is possible? What should be possible? How do we write, code, and interact in digital spaces? Such questions can and should be addressed by scholars from multiple disciplines and by a procedurate public.

PART 2

Hospitable Databases

FOUR

Database Integrity: *Ethos* and the Archive

The July 31, 2006, issue of *The New Yorker* featured an article by Stacy Schiff on Wikipedia. As part of the piece, Schiff interviewed a Wikipedia bureaucrat named "Essjay."[1] Essjay was this Wikipedian's username. Like many others he chose to use a pseudonym, and he chose this particular pseudonym because it reflected his specialization in theology (the abbreviation S.J. after a name indicates that one is a Jesuit priest). In Essjay's case, he claimed he used this name because "he routinely received death threats." Schiff's story details Essjay's online and offline credentials:

> One regular on the site is a user known as Essjay, who holds a Ph.D. in theology and a degree in canon law and has written or contributed to six-teen thousand entries. A tenured professor of religion at a private univer-sity, Essjay made his first edit in February, 2005. Initially, he contributed to articles in his field—on the penitential rite, transubstantiation, the papal tiara. Soon he was spending fourteen hours a day on the site, though he was careful to keep his online life a secret from his colleagues and friends. (To his knowledge, he has never met another Wikipedian, and he will not be attending Wikimania, the second international gathering of the ency-clopedia's contributors, which will take place in early August in Boston.)[2]

Schiff also noted that Essjay was a member of the Wikipedia mediation com-mittee and had the ability to trace user IP addresses (something reserved for only certain Wikipedians). By all accounts, Essjay was a model Wikipedian who had been acknowledged by others within the community for his work. His Wikipedia user page showed several Barnstars—awards that Wikipedians give to one another for diligent work.

Regardless of Essjay's hard work on Wikipedia articles, his credentials turned out to be fraudulent. Nearly five months after the piece in *The New Yorker* was published, Daniel Brandt—an outspoken critic of Wikipedia and founder of the watchdog site Wikipedia-watch.org—told *The New Yorker* that Essjay was actually Ryan Jordan. Jordan was not, in fact, a professor. Brandt knew this because Jordan had recently been hired by Wikia (a for-profit company started by Wikipedia cofounder Jimmy Wales) and had posted an online profile stating that he was Essjay and that he was 24 years old. The profile made no mention of graduate degrees. Jordan's ability to maintain this constructed identity while rising to an influential position within the Wikipedia community stems from one of the central tenets of the Wikipedia constitution—anonymity. Users are allowed to remain "anonymous." I use scare quotes because Jordan was not really anonymous. Rather, he created another identity that would help him navigate Wikipedia. Thus, these edits were not written anonymously— they were written by Essjay. Further, even those Wikipedians who do not register for a username can still be traced to an IP address (an IP address is included next to each edit on Wikipedia).

In many ways, anonymity on Wikipedia (or on the web in general) is a fiction. Some identity or IP address is linked to each edit, meaning that every click or inscription leaves some piece of evidence linking writing to a writer, even if that information is sometimes difficult to link to a specific person. Still, critics of Wikipedia complain that anyone can anonymously edit Wikipedia, and what these critics mean is that Wikipedians cannot always be linked to "real life" (RL) identities. That is, Wikipedian identities are virtual identities built for a virtual reality (VR). Many critiques of Wikipedia are based on the assumption that RL identities afford more credibility than VR identities. As we will see, this controversy about anonymity can also be framed in terms of *ethos*—in terms of the credibility that one constructs in the course of writing and arguing and the credibility that is attached to credentials. Regardless of its problems, I will retain the word "anonymity" at points in this chapter since it is a term that grounds so many critiques of Wikipedia. When I use this term, I am using it in the sense that critics use it. For these critics, even those who construct a VR identity are anonymous because that identity does not necessarily line up with an RL identity.

In a space where VR identity is only loosely connected to RL identity, *ethos* becomes an increasingly important rhetorical resource. In *The Laws of Cool*, Alan Liu reminds us that *ethos* is the "inchoate coming-to-be or basis of identity; it is identity at the point of emergence from collective, undifferentiated doxa."[3] While Liu's discussion of *ethos* would seem to address a different situation than I do in this chapter, his theorization of "an *ethos* of the unknown" is helpful as we consider how *ethos* is wielded as an ethical program in hospitable databases. Liu is concerned with how a corporate culture of "teamwork" in late capitalism erases the identity of the worker, removing the solidarity of traditional class identity and replacing it with an ahistorical, "multicultural" worker. The "team" of information workers, skateboarding through rows of cubicles, "deleted the entire apparatus of classification earned through class struggle by flattening everyone to the status of all-purpose, anonymous worker in an ant hive."[4] Given this situation, Liu seeks out a new way of understanding identity and collective action, but he asks: Is this project possible "without being nostalgic for foreclosed group and class identities in a manner that would inauthentically mime the great fundamentalist, nationalist, and ethnic reactionisms of people of the world *excluded* from 'knowledge?'"[5] For Liu, an *"ethos* of the unknown" might (this "might" is crucial—Liu admits that he is more elegiac than optimistic) offer a way to subvert corporate culture from within, offering the information worker not a stable identity but instead a reconsideration of solidarity in terms of finitude rather than essence. He points to the work of Jean-Luc Nancy to explain this unknown *ethos*: "'We' are no more than this transient moment when we have nothing more in common—as Jean-Luc Nancy might say in his *Inoperative Community*—than our finitude, our extinction, our 'death.'"[6] Liu cites Nancy's theorization of community as finitude rather than essence in an attempt to combat corporate culture without returning to an essential identity.

Interestingly, the postindustrial rhetoric of "teamwork" and the erasure of class identity finds expression in Wikipedia as well, from its discussion as a free and open enterprise (its slogan is "the free encyclopedia that anyone can edit") to its official roles for writers (bureaucrats, editors, stewards, and so on). The patterns Liu identifies in management literature and "the new corporatism" appear in the world of Wikipedia and its software platform, MediaWiki, offering support for his argument that finding a place for the arts and the literary in contemporary culture means recognizing that "the academy can no longer claim supreme jurisdiction over knowledge" and that we require a full engagement with "business as an intellectual and practical partner in knowledge work."[7] This blurring of the worlds of business and knowledge production and the location of the "knowledge worker" both inside and outside of corporate structures is a result of networked hospitality, which makes situating knowledge work in any single location nearly impossible. Rather than separating business from academic work, we can instead seek out ethical programs that determine how writing can or should happen in networked spaces that cannot escape these ideologies and structures. In fact, such ideologies end up coded into the very computational infrastructures that shape knowledge work. If education is a "decentralized field where no one institution individually corners the market and where we encounter a dizzying dispersion of the kinds and scales of learning," then examining how *ethos* and identity operate in textual spaces like Wikipedia and computational infrastructures like MediaWiki becomes critical for understanding the complexities of networked life in multiple, intersecting spaces.

Like Liu's "knowledge worker" who is attempting to work within a culture of information that erases stable identities, Essjay's *ethos* sits in the uncomfortable space of the "*ethos* of the unknown," and this is because it is a product both of his claims to certain credentials and his attempt to construct *ethos* in arguments about Wikipedia articles. But while Liu's method involves the cultural critique of business and management literature, I am turning my eyes to the computational infrastructures that enable or constrain the *ethos* of the unknown. My aim is to track how the *ethos* of MediaWiki (*ethos* as a dwelling that shapes and constrains rhetorical action) links up with the *ethos* of Wikipedians (*ethos* as the "coming-to-be of identity"). This requires a textured understanding of *ethos*, one that accounts both for how writers cultivate an *ethos* and how *ethos* is attached to writers over and beyond their own intentions. When Aristotle's *Rhetoric* presents *ethos* along with *pathos* and *logos* as rhetoric's proofs, he also divides these proofs into two different types: artistic and inartistic. Artistic proofs are constructed by the rhetor; inartistic proofs are not. Thus, *ethos* can operate both artistically and inartistically. If a rhetor's credibility is established by reputation, it is inartistic. This is often referred to as *situated ethos*, and it is a type of credibility that is not necessarily created by the rhetor. A rhetor that uses certain kinds of claims and appeals to build credibility is using an artistic proof; she or he is using an *invented ethos*. Essjay's case is interesting because he invented a situated *ethos*, something we'll return to later in this chapter.

As I discussed in chapter 1, this understanding of *ethos* as a rhetorical strategy is always tied to the notion of *ethos* as dwelling place, as an ethical space constructed, maintained, and experienced by rhetor, audience, and community. This second notion of *ethos* is often at work when we consider Wikipedia as rhetorical dwelling, and the idea that this dwelling place's ethical programs are always being reconfigured became a major concern when Wikipedia began testing its "flagged revisions" policy. This policy was first tested in early 2009 and was an attempt to have administrators edit and approve the contributions of less-established editors. Noam Cohen of *The New York Times* was one of many who suggested that this ethical program would "mark a significant change in the anything-goes, anyone-can-edit-at-any-time *ethos* of Wikipedia, which in eight years of existence has become one of the top 10 sites on the Web and the de facto information source for the Internet-using public."[8] Here, Cohen is specifically invoking the use of *ethos* as dwelling, as a way of describing a space rather than the characteristics of a rhetor. What this chapter will articulate is how these two notions of *ethos*—*ethos* as dwelling and *ethos* as rhetorical tactic—are related and how software plays a crucial role in mediating the two.

In fact, what's most important for our purposes is that "flagged revisions" was more than just a policy shift—it was a MediaWiki extension. Extensions are software modules used to customize MediaWiki software. While this chapter focuses on a different aspect of the MediaWiki software—its deep textual archive—it is worth pausing here to understand how software played a role in the "flagged revisions" policy shift. The discussions surrounding "flagged revisions" as well as the MediaWiki Extension itself offer a key example of how ethical programs can sit at two levels simultaneously, the level of discourse and the level of computational procedure. Popular discussion of "flagged revisions" focused on how this policy shift would change the dwelling of Wikipedia, and here the concern is with the ethical program being enacted by the policies that determine how Wikipedia's editing process is carried out. However, that same popular discussion was less focused on the computational artifact called FlaggedRevs, which actually changed the MediaWiki infrastructure in a number of versions of Wikipedia. This extension was installed in the English version of Wikipedia in December 2012, while most other versions enabled the extension between 2008 and 2010. A deeper consideration of the ethical program enacted by way of computational procedure might have examined the way the extension handles the flow of articles through the editorial process or the default tags coded into the extension, which allow editors to describe the quality of a particular edit. The default values for these tags—accuracy, depth, and tone—are reconfigurable, and any administrator of a MediaWiki installation can determine whether or how these tags are used. However, the defaults make arguments about what constitutes a valid and useful edit. Further, the extension allows site administrators to make a number of choices about configuration. One configuration of note is the setting of parameters—number of edits, whether certain benchmarks are reached, time between edits—that determine when a user is automatically promoted to "editor status."[9]

Wikipedia's consideration of flagged revisions was seen as a tectonic shift that would forever alter its *ethos*, and a closer look at the software that accompanied this shift demonstrates that these tectonics involve the enacting of ethical programs at multiple levels. This more architectural notion of *ethos* provides a useful point of intersection between rhetorical studies and software studies, and it also serves as a starting point for this chapter's discussion of how Wikipedia's software platform, MediaWiki, creates a certain kind of dwelling that sets the stage for rhetorical claims about credibility. These two notions of *ethos* allow us to account for how software plays a part in shaping the dwellings in which digital rhetors write, argue, and communicate. Further, a broad understanding of *ethos* provides one more framework for understanding the laws of hospitality that are built in response to the demands of the Law of hospitality. Recent work in software studies has insisted on the expressive potential of software, and this chapter extends that work by examining rhetorical activity at two levels: (1) The code and structure of MediaWiki and Wikipedia, which establishes a networked dwelling, and (2) the wiki writers who dwell in (and therefore reshape) the space provided by that structure.

While this discussion of MediaWiki is part of my attempt to describe how ethical programs shape, constrain, and enable rhetorical activity, it should also be read as a corrective to attempts to dismiss Wikipedia as "unethical." Those who believe that Wikipedia does not allow for a responsible tracing of textual origins (and thus does not credit a responsible party) are assuming that the tracing of texts to the proper RL identity is a relatively unproblematic (and a more ethical) way of grounding a text. This is the claim of Larry Sanger, a cofounder of Wikipedia. Sanger's competing encyclopedia project—Citizendium—is an open-content encyclopedia that requires writers to provide their RL identities. In an essay entitled "The New Politics of Knowledge," Sanger argues that communities like Wikipedia wield a great deal of power as their articles shape Google searches and help to define people and places, and Sanger believes that such sites must consider the far-reaching ramifications of their policies. As Wikipedia monopolizes more prime real estate atop Google search results, Sanger argues, its community needs to recognize that its internal governance has immense external ramifications. Pointing to situations where governments have regulated online environments—such as the U.S. government intervening to make sure that MySpace is not a haven for sexual predators—Sanger worries that governments might eventually see fit to intervene in projects like Wikipedia:

> I think cyber-polities can generally regulate themselves. But communities with poor internal governance may well incur some necessary correction by governments, if they violate copyright on a massive scale or if they permit, irresponsibly, a pattern of libel. Why should this be disturbing to me? Government intervention is perhaps all right when we are talking about child molesters on MySpace; but when we are talking about projects to sum up what is known, that is when more serious issues of free speech enter in.[10]

Sanger's essay points to Citizendium as a potential answer to the shortcomings of Wikipedia. By seeking out experts and by requiring contributors to prove their RL identities, Sanger hopes to avoid the pitfalls of Wikipedia's less stringent policies. He also believes that digital communities should do all they can to avoid government intervention.

Though some might argue that Sanger's discussion of government intervention offers an unrealistic doomsday scenario, his larger point is well taken.

Cyberpolities such as Wikipedia wield a great deal of power, and this means that such communities will need to consider the far-reaching consequences of their structure. But a true engagement with such issues will have to account for (and not merely dismiss) the ethical programs that lie beneath such cyberpolities. According to Andrew Orlowski, writer for *The Register* and vocal Wikipedia critic, Wikipedia will never be able to adequately address its ethical problems because "failure is genetically programmed into its mechanisms."[11] This assertion that Wikipedia is programmed to fail makes a number of ethical assumptions, and we could quibble (or agree) with these assumptions. For one, we might suggest that failure might not be the worst kind of ethical program and that it allows for discussion and revision. But my task here is not to argue whether or not Wikipedia offers an ethical approach to the creation of knowledge. Instead, I aim to understand MediaWiki as an ethical program that engages with the difficulties of databases that are hospitable to writers and information and to examine how Wikipedians operate in this digital dwelling.

This chapter will examine what kind of dwelling MediaWiki creates for writers in order to address the following question: How do our rhetorical dwellings ground our rhetorical exchanges, and how do they face up to the challenges of the Law of hospitality? First, I discuss how MediaWiki software deals with user accounts and permissions. By examining the software's assumptions with regard to users, we can begin to see the kind of dwelling this software establishes. Next, I return to the story of Essjay in order to understand how MediaWiki software influences the rhetorical practices of Wikipedians. The Essjay incident was covered by media outlets and serves as one among many Wikipedia scandals. But this chapter examines Essjay with an eye toward the MediaWiki software and its ramifications for the *ethos* and identity of digital writers. Finally, the chapter examines Citizendium and its policies with regard to RL identity. Though Citizendium and Wikipedia have very different sets of rules, particularly with regard to RL and VR identity, they both make use of MediaWiki software. In comparing these two projects, we can begin to see how computational ethical programs affect rhetorical activities in different ways and how the affordances and constraints of software leave a mark on those activities. The *ethos* of Wikipedia is influenced by its rules, regulations, and assumptions about identity and authority, but it is also shaped and constrained by MediaWiki's ethical programs.

MediaWiki: The Username and the Archive

Like any piece of software, MediaWiki has its quirks. One of these quirks seems innocuous enough—MediaWiki has idiosyncratic capitalization rules.

In fact, even explaining these rules (let alone navigating them in a MediaWiki installation) can make your head spin. As Daniel Barrett explains in his *MediaWiki (Wikipedia and Beyond)*, MediaWiki's capitalization rules cause confusion when it comes to article titles. Consider an article entitled "Hello World." MediaWiki software treats "hello world" the same as "Hello world." That is, both of these phrases would link to the same article. But the article entitled "Hello World" (both "H" and "W" capitalized) links to an entirely different article.[12] This problem can be fixed with a "disambiguation page" that serves as a place to sort out similarly named articles. Most visitors to Wikipedia are familiar with this concept. For instance, Wikipedia's disambiguation page for "Interpol" provides links to, among other things, articles for an indie rock band, a video game, and International Criminal Police Organization. A "Hello World" disambiguation page could link together the three titles mentioned above regardless of their capitalization. Barrett argues that these capitalization rules are in place for aesthetic reasons: "MediaWiki displays a title with its first letter capitalized because it looks nicer than using all lowercase."[13] This aesthetic choice makes for confusion, but it also stands as an ethical choice, one that has farther-reaching ramifications than the look of article titles.

These capitalization rules present challenges when it comes to usernames. Because of these rules, usernames must begin with a capital letter. Brion Vibber, chief technology officer of the Wikimedia Foundation, which hosts Wikipedia, explains that these capitalization rules extend to usernames because usernames are "a subset of page titles, and must follow the rules for page titles."[14] Because usernames are incorporated into certain page titles—each user has a "user page" that is automatically generated when they set up an account—these usernames are subject to the same capitalization rules as articles. This reveals one of MediaWiki's assumptions with regard to user identity and permissions. As far as MediaWiki software is concerned, usernames are part of a larger grouping called "page titles." In many ways, the MediaWiki database sees little difference between the article for "Rafting" and my Wikipedia username (Jamesjbrownjr). Both are lines in the relational database structure, and both are subject to the same capitalization rules (if I manually enter the URL to either of these entities with a lower-case letter, MediaWiki will automatically capitalize it). The capitalization rule's effect on usernames would seem to be minimal. Who, after all, really cares if their username is capitalized? But it has proven to be enough of an annoyance that a MediaWiki developer named "GhostInTheMachine" designed a solution that he says "is not *nice* enough to be called an extension" (he calls it a "hack").[15] This hack is incomplete, and this is most likely because "GhostInTheMachine" and other programmers extending the MediaWiki platform are up against the difficulties of MediaWiki's database. As much as some MediaWiki users and developers would prefer to have more control with regard to usernames, changes to these capitalization rules prove to be more trouble than they're worth.

This capitalization quirk shows us that usernames are one piece of data among many in a MediaWiki database, and it reveals some of the assumptions of the *ethos* (dwelling) established by MediaWiki. Everything is data in a MediaWiki installation, making for an interesting ethical program: all of that data is worth archiving. MediaWiki's database structure is not flat—there are important hierarchies built into the database structure. And in certain ways articles and users are treated differently. The most obvious difference would be that articles cannot "edit" other articles. However, the existence of "bots" in Wikipedia—computer programs designed to automatically edit articles— would indicate that while articles might not be editing one another, the line between human users and other database entities is at least somewhat unclear. At bottom, MediaWiki is an interface to a database, and each piece of data plays an important role in building a deep and wide textual archive. That archive is visible to any user of MediaWiki who clicks on the "history" link of an article, but it is also present in the logs that MediaWiki administrators can track. These logs keep track of things such as deleted articles, renamed articles, or users who have been blocked. Usernames become a part of these logs the instant a user begins to write in the wiki. In the dwelling of MediaWiki, usernames are data points.[16]

Like the iterations of a Wikipedia article, a username is logged, tracked, and archived. The username is an important piece of data for a MediaWiki user trying to parse an article or an edit—it is a triangulation point for users and writers trying to determine the motives behind a particular piece of writing. MediaWiki's database structure means that users are inserted into the database from the first moment that they edit an article, and this means that it's very difficult to remove a user from that database. As MediaWiki programmer Rob Church explains, removing a user from the database is not impossible, but it is typically not worth the effort:

> If the user has made edits, then removing rows from the user table cause [sic] theoretical loss of referential integrity. Now, to be honest with you, I can't think of any conditions where this would cause an actual problem; "undefined behaviour" is the phrase we use. What I'd suggest doing, to be on the safe side, is running a couple of quick updates against the database:

```
UPDATE revision SET rev_user = 0 WHERE rev_user = <current_user_id>
UPDATE archive SET ar_user = 0 WHERE ar_user = <current_user_id>
```

What this will do is cause MediaWiki to treat the revisions as having been made anonymously when generating things like page histories, which should eliminate any problems caused by these routines attempting to check user details from other tables. If the user has caused log entries, i.e. rows in the logging table, or uploaded images, then the situation becomes trickier, as you'll have to start mopping up all the rows everywhere and it could become a bit of a mess, so if the user's done anything other than edit, I would strongly recommend just blocking them indefinitely. If the username is offensive or undesirable, then you could consider renaming it using the RenameUser extension.[17]

In order to avoid "undefined behaviour," MediaWiki developers suggest that users be blocked instead of deleted. More than this, the software itself suggests this course of action through its very structure. A malicious user may have trashed your wiki, but that user is also a data point. That data point will most likely have insinuated itself into various places in the database. Deleting that data point may or may not corrupt the database, but MediaWiki is designed so that administrators can avoid this decision altogether. In a kind of "passive-aggressive" administrative move, MediaWiki administrators are encouraged to respond to the Law of hospitality by blocking "trolls" rather than deleting them. This avoids any interruption of the database, and it provides MediaWiki with one way of addressing the arrival of the other.

As Church explains, programmers have also designed a "RenameUser" extension to MediaWiki. The RenameUser extension follows the same archive logic—rather than deleting an offensive username, a MediaWiki bureaucrat can just rename the account. Another extension called "Merge and Delete" allows a bureaucrat to merge two different user accounts. However, a closer look at the "talk page" for this MediaWiki extension (a space where users can get help or ask for additional features) reveals how difficult it is to merge two accounts. Users explain that this extension "leaves residues of the removed users in the database in places like searchindex [sic] and recentchanges [sic] (among many others)."[18] The author of the extension, Tim Laqua, responds to this concern by saying that he'll "take a look" at the problem but that "the true intent of the extension is to allow removal of users while maintaining the referential ingegrity [sic] of the database."[19] Again, the archive is to be kept intact—this is a foundational assumption of MediaWiki's ethical program. MediaWiki's *ethos*—the dwelling that it creates for wiki writers—is defined by this archiving impulse. This logic means that usernames are, first and foremost, data, and it means that this dwelling forces rhetors to carefully consider how they write and interact in an archive that attempts to remember all.

In the most famous MediaWiki installation in the world, this logic plays out in interesting ways. Wikipedians spend a great deal of time maintaining their wiki-credibility, and this often means attempting to merge accounts or asking that their username be changed. But Wikipedia policy pages continually remind contributors that certain data about their contributions can never be altered or removed from the database. Even username changes are listed in a "user rename log."[20] With a little bit of sleuthing, anyone can connect the dots between an old and new username, and exerting any final control over one's wiki *ethos* by changing a username or disappearing from Wikipedia is nearly impossible. Why is it so hard to control your username? Why is MediaWiki so inflexible? Because the software tracks as much as possible, and deleting a user corrupts the archive. The archiving of content on MediaWiki is paramount, and it begins from the moment the software is installed. Every action is logged, every edit is tied to a user (via a username or IP address).

MediaWiki lays the groundwork for an extensive archive, and this gives usernames a kind of permanence, providing readers and writers with an archive from which to gather information about the credibility of a wiki writer. As we have seen, there are some workarounds for this predicament, but they often mean headaches for both wiki administrators and wiki writers. Managing one's *ethos* in such a situation becomes both extremely difficult and of the utmost importance. If all of my actions in a MediaWiki installation are attached to a username that is a permanent fixture in the database, then my *ethos* is my most important rhetorical asset as a wiki writer. In a space like Wikipedia, this means that the maintenance and management of one's *ethos* is crucial, and this is directly linked to MediaWiki software and its approach to the predicament of hospitality. A user's ethical programs—her attempts to manage how others interact with her or to determine the credibility of other writers—are tied directly to the ethical programs of MediaWiki, which establish and maintain a hospitable database.

Essjay's *Ethos*

Ethos management is of great import to the Wikipedian due to the encyclopedia's hospitable archive. As we think through how Wikipedians maintain credibility, we can make use of the distinction between a rhetor's situated and invented *ethos*. One's situated *ethos* precedes his or her argument. It is tied to a reputation that has been built up over time, and it has to do with the ethical or moral attributes assigned to particular human bodies. So, along with the reputation that a rhetor builds within a community, one's race, gender, and class can be part of a situated *ethos*. In addition to situated *ethos*, a rhetor is able to construct *ethos* within a speech or text (or with code). Through the use of certain strategies such as appearing unbiased, fair, and knowledgeable, a rhetor can build an *ethos*. This latter form is called "invented" or "constructed" *ethos*, and in a space like Wikipedia it is often built with a collection of citations.

Given that Wikipedia is an encyclopedia, the *ethos* of Wikipedians is often tied to their claims to expertise. Wikipedia's stance regarding expertise is probably best exemplified by its "no original research policy," a policy that insists that Wikipedia is a place to summarize previously published (or "verifiable") research and not a place to publish new findings. When it comes to knowledge, Wikipedia is interested in gathering citations of experts—via an obsessive archive—and not in the RL expertise of wiki writers. The obsessive archive of MediaWiki is mirrored by this same ethic among Wikipedians— the goal is to collect and archive as much as possible, making the writers in this space something more like conduits than authors. Rather than relying on a situated *ethos* of expertise, Wikipedians are asked to rely on an invented *ethos* by citing other texts. Many Wikipedians build up reputations within the community, and this means that they enter any dispute or discussion with a certain amount of situated *ethos*. The trail of citations required by Wikipedia's constitution does in fact lead to printed texts that have undergone traditional vetting processes—to texts that are ostensibly written by experts. That is, expertise itself is not banned from Wikipedia by its citational ethic. Rather, it is the use of the RL expertise of the Wikipedian that is not supposed to be in play. Instead of pointing to "me" or "my expertise," the Wikipedia rules ask that I help build the archive by pulling in a trusted source. Again, Wikipedia rules line up nicely with MediaWiki's determinations about the value of data. The goal is to accumulate data. As I edit Wikipedia, any attempt to invoke my own situated *ethos* of RL expertise operates in opposition to both Wikipedia and MediaWiki's *ethos* of data collection, citation, and archiving.

To further complicate things, networked environments make it difficult to hold a situated *ethos* and an invented *ethos* apart. That is, in many situations, digital rhetors invent their situated *ethos*, and Essjay is a perfect example of this. By presenting himself as a credentialed theologian, Essjay was able to invent a situated *ethos*. All of this suggests that *ethos* is a bit more malleable on the web and that it is of particular importance in a digital space that archives nearly everything. In the following discussion of the Essjay controversy, we will see how *ethos* is what drives rhetorical exchange in Wikipedia. Whereas RL interaction allows a writer to rely on reputation and expertise via a situated *ethos* based on credentials, VR changes the rules of the (rhetorical) game. These rules of engagement are a direct result of MediaWiki's ethical programs.

We can now return to the story that opened this chapter—a story that tells us a great deal about how the dwelling of MediaWiki sets the stage for certain kinds of rhetorical exchange. The outing of Essjay as Ryan Jordan and the subsequent scandal began well before the *New Yorker* published an editorial note regarding Stacy Schiff's piece about Wikipedia. While Wikipedia critic Daniel Brandt was largely responsible for the "outing" of Essjay, others had noticed this inconsistency as well. A fellow Wikipedian posed this question to Essjay on his Wikipedia "User Talk" page (a page on which Wikipedians provide personal information):

> Essjay, I'm kinda puzzled. Your Wikia profile says that you're 24 years old, work as a Community Manager for Wikia, and used to be employed by a Fortune 200 company. But your Wikibooks profile says you're over 30 and currently work as a Theology professor. Is the Wikia profile someone else? I hope you can shed some light on this matter.[21]

Jordan responded that he had, in fact, created a fake persona for Wikipedia to avoid "the attention of an unsavory element."[22] He claimed that stalkers often made death threats to high-profile Wikipedians, and that rather than worry about such threats he had created the "Essjay" identity. Yet, for Jordan, this fake identity was not necessarily a way of hiding something. In fact, it was just the opposite. Jordan argued that those Wikipedians who attempted to hide their RL identity would inevitably let a detail slip, allowing others to find out their RL identity. Rather than having to carefully guard personal information, he created a new persona. In his mind, this allowed him to avoid the paranoia that can follow from trying to maintain complete anonymity:

> I decided to be myself, to never hide my personality, to always be who I am, but to utilize disinformation with regard to what I consider unimportant details: age, location, occupation, etc. As a result, I've made many strong friendships here, because I've always been the person I am, but the stalkers have spent the last two years searching for middle-aged college professors with the initials "SJ" (which are, by the way, my initials) who live in the Northeast; I never had to worry that anything I said would lead back to me, because the areas they focused on, the unimportant statistical information, was a cover.[23]

Essjay's cover provides some insight into how MediaWiki's penchant for archiving every bit of information shapes rhetorical activity in Wikipedia. Knowing that others could piece together small bits of information in order to construct a picture of his offline identity, Jordan decided to avoid this trap altogether. By building the identity of Essjay, he was able to carefully construct an *ethos* without having to worry about an accidental reference to his or her RL life—a reference to what Matthew Fuller might call a "fleck of identity"— cracking the façade.[24] He goes on to say that he thought stalkers "were the only people who actually believed the story" and that a glance at his edits should have made it clear that he was not a theologian: "most everybody who is particularly close to me knew it was a cover."[25]

And MediaWiki's ethical program with regard to database integrity had important implications for the ethical programs of Wikipedia. Jordan's choice to hide his "real name" is a reflection of the Wikipedia community's ethical program with regard to RL identity. Wikipedia policy pages caution against using one's real name when setting up an account: "Your username is a nickname that will identify all of your contributions to Wikipedia. It can even be your real name, if you so choose, but you should be aware of the risks involved in editing under your real name."[26] In fact, Wikipedians will often go so far as to stop users who choose to use their real names: "Using your real name as a username may put you at risk for harassment. Your request to use your real name will be delayed unless you state explicitly that you are aware of the implications of using your real name."[27] Such concerns seem odd to Wikipedia outsiders, but those who edit often and who take an administrative role are insistent that pseudonyms are necessary, and Jordan was part of this culture. Jordan built this situated *ethos* of expertise for "outsiders" and "stalkers," believing that those Wikipedians who dealt with Essjay on a regular basis did not believe that he held such credentials.

After he was hired by Wikia, Jordan revealed his RL identity to Jimmy Wales and others within the company, and this raised no problems for his new employers. For Essjay and many in the Wikipedia community, this truly was not a major event. He describes the reactions of those he talked to after the "came out":

> Nothing really has changed any; I'm still the person everybody has known for the past two years, I just have a different job. I've never been disingenuous in my interactions with others: I've always been myself, and have every intention to continue being myself, people just know a bit more about what I look like and where I live now. Of the dozens of people I've talked to since I "came out," all have been happy to have a face to associate with the person they know, have understood the need to be protected, and have no doubts that nothing has changed about the person they have come to know. I don't expect anyone who knows me to feel any different.[28]

This reaction held true for many Wikipedia insiders. This is revealed in the nonchalant reaction of Dev920, the Wikipedian who initially raised the question of RL identity to Essjay: "That makes a lot of sense. I didn't think you had the time to be everything you said you were. :) Thanks for taking the time to write such a lengthy reply, and congratulations on getting the job at Wikia!"[29]

But this kind of understanding response seems to have been confined only to certain contributors. Upon receiving information from Brandt about Jordan's true identity, the The New Yorker published an editorial note:

> Essjay was recommended to Ms. Schiff as a source by a member of Wikipedia's management team because of his respected position within the Wikipedia community. He was willing to describe his work as a Wikipedia administrator but would not identify himself other than by confirming the biographical details that appeared on his user page. At the time of publication, neither we nor Wikipedia knew Essjay's real name.[30]

The editorial note closes with a quote from Wales: "I regard it as a pseudonym and I don't really have a problem with it." Such reactions were baffling to bloggers and other commentators: "The reaction from Wiki devotees to this scandal is bizarre to outsiders. Jordan pointed the finger at The New Yorker for not being wise to his game. Others attacked Brandt [the person who outed Jordan]—a popular Wiki pastime."[31] However, as time wore on, a number of Wikipedians expressed their displeasure with Essjay's use of fraudulent credentials. A "Request For Comments" page—"an informal, lightweight process for requesting outside input, consensus building, and dispute resolution, with respect to article content, user conduct, and Wikipedia policy and guidelines"—shows hundreds of responses by Wikipedians, many of whom were upset with Essjay's conduct.[32] A straw poll initiated around the same time shows a range of opinions on the matter.[33] Within days of the publication of The New Yorker's editorial note, even Wales was having second thoughts: "When I last spoke to The New Yorker about the fact that a prominent Wikipedia community member had lied about his credentials, I misjudged the issue. It was not O.K. for Mr. Jordan, or Essjay, to lie to a reporter, even to protect his identity."[34] Jordan's suspect behavior was not confined to this claim of false credentials. He also claimed that Schiff offered to compensate him for his time—an ethical no-no for journalists. Schiff denied this.[35] Wales asked Jordan to step down from Wikipedia. He did, and he also resigned from his position at Wikia. The pressure of media attention (the story was covered by many major media outlets) had forced Wales to change his tune.

In the wake of this controversy, both Wikipedians and the community's critics took advantage of the massive Wikipedia database and began to dig through some of Essjay's edits and contributions. In doing so, many found that Essjay spent most of his time "ensuring that the encyclopedia was as free as possible of vandalism and drawn-out editing fights."[36] Wales made similar claims, and pointed out that Essjay was a very likable Wikipedian:

He spent most of his time reverting vandalism, mediating disputes and was always a very kind and loving and thoughtful person who, you know, anytime people were having a dispute it was always good to see Essjay show up because he was quite good at getting all parties on the same track.[37]

Yet Essjay's claim that he had "never been disingenuous" turned out to be somewhat disingenuous. In certain situations, Essjay used the situated *ethos* of a credentialed professor to guide a discussion or claim expertise. One such instance involved Essjay's contribution to the article for "Imprimatur." By following edits on the discussion page for this article, we can see how Essjay guided the discussion by using claims of expertise. He did this by using a situated *ethos* to guide a discussion about Catholic doctrine. But we can also see that Wikipedians continue the rhetorical exchange regardless of claims to RL expertise. No one in this discussion actively questions Essjay's credentials, but none of these Wikipedians allow that claim to halt discussion either. As they piece together their arguments, all parties to this discussion draw from whatever rhetorical resources the database offers them. Essjay's decision to cite his own credentials is treated as one data point in this debate, one bit of information archived by MediaWiki. It is not ignored, but it is also not treated as an unquestionable claim.

The following discussion about the word "imprimatur" offers a particularly relevant example of how this works. An imprimatur is issued by a bishop of the Catholic Church in order to approve the publication of some work. From March 28, 2005, through September 2, 2005, the discussion page for Wikipedia's "Imprimatur" article shows an exchange between Essjay and other Wikipedians:

March 28

A user notes a problem with the article:

> The explanations of Imprimatur and Nihil *Obstat* presented here are confused. The following Web page apparently gets it right: http://www.kensmen.com/catholic/imprimatur.html

March 29

A day later, this same user adds a more specific discussion of the problems with this article and asks for help editing the article:

More specifically, the current article seems to reverse the roles of imprimatur and *nihil obstat*. It would probably be more accurate to write, "While the *nihil obstat* certifies there is no moral or doctrinal error, the imprimatur is an express permission from the bishop for the text to be printed." (That is, the censor does the legwork, then the bishop confers his authority on the censor's decision.)

In addition, *nihil obstat* is better translated "nothing hinders" [publishing the reviewed work].

I would edit the actual Imprimatur article directly, if I trusted my ability to do so successfully. There are MANY rules and conventions I have not learned!

April 12

Essjay enters the discussion arguing that the article is correct as is and cites *Catholicism for Dummies*, a text that he claims he often requires for his students:

> I do not believe this to be correct. An individual bishop has no power outside his diocese to forbid anything to be printed, thus he cannot offer a *nihil obstat*, only an imprimatur, which certifies that the text is free from moral error. . . . Unless of course he is the Bishop of Rome. However, the censor, who is an agent of the Roman Curia/Holy See may certainly place a text on the "blacklist" of heretical publications. I believe the entry to be correct as it reads, and I offer as my reference the text "Catholicism for Dummies" by Trigilio (Ph.D./Th.D.) and Brighenti (Ph.D.). The text offers a *Nihil Obstat* from the Rev. Daniel J. Mahan, STB, STL, Censor Librorum, and an Imprimatur from the Rev. Msgr. Joseph F. Schaedel, Vicar General. This is a text I often require for my students, and I would hang my own Ph.D. on it's [sic] credibility.

April 21

Another Wikipedian enters the discussion and also claims that the article is flawed: "Imprimatur translates as 'let it be printed.' I think this text is the wrong way round, too."

April 23

A third Wikipedian agrees with the first two and makes changes to the article: "The text is totally the wrong way round. I'm changing it."

April 25

Essjay backtracks, saying that he has consulted with "the Curia"—an official ruling body of the Roman Catholic Church—and admits that he was at least partially wrong:

> After consulting with the Curia, I amend my above-comments. Imprimatur is a permission to print, about this I was incorrect. However, it can only be issued by a bishop. *Nihil obstat* is a certification that no error exists, and is issued by the censor.

September 2

More than four months after Essjay's partial retraction, another Wikipedian updates the article and adds this comment to the discussion page:

> I've updated this document significantly; I work for a Catholic book publisher as well as for the bishop of the local diocese, and have worked to get the imprimatur on several books—no offense to "Catholicism for Dummies," but it was definitely unclear (a Ph.D. doesn't necessarily mean someone understands Catholic practices very well . . .)

This final jab—"a Ph.D. doesn't necessarily mean someone understands Catholic practices very well"—might be taken by some as evidence of Wikipedia's hostility to expertise. However, in this particular case, the expert is not really an expert, and healthy skepticism has made for a more accurate article. This skepticism has made for a fruitful rhetorical exchange that plays out because MediaWiki's structure provides the space in which these writers develop an article. That structure and its archiving impulse not only allowed me to dig through the archival material to reconstruct this rhetorical exchange, it also ensures that all information can be part of the conversation. If an author chooses to claim RL expertise—something that Wikipedia rules discourage—that expertise is considered to be one line in the database, one piece of evidence in the argument at hand. The expert's credentials are not the starting point for the conversation but are instead part of a deep textual archive enabled by MediaWiki.

Credentials are not attached to a rhetor, and they do not grant the rhetor a higher rank in the discussion. Instead, *ethos* and credentials become one more citation among all the citations that drive this rhetorical situation. Rather than seeing RL identity as a starting point for this discussion, these Wikipedians incorporate all the information at their disposal into their arguments.

Essjay invoked an *ethos* of RL expertise, but the *ethos* (dwelling) established by MediaWiki means that this data (whether or not the other writers involved believed it) was but one part of a complex rhetorical and ethical matrix. Regardless of its fraudulence, Essjay's claim of expertise fails to stop the discussion. Undaunted by Essjay's claim of expertise, these writers provide citations and sources in order to better the article.

Essjay Fallout

The Essjay controversy caused a great deal of public outcry. In a March 7, 2007, blog post, Andrew Keen compared Wikipedia's dealings with Essjay to the Czechoslovakian Communist Party's ability to make people vanish: "The communists, of course, were particularly adept at forgetting."[38] Keen argued that Wikipedia has done the same with Essjay: "Jimmy Wales fired loyal Jordan/Essjay and, all of a sudden, the kid/theologian is history. One minute he's everywhere and then he's nowhere . . . Now Wikipedia just says: RETIRED: This user is no longer active on Wikipedia"[39] Keen is an outspoken critic of communities like Wikipedia that valorize the amateur at the expense of the expert. His book, *The Cult of the Amateur*, argues that blogs destroy traditional journalism and that communities like Wikipedia eliminate any hope of obtaining reliable information online.[40] Ironically, Keen (whose text expresses concern for the loss of in-depth reading and research) is completely wrong when he claims that Wikipedia attempted to "disappear" Essjay. Certain information (such as the form letter that Essjay sent to professors) was deleted from the site, but had Keen done more investigating he would have realized that, thanks to MediaWiki's drive to archive as much information as possible, Essjay's exploits were being obsessively documented. Further, Wikipedia's database is archived by several external sites, some of which are critical of the project. That is, Wikipedia's structure leaves itself open to anyone who chooses to archive its information. Much of the information that Essjay or other Wikipedians attempted to delete from the record was archived by sites such as Wikitruth.info. Further, as with most websites, Wikipedia is continually archived by the Internet Archive, a site that should remind us how difficult it is to "disappear" online.

On March 2, 2007 (five days prior to Keen's blog entry about Wikipedians "disappearing" Essjay), a "request for comments" page had been initiated that would allow Wikipedians to discuss the Essjay controversy. On that same day, the "Essjay controversy" Wikipedia article was a mere "stub"—the name Wikipedia gives the brief chunk of text that initiates an article—but it existed. This first version of the article explained who Ryan Jordan was, referenced the article in *The New Yorker*, and explained that Jordan lacked the degrees he claimed to have.[41] And this was not the only space in which Wikipedians were discussing Essjay. There is a great deal of evidence that not all in the community thought Essjay's transgression was minor, and many wanted to discuss the issue out in the open. These extensive conversations seem to conflict with Keen's account that Wikipedia was looking to forget that Essjay ever existed. A piece by Noam Cohen in the *International Herald Tribune* reports that "[m]ounting anger was expressed in public forums like the user pages of Wales and Essjay" and that after some initial understanding responses by Wikipedia insiders, the sentiment eventually shifted: "the prevailing view was summarized in subject lines like Essjay Must Resign, and notes calling the actions by Jordan 'plain and simple fraud.'"[42] Of course, it should not be forgotten that initial reactions were indeed less harsh, and that much outcry happened only after the story began to circulate widely.

Nevertheless, some of the discussion happening in the wake of the Essjay scandal revolved around developing a policy by which Wikipedians would have to provide RL credentials. These were issues that had been raised before, but the community had been resistant to such a change. Wales himself pushed for this change, but the discussions and straw polls mentioned above resulted in no change of policy.[43] Unlike the example in the previous chapter, in which an exploit was successfully used as justification for using the Twitter platform differently (suggesting that people move away from the Twitter website and toward third-party applications), this situation resulted in no immediate changes to Wikipedia policies. While ethical programs are reprogrammable, there is no guarantee that they will be rewritten in the face of new reminders of the Law of hospitality. Regardless of arguments that Wikipedia needed a policy for validating credentials, Wikipedians like Misza13 continued to argue that "nobody cares about your credentials."[44] In response to pleas from academics that their degrees do in fact "mean something," this Wikipedian expresses the citational ethic of Wikipedia succinctly:

> As a qualified academic you should be at an advantaged position for finding external sources for articles. Use that! Make Wikipedia a better encyclopedia and everyone will be grateful . . . however, your credentials will not give you any upper hand in content disputes (unless of course you manage to find external sources backing up your claims, but how's that different from anyone else providing them?).[45]

If anything were to persuade Wikipedia (the text) and Wikipedians (the writers) that a change in policy was necessary, one would think it would be the Essjay controversy. The Wikipedia community spent a great deal of time talking about Essjay and the issue of credentials, but in the end they did not change the site's ethical program with regard to RL identities, and it did not result in any immediate changes to the MediaWiki software. The Essjay scandal shows us how MediaWiki's attempt to write the laws of hospitality, its particular answer to the network's Law of hospitality, is difficult to dislodge. Though MediaWiki and Wikipedia are not static artifacts and though they continue to shift their ethical programs, the Essjay scandal did not cause the immediate changes that many assumed it would. An ethical program (computational or otherwise) can always change, but even in the face of a number of difficult situations Wikipedia has retained MediaWiki's archival impulse—an impulse that ends up discouraging the use of RL credentials in favor of citation and curation—as one of its primary ethical programs. However, while MediaWiki may rely on an archiving impulse, it can still be used to construct very different kinds of dwellings.

Citizendium: Another Kind of Dwelling

Wikipedia welcomes arguments and conversations among writers, and it considers such exchanges to be part of its text. The Wikipedia article certainly sits atop this messy process, and each article is accompanied by a "discussion" page in which visitors debate its content. Still, Wikipedia's database runs deep, and its articles are but one of its many different types of data. It is a project that thrives on debate and disagreement, and these rhetorical underpinnings are especially interesting considering that one of its cofounders is a philosopher. Larry Sanger earned his PhD in philosophy at Ohio State University.[46] We can view Sanger's struggles with Wikipedia as one version of the philosopher struggling with the contingencies of rhetoric. Seeking to build a "compendium" of knowledge is very different from building a wiki that welcomes and documents debate. Initially, Sanger was looking for a stable way to document knowledge, but Wikipedia actually resists stability at every turn by allowing edits from multiple users, regardless of credentials. Even if the "flagged revisions" policy (and software extension) described above build an infrastructure of editorial approval, such approvals always come after Wikipedia has invited authors to contribute.

Sanger's struggles with Wikipedia are especially interesting, given that he had a hand in creating it. Sanger and Wales established Wikipedia in January 2001 on a whim, or as a result of what Joseph Reagle has called a "happy accident."[47] The two were collaborating with a group of volunteers to create Nupedia, a free encyclopedia that was to be written by experts. Sanger and others were developing a seven-step editorial process, and a group of programmers were building software that would allow articles to move through this process. That software was created under an open source license, and it underwent many iterations as Nupedia attempted to tackle various problems. Among its developers was Magnus Manske, who also designed an early version of MediaWiki. One of Nupedia's early problems was the sorting of content. Early in the software development process, programmers attempted to design a workflow that would allow for XML markup of documents. One developer, Peter Saint-Andre, frames the problem clearly when he argues that "it's dubious at best that PhD historians (or whatever) will take the time to learn any XML, let alone mark up their documents correctly. One missing </place> tag and the doc isn't valid."[48] While this is only one problem that the Nupedia software developers were working on, it stands as a kind of synecdoche for the difficulties of this project. As Nupedia's software developers determined how best to build its collaborative tool, a central concern was how to build and maintain its database. In early stages, content was transferred via e-mail, and Wales believed that this was a part of the process that might endure. However, he wasn't entirely sure: "Communication among authors and reviewers/editors is through email. For now, this is the best way, and I *think* this will always be best, because it is infinitely flexible, and lets everyone use their own favorite tools."[49] Still, the question of how content would be compiled, edited, and sorted continually plagued those designing the software.

Many of the discussions on Nupedia's "tools-l" LISTSERV (a list devoted to conversations about "NupeCode" software development) were concerned with developing procedures for the problem of workflow. How would articles be submitted? How would they be reviewed? How would content be sorted and tagged? In the same e-mail cited above, Saint-Andre suggests a "web front-end for article submission":

> The beauty of this is that the person who is taking over from me in the task of building out the vocabulary doesn't know XML and doesn't need to— all she has to do is go to the web interface I built, type in the appropriate information (which is checked for validity on submission), and the form input is parsed out by a Java servlet into valid XML that conforms with the DTD [Document Type Definition documentation].[50]

While Saint-Andre is not necessarily describing a wiki, we can see that his description is not too different from what Wikipedia would eventually become. A writer submits content and the task of inserting XML tags is left to a computer program that ensures that the document conforms with the DTD (a "dictionary" that defines the XML tags for a given system) developed by Nupedia programmers and editors. Volunteer software developers were attempting to deal with this problem and many others, and Nupedia was slowly trying to get a handle on how to build and sort its database. In the midst of this work,

Sanger learned of Ward Cunningham's wiki software from his friend Ben Kovitz.[51] Sanger was intrigued, and he started a wiki on January 15, 2001. He sent a message to the Nupedia mailing lists: "http://www.wikipedia.com/ Humor me. Go there and add a little article. It will take all of five or ten minutes."[52] The text began to grow instantly, largely because many of the issues that Nupedia was attempting to solve—workflow, the sorting of content, a linear process of article review—were pushed to the side by a web-based interface that put fewer restrictions on authors and that allowed wiki writers to edit articles on the fly. The choice by Sanger to open the floodgates with what he saw as little more than an experiment laid the groundwork for what would later become MediaWiki and Wikipedia. While the problem of sorting data had not been solved, a lack of articles (that is, populating the database) was no longer an issue.

The instant success of the wiki—within two weeks Wikipedia had 600 articles—meant that Nupedia was abandoned.[53] This was something that Sanger lamented:

> We always suspected that we would wind up scrapping our first attempts to design an editorial system, and that we would learn a great deal from those first attempts; and that's essentially what happened. But Nupedia could have evolved, and would have, had we continued working on it.[54]

Sanger believed that the Nupedia model of involving experts was a strong one, and he assumed that Wikipedia would eventually incorporate this model in some way. As the Wikipedia project grew, Sanger began to have second thoughts. A wiki-based encyclopedia addressed the shortage of content, but its willingness to welcome so many writers from so many different angles created an entirely new set of problems by inviting many voices to the conversation. Such cacophony meant a loss of control for Sanger, who was a kind of editor-in-chief for Nupedia. He also served in this capacity in the early days of Wikipedia, but the chaos of the fast-growing community (and run-ins with Wikipedians who viewed the project differently) eventually forced him to leave the project. In writings published after he left, Sanger has voiced his displeasure with the community's alleged "anti-elitism."[55] Wikipedia eventually became too sprawling for Sanger, the philosopher, who grew to despise how debates were carried out in this virtual community.

This all-too-brief history of Wikipedia, Nupedia, and NupeCode is not meant to be all inclusive but rather to provide context for the ethical programs that helped shape the MediaWiki platform. Wikipedia's "edit me" *ethos*—its status as a particular kind of digital dwelling—emerged from a complex set of historical forces, and the early discussions surrounding Nupedia offer evidence that the software might have been designed differently. Sanger's decision to set up wikipedia.com and welcome writers with a quip of "Humor me" was a response to the Law of hospitality, one that he never imagined would become essentially irreversible. The Wikipedia we know today largely began with (if we take Sanger at his word) an impulsive decision to roll out the red carpet, a decision that set up a clash between Sanger the philosopher and the obsessive archiving impulse of a hospitable database:

> On a wiki, contributions exist in perpetuity, as it were, or until they are deleted or radically changed. Consequently, anyone new to a discussion sees the first contribution first. So, whoever starts a new page for discussion also, to a great extent, sets the tone and agenda of the discussion. Moreover, nasty exchanges live on forever on a wiki, festering like an open wound, unless deliberately toned down afterward; if the same exchange takes place on a mailing list, it slips mercifully and quietly into the archives.[56]

Sanger envisioned Wikipedia as a way to generate content for Nupedia, a text that would be a stable offering of the most important (or encyclopedic) information, and in its earliest stages Wikipedia was relatively stable. However, the wiki structure meant that this stability shifted significantly as the text and its number of contributors grew. Wikipedia is less a compendium of the encyclopedic than a conversation about what is or is not encyclopedic. It is a rhetorical, deliberative space that relies on the network's Law of hospitality—a space that came to be shaped by MediaWiki's archival impulses. As Wikipedia shifted to a site of debate, Sanger got exceedingly uncomfortable with the community's direction. Debate called for a shift away from the more manageable exchanges via e-mail to messier exchanges encouraged by a wiki. Sanger's metaphor of "festering wounds" offers a particularly vivid image of Wikipedia articles as messy sites of strife.

Sanger was happy to have debate and conversation, but he didn't view it as part of the encyclopedic article. Instead, he believed it should happen in closed off spaces (like e-mail lists) where particularly difficult opinions can disappear "mercifully and quietly." For Sanger, such conversations need not necessarily be part of the archive, and this is our first clue that Sanger's view clashes with the ethical program of MediaWiki. In a space where all information is welcomed and archived—including the naggings of trolls—it's difficult to get things to slip "mercifully and quietly into the archives." Information may certainly drop from prominent view, but it will remain available for anyone who chooses to seek it out. Beyond Sanger's desire to draw a line between public and private rhetorical exchanges, we also see a major difference between his view of the role of *ethos* in the construction of an encyclopedia and the assumptions encoded in MediaWiki. The MediaWiki structure complicates any attempt to stem the impulse to archive. MediaWiki can be configured in multiple ways, but it seems to contain a certain drive to archive, one that Sanger attempts to augment.

It is against this backdrop that we can better understand Sanger's attempt to build a new kind of encyclopedia, one that would use MediaWiki software but would attempt to build a dwelling that was quite different from Wikipedia. As we have seen, Wikipedia considers user identity to be a piece of information to be scrutinized in the midst of conversations about content. That information is on the same plane as Wikipedia's bits of information or other citations offered by Wikipedians. Credentials are but one text a Wikipedian can cite, even if the citation of credentials is discouraged by Wikipedia policies. However, Sanger's Citizendium takes a different approach by sifting through writers prior to allowing them to contribute. User identity in Citizendium is determined outside the space of the encyclopedia. In this dwelling, situated *ethos* (one's credentials and identity) is determined prior to entering into discussion. Situated *ethos* is held apart from constructed *ethos*, something that Wikipedia does not necessarily encourage.

But this attempt to determine situated *ethos* on the front end is still done within the same software platform, MediaWiki, meaning that Citizendium must build an entire credentialing mechanism into the software. Citizendium requires all authors to fill out a form that lists their real name, a biography, and some way of verifying that identity.[57] In addition, if that author would like to apply to be an editor, he or she must provide a CV or resume along with "some links to Web material that tends to support the claims made in the CV, such as conference proceedings, or a departmental home page." Authors and editors are approved by "constables." All users are also required to be at least 13 years old, and any authors between 13 and 16 years of age are asked to not include any "personal identifying information." The site provides stern (but contradictory) information about pseudonyms:

> No pseudonyms: if you want to apply for a pseudonym, do not use this form. Instead, send your information topersonnel@citizendium.org, addressed to the Chief Constable, explaining the reasons for your request. We grant pseudonyms only for very rare and exceptional reasons.[58]

This provides the kind of space that Sanger wants—a solid ground of RL expertise on which to build his encyclopedia.[59] In the space of Citizendium, user identity and *ethos* are not part of the debate. As users debate and write articles in this space, they can take a writer's *ethos* for granted since it is linked to an RL identity.

Sanger longed for an infrastructure that allowed noise to be filtered. He hoped that debate could happen in more controlled way (or, in words he might use, a more civil way). He hoped that at least some of the messier conflicts could happen out of sight and behind the scenes, something that the MediaWiki structure resisted. As a perpetually open conversation, Wikipedia's use of MediaWiki invites debate and disagreement. As much as we might object to Sanger vilifying the openness of a text like Wikipedia, such openness is not necessarily always a good thing. Festering wounds stink. Debates can devolve into flame wars, and libelous statements can live on unnoticed.[60] But the structure of Wikipedia assumes that such wounds are still preferable to the alternative. Given the opportunity to require RL identities in the wake of the Essjay scandal, Wikipedia's answer to the predicament of hospitality remained in place. It was this approach that drove Sanger away from the unwieldy text of Wikipedia and toward building a project with a different kind of constitution.

The Citizendium project uses MediaWiki, but it does so in a very different way. There is evidence that Citizendium has customized its MediaWiki software—the community has created a page to track such customizations. But there has been little activity on this front.[61] Most of Citizendium's customizations have been built "on top" of the MediaWiki software. Citizendium has built in a number of rules and regulations that serve as modifications to MediaWiki's software. It has built a different dwelling, and this difference serves as a reminder that any study of software has to account for multiple factors. Citizendium's "citizens" use a number of rules and regulations that do not necessarily alter the MediaWiki software. This is evidence that the MediaWiki dwelling can be both resistant to change and hospitable to it, depending on the angle of our analysis. The *ethos* (dwelling) of MediaWiki makes certain assumptions about users and permissions, and those assumptions can often be difficult to unseat. Software never completely dictates practice, and Citizendium's ability to build a different structure that incorporates MediaWiki is evidence of this. Wikipedia and MediaWiki offer one kind of dwelling, but when MediaWiki is paired with Citizendium, rhetorical exchange is shaped and constrained in different ways.

Citizendium's archive is just as obsessive as Wikipedia's, but Citizendium builds a set of rules that shapes rhetorical exchange differently. First, by filtering and approving users on its front end, Citizendium institutes a space that values RL credentials. This lays the groundwork for certain kinds of rhetorical exchange. Users have been vetted, and they use their RL names, and this means that their expertise is not necessarily up for debate. Nonetheless, MediaWiki's user page function has not been disabled by Citizendium, and any Citizendium "citizen" can visit any other user page (in fact, anyone can view a

Citizendium user page). Thus, while the credentials offered by the writers in this space are not up for debate, they are part of the archive. In a debate about content on Citizendium, one can certainly view credentials and judge an interlocutor's *ethos* by visiting a profile page or reading a CV, but Citizendium does not encourage the questioning of those credentials and it takes pains to verify them. On Citizendium, RL expertise is a key to entry, and RL credentials are given more rhetorical weight.

Wikipedia welcomes contributions regardless of a writer's credentials and then immediately begins archiving information about both the writer and his, her, or its (if the writer is a bot) contributions. The *ethos* of a writer is not in question when it comes to Citizendium's policy—the goal is for that *ethos* to be determined outside of the text, prior to any contributions. Still, once beyond the Citizendium gatekeeping mechanism, the archive begins its work of tracking and logging the actions of users. Both Wikipedia and Citizendium invite collaboration and rhetorical exchange, but Citizendium attempts to exclude certain kinds of information from those exchanges and thus ensures fewer "festering wounds." Those attempts are, in some sense, thwarted by MediaWiki's archiving impulse. The rules and regulations built on top of the MediaWiki software (the ethical programs it institutes with regard to credentials) are a way of augmenting the software in the interest of policing its archive differently than Wikipedia does.

Citizendium's desire to control its archive is also reflected in its dealings with Wikipedia content. Citizendium policy discourages writers from incorporating content from Wikipedia. Instead, it asks that they "start over from scratch." Citizendium offers tips for those wanting to edit a Wikipedia article in the interest of differentiating between Citizendium and Wikipedia: "To the extent that Wikipedia articles themselves encode a navel-gazing, user-unfriendly culture that we want to reject, we absolutely must revise these articles entirely—or start over from scratch."[62] The explicit mention of code here is instructive, and it indicates that Citizendium is very consciously attempting to recode MediaWiki in the interest of instituting a different kind of ethical program. In addition to carefully tracking the RL identities of its writers, it attempts to police the boundaries of its database a bit more carefully. Rather than welcoming all content, it instructs its writers about what should and should not be cited. What are the advantages of starting an article "from scratch"? Citizendium offers a number of reasons including the poor writing and inaccuracy of Wikipedia articles, the constraints of dealing with the structure of a preexisting article, and the more enjoyable experience of writing your own article. Citizendium's dwelling is concerned with a much different kind of archive—one that does not welcome all writers and one that seeks only a certain kind of content. In order to build this dwelling, it makes modifications to MediaWiki by encouraging writers to start from scratch, building a credentialing process for users, and disallowing anonymous edits.

Regardless of the fact that both Citizendium and Wikipedia use the same software platform, these two projects attempt to construct very different dwellings. This difference, in the case of Citizendium, is a conscious choice. Its documentation continually attempts to differentiate Citizendium from "that other community" and to identify as a more grown-up text: "Several people, independently, have said that we're 'Wikipedia for grown-ups.' That's because we require real names, at least a brief (and accurate) bio, and the contributor's agreement to follow our 'Statement of Fundamental Policies.'"[63] These policies can tend to put Citizendium *above* Wikipedia:

> Citizendium will have a set of persons of mature judgment specially empowered to enforce rules, called (at least tentatively) "constables." The enforcement of project rules—up to and including the ejection of participants from the project—is to be carried out using common sense and leniency while following "the rule of law."[64]

The constables will exercise "mature judgment," especially when "ejecting" authors. The implication here is that Wikipedia allows for a great deal of juvenile behavior. Indeed, a view of the Wikipedia article on "Sex" on October 11, 2007, would have revealed two lines of text: "A boy whos [sic] name is Jon will put you on cloud 9 and will be good with his fingers and tongue. I have a nosebleed."[65] Obviously, this is juvenile behavior. However, considering Sanger's comments about "festering wounds" and his concerns about Wikipedia's "anti-expertise bias," one wonders whether rhetorical exchange is lost in the attempt to cut out "juvenile behavior."

Yet the point here is not that these requirements are unfair or even inhospitable. Any filter is an imperfect attempt to write the laws of hospitality, and even Wikipedia is unable to avoid this. While Wikipedia allows "anonymous" edits, the development of a tool that tracks edits to physical locations through the use of IP addresses is an indication that web anonymity is a myth.[66] But the requirements Citizendium has established are different from what is required of a Wikipedian. By making sure that people provide their RL identities, Citizendium tries to set up a situation in which credentials or RL expertise are not part of the conversation. But MediaWiki's ethical program always presents the possibility that those credentials will be pulled into the discussion, and this is perhaps what is most important to notice as we examine these two encyclopedias. While the ethical programs of Wikipedia and Citizendium are different, they share a common root in MediaWiki. The ethical programs of the latter rear their heads often, regardless of what kinds of policies have been put in place by those using the software.

Cunctation

Sanger made no secret of the fact that he saw the Essjay scandal as evidence that the Wikipedia model was a failure. Most of his discussion of the situation—he posted his thoughts on his own blog—dealt with Wales's response to the Essjay affair. Sanger was bothered that Wales seemed unfazed by Essjay's use of a pseudonym. Wales eventually backtracked on his comments and claimed that he did indeed disapprove of Essjay's use of false credentials. However, he insisted that the use of a pseudonym was not, by itself, a concern. Sanger vehemently disagreed:

> All right, perhaps it was only this morning that Jimmy saw evidence that Essjay used his false credentials in content disputes. But why is evidence necessary. Why else would someone claim to have advanced degrees, as opposed to making up some other story? It is quite obvious in itself that someone who claims to have impressive credentials that he hasn't got intends to use them to get ahead. No one needs to see the "diffs" ["diffs" is wiki slang for comparisons between various page versions in the wiki archive]. And so it ought to be evident on its face that claims to have advanced credentials is a "violation of people's trust." Particularly when the liar has risen through Wikipedia's ranks, the reasonable assumption is that the claimed credentials played a positive role in Essjay's rise. This is, again, something that needs no special evidence.[67]

It is this issue of trust that most concerns Sanger. He believes that Wikipedia has a responsibility to ensure that its writers are who they say they are, and it is here that we can best understand Sanger's views with regard to how Wikipedia's structure is flawed. Sanger sees Wikipedia as a publication. He discusses the Essjay situation by comparing Wikipedia's *ethos* to that of *The New Yorker*:

> Of course, the moniker "Essjay" is obviously a pseudonym. But Essjay's *invented persona*, as the *New Yorker* described it, or in other words his lies about being a different person, cannot be regarded as a pseudonym by anyone who knows what "pseudonym" means. A pseudonym, or pen name, is just a *name*, not an *identity*. Responsible publications that permit pseudonyms don't permit misrepresentation of the actual qualifications of the person with the pseudonym. *That* would be a breach of the readers' trust.[68]

In essence, he assumes that these two dwellings—Wikipedia and *The New Yorker*—are (or should be) similar. Wikipedia is, for Sanger, a publication, and a publication should offer a certain kind of dwelling. This is why Citizendium deals with questions of expertise with "constables" who decide which writers are allowed to enter. Most important, for our purposes, these constables are necessary because the software that Sanger chose for the Citizendium project is built to welcome writers regardless of credentials, authority, or credibility. MediaWiki carries with it certain assumptions about how a wiki should operate. It is an ethical program, establishing a particular kind of networked space. While the ethics of MediaWiki institute a somewhat fluid program—it can always be reconfigured and reprogrammed—the archiving impulse is difficult to shake. And because of MediaWiki's version of the laws of hospitality, Sanger's Citizendium requires vigilant constables to police identities and content.

After the Essjay scandal broke, Wikipedia critic Nicholas Carr asked an apt question: "If credentials don't matter, why bother faking them?"[69] What was the purpose of Essjay's faked credentials in a space that does not require (or, as some might put it, in a space that does not *respect*) expertise? The answer that this chapter has offered lies in part in the MediaWiki's software and its desire to archive all information. Wikipedia may discourage reverence for experts, but MediaWiki's penchant for obsessively archiving all information makes *ethos* the primary rhetorical resource in conversations about content. It is difficult (if not impossible) for a user to hide from their trail of writing and the keystrokes that have been logged by the software. Managing that trail is one task of the Wikipedian, and credentials helped Essjay with this task. MediaWiki is foundational to both of these two encyclopedia projects, and its archiving impulse does seem to continually reassert itself, even in the case of Citzendium.

But the larger question of rhetoric and ethics in the network is this: Does Citizendium address the network's Law of hospitality adequately? The word "adequately" here does not refer to the project being wrong or unethical. Rather, I mean to suggest that a structure like Citizendium—one that attempts to filter and control its database and to establish common ground—assumes that it is possible to police the boundaries of the database. Given the complications of a hospitable network, how would any ethical program adequately settle the questions of ethics and rhetoric through an agreed-upon constitution? Such a constitution determines who or what can be a party to the conversation and how rhetorical exchange happens. It would determine what portion of the database can be marshaled in the creation of arguments. But does this approach measure up to our contemporary rhetorical environment, one that must constantly come to terms with a globalized network in which our audiences, our collaborators, our interlocutors are not necessarily the ones we choose?

The inquiries of Wikipedia trolls and gadflies might be malicious and irrelevant, but the MediaWiki infrastructure asks us to consider the ethical (and practical) implications of silencing even the most irritating of "wikitrolls," Wikipedians whose main goal is to nag, delay, and slow down the process of knowledge production. One of Sanger's most famous Wikipedia opponents went by the name "Cunctator," a reference to the Latin term for "procrastinator" or "delayer."[70] The impulse to archive everything and to offer any bit of information as fodder for rhetorical exchange certainly tends to slow things down, and we have seen how that process can lead to festering wounds. But networked life continues to remind us that the problematic of hospitality is thrust upon us, and that we are in contact with others over and beyond our choice to engage. MediaWiki is but one tool for building rhetorical dwellings that raise and address such questions. The two iterations of it covered in this chapter show us how software can be adapted to different ethical programs, but they also demonstrate how the platform often holds stubbornly to its own agendas.

// FIVE //

Rhetorical Devices: Database, Narrative, and Machinic Thinking

Major League Baseball is obsessed with numbers. Since at least 1859, when Henry Chadwick invented the box score (the statistical record of a baseball game that lives on in newspapers and on websites today), the game has revolved around batting averages and home run totals. Baseball statistics are sacred, so much so that as Roger Maris approached (and eventually surpassed) Babe Ruth's single season home run record of 60, he received death threats. These statistics emerged once again as a site of libidinal energy in 2012, as journalists and fans debated the American League Most Valuable Player award. In November of that year, the Baseball Writers' Association of America (BBWAA) awarded the MVP to Detroit Tigers third baseman Miguel Cabrera. To many, Cabrera was a no-brainer when it came to choosing an MVP, since he had become the first player since 1967 to win the Triple Crown: he led the league in batting average, home runs, and runs batted in (RBI). The Triple Crown, like Ruth's 60 home run season, is mythical. It is one more example of baseball's number mania.

However, this number mania has ramped up in recent years, and this is why Cabrera's MVP award is of interest to us. For in the same year that Cabrera won the Triple Crown, Mike Trout had what many considered a superior season. In fact, some called Trout's season one of the best in the history of the game. Trout finished behind Cabrera in batting average, home runs, and RBI, but he stole 48 bases and was by anyone's account much more valuable than Cabrera defensively. Cabrera's defense likely cost his team, and he is not known as a good runner (he stole only 4 bases). But beyond his value on the base paths and in the field, Trout also far exceeded Cabrera in a statistic called Wins Above Replacement (WAR). WAR is a stat that attempts to calculate a player's individual contribution to his team's total number of wins.[1] In 2012, Cabrera's WAR was around 7 while Trout's was somewhere between 10 and 11.[2] An MVP candidate would typically have a WAR over 6, so it's clear that both of these players had superb seasons. However, Trout's WAR was the highest of any player in a decade, and many argued that he was easily that season's MVP.

This debate led many fans and journalists to ask: How is it possible that a player who won the Triple Crown was not the unanimous choice for the American League MVP? In 2012, Cabrera received 22 of 28 first place votes, and he finished only 81 points ahead of Trout in the voting (each ballot lists three names, and points are awarded for first-, second-, and third-place votes). If this same scenario had played out 20 years prior (before statistics like WAR were part of the conversation), it's unlikely this would have been a debate at all. But the baseball "stats geek" would ask a different question: How is it possible that Trout was passed over for the award, given that he seems to have had not only a superior season but a landmark season, historically speaking? There are many, many possible reasons for this. For one, Cabrera's team made the playoffs and Trout's did not. Historically, the MVP award has gone to the best player on the best team and not necessarily to the best all-around player. The BBWAA's criteria are notoriously fuzzy, and the organization does little to clear things up in its documentation: "There is no clear-cut definition of what Most Valuable means. It is up to the individual voter to decide who was the Most Valuable Player in each league to his team."[3]

But this debate was not really about Trout and Cabrera. It was, in the words of one writer, "a proxy battle in a larger cold war."[4] We could call it a battle between "writers" and "stats geeks," or "scouts" and "computers," or those who trust their "gut" and those who discuss "small sample sizes" and WAR. Baseball has become a key site for figuring out which tasks are better suited for humans and which are better suited for computational machines. On one side, we have those who trust human intuition and interpretation, and on the other those who believe that computational analysis of "big data" can offer perspectives that are otherwise invisible to humans. Michael Lewis's *Moneyball*, a 2003 book that is largely credited with raising awareness about this debate, describes the situation as one in which grizzled baseball scouts who spend their lives in the stands of minor league ballparks are suddenly battling mathematicians with computers, statistical models, and Ivy League degrees. When the scouts in Lewis's book see a baseball prospect named Jeremy Brown, they see what they call a "bad body" catcher. To these scouts, Brown doesn't look like an athlete. But the stats tell a different story, suggesting that Brown has a rare set of skills (the ability to get on base more often than most players) that we see only if we use statistics to question the scouts' eyeball tests.[5]

We can put this debate yet another way by suggesting that it is a debate about the relationship between database and narrative. In one of the texts that launched software studies, Lev Manovich provided this useful (if also controversial) theoretical construct: the competing worldviews of narrative and database. In The Language of New Media, Manovich argues that these two worldviews compete in the world of new media. If narrative presents a single and ordered path through information, database allows for multiple (even contradictory) paths to exist at once: "As a cultural form, the database represents the world as a list of items, and it refuses to order this list. In contrast, a narrative creates a cause-and-effect trajectory of seemingly unordered items (events)."[6] One might argue that the argument for Cabrera, while rooted in statistics, is one associated with the worldview of narrative. Yes, there are numbers to support a vote for Cabrera, but those numbers are more about a particular narrative—he was the first Triple Crown winner in 45 years. Questioning that argument is ridiculous from the perspective of narrative, since the Triple Crown is hallowed. The case for Trout, this same person might say, emerges from the worldview of database, from an attempt to evaluate player success by taking advantage of more data. The hospitable database welcomes more data and more statistics, more information and more procedures for generating narratives. While the worldview of narrative might put more stock in the idea of the Triple Crown, the worldview of database tries to establish a different kind of ethical program—it attempts to take on a swarm of data by developing new analytic tools and generating new narratives. But the distinction between database and narrative is not a clean one. We can see narratives driving the case for Trout just as we can see data marshaled in support of a vote for Cabrera. A vote for Trout is certainly supported by a narrative, and WAR (as with any statistic) tells us a "story." This suggests that narrative and database are not separable, a point that Katherine Hayles makes in her response to Manovich.

We'll return to Hayles's arguments in a moment, but for the time being we should recognize that the very existence of the Mike Trout camp in this "cold war" is an indication that the relationship between database and narrative is in the midst of a shift, that the database is now hospitable to both more data and more narratives, and that this situation calls for an understanding of how to generate multiple narratives from data and how to make sense of competing, conflicting narratives. In other words, the ethical predicament of hospitality calls not for picking a side (database or narrative) but rather for methods and strategies that allow us to shift between these two worldviews.

While The Language of New Media does not explicitly address how ethics intersects with database and narrative, Manovich has speculated (albeit briefly) about the different ethics of database and narrative. In an interview, he offers a brief statement that helps frame the discussion of narrative and database in this chapter:

Like new media in general, databases allow for coexistence of different points of view, different models of the world, different ontologies and, potentially, different ethics. Narrative, in contrast, offers a singular interpretation of the world, a single model. Of course, this is an extremely schematic opposition, which often does not hold. A classical Hollywood film may indeed offer a singular model, but novels by Dostoevsky, as analyzed by Bakhtin, allow for exactly the opposite: coexistence of different world views. So we should be careful not to assign any essential qualities to a database.[7]

Manovich hedges a bit, insisting that narrative and database cannot be essentialized, but he does suggest that these two worldviews imply different sets of ethical assumptions. And while we might choose to call narrative less hospitable, and thus less ethical, than database, this argument would ignore that any attempt to make sense of data requires a narrative. Choosing a side, by arguing that our contemporary environment demands a database worldview, oversimplifies a difficult ethical predicament. If the ethical programs we enact with computation and with language are to address the particularities of situations (if they are to embody what Jim Porter calls a "rhetorical ethics"), then they will have to move between these two ethical approaches. The most useful ethical program is not one that chooses narrative or database but rather one that is agile enough to move between these worldviews, understanding how humans and computers translate data into narrative and vice versa. As Manovich argues, narrative and database are best understood as approaches to information rather than as specific genres or forms. One can write in a way that falls at places along the narrative-database continuum, and one can do so by way of language, computation, or various other media.

As Katherine Hayles argues in *How We Think*, our contemporary access to data means that "no one narrative is likely to establish dominance as the explanation, for the interpretive possibilities proliferate as databases increase."[8] For Hayles, this means that the worldviews of narrative and database require each other. Hayles presents a convincing argument in response to Manovich that neither database nor narrative will "win" but that they are "natural symbionts." If Manovich sees narrative and database as competing, Hayles offers a corrective by suggesting that narrative and database work in concert:

This symbiotic relationship presents us with a proliferation of narratives:

No longer singular, narratives remain the necessary others to database's ontology, the perspectives that invest the formal logic of database operations with human meanings and gesture toward the unknown hovering beyond the brink of what can be classified and enumerated.[9]

Here in addition to arguing that narratives are proliferating, Hayles also suggests that narratives are within the realm of "human meanings and gesture." This chapter will call this claim into question by examining some robots that use data to generate narratives, but Hayles's larger point still stands.[10] Most important, the Law of hospitality that defines networked life invites more data, shifting how we move between the worldviews of narrative and database. It's crucial that we toggle between these two, rather than making arguments that we have somehow progressed from the regressive world of narrative to the more sophisticated world of database (or that we require a "return" to narrative). This was largely how the Trout vs. Cabrera debate was couched, as a fight between crusty, old newspaper writers and geeky, stat-head bloggers. But given that arguments for Cabrera used data as evidence and arguments for Trout built narratives to explain data, this framing conceals more than it reveals. The interpretation of data will always require narratives. The question becomes the following: How do we navigate the increasingly complex relationship between database and narrative as the amount of data increases?

Baseball's recent identity crisis is but one way of understanding the exigence for this chapter, since it stands in as a microcosm for a larger set of cultural and rhetorical shifts. The multiple contemporary conversations surrounding big data demonstrate that we require new ways of understanding the shifting relationship between database and narrative, and these new modes of understanding can be aided by work in software studies that examines how computational machines mediate these two worldviews. Further, as this chapter will argue, the rhetorician is particularly well equipped for tackling this problem, since rhetoricians study and develop procedures for generating and analyzing narratives. In short, the tools of rhetoric provide procedures for moving back and forth between the worlds of database and narrative. In this chapter, I examine the robot writers of a company called Narrative Science, algorithms that generate narratives about large datasets (including baseball game data). The existence of these robots has led many to question whether computers can write as effectively as humans. However, this line of questioning, like the battle between scouts and statistics, offers a false choice. Instead, I ask what Narrative Science's computational machines can tell us about the shifting relationship between data and narrative and also what strategies they might reveal as we attempt to learn how to most effectively toggle between these two worldviews. I examine some of the code behind an early prototype of Narrative Science's robot writers, a system called Stats Monkey, in order to see what kinds of procedures are applied to data to generate admittedly simple recaps of MLB games. What we learn when taking a look "under the hood" of Stats Monkey is that its algorithms are motivated. They are not "mere machines" but are rather *rhetorical devices* that sit between database and narrative, making decisions. In short, they are ethical programs.

If both human and machine are generating narratives in order to aid (or, sometimes, sabotage) our attempts to make sense of interlocking and intersecting databases, we are reminded twice over that no single narrative can be trusted. Most important, the proliferation of both databases and narratives demonstrates the utter impossibility of cleanly separating the concerns of narrative and database. It is not enough to comfort ourselves with the worldview of narrative, assigning the database work to the machines that continue to welcome more and more data. Instead, networked life will require that we continuously move back and forth between database and narrative, finding ways to sort out how data gets funneled into narratives and how to decide what to keep and what to filter out. Narrative Science's "robot journalists" present a possible method for addressing this set of problems—the cultivation of machinic thinking. This approach to problem solving—which goes by multiple names, including computational thinking, algorithmic thinking, and systems thinking—is a key strategy for living in a world of hospitable databases. I use the term machinic in this chapter because it accounts for a range of the different ways that procedures "machine" data. Whether we consider algorithms or heuristics (the former involving a defined set of procedures that achieve a discrete goal and the latter offering a more open-ended method for solving computational problems), we're discussing *machines* that enact ethical programs to solve problems. In this chapter, the problem I am most interested in is the translation of narrative into data and data into narrative.

In order to understand Narrative Science's robots, we need to understand how computational machines work and how they can be used to author narratives. If we see the world from the viewpoint of these machines, we find ways of toggling between the worldviews of database and narrative. Computational machines sit in the liminal space between database and narrative and represent a set of processes for transforming data into narrative. Further, those same machines bear resemblance to the theoretical tools of rhetoric, which apply procedures to language to both generate and interpret arguments. From this angle, rhetoric becomes not just a tool for mediating disputes like those between supporters of Trout and Cabrera but also a tool for *mediating the worldviews of database and narrative*. We typically think of rhetorical theory in terms of discourse, in terms of how to judge, analyze, or create arguments. However, to limit rhetoric to this realm is to miss that rhetoric is concerned not only with the output of machines (text, image, and so on) but also with the machines themselves. Rhetoric, even in its predigital permutations, is concerned with the machines that machine discourse. That is, rhetoric cuts across the concerns of database and narrative. The movement between database and narrative requires that we think machinically. Rhetoric, which has always been machinic, is of great use when approaching this task.

Narrative Science's Robot Journalists

In early 2012, just months before the Trout vs. Cabrera debate, robot writers began threatening the livelihood of journalists everywhere. Actually, it is perhaps not fair to blame the robots. Instead, it was Kristian Hammond, chief technology officer of a company called Narrative Science, who was firing shots across the bow. Hammond claimed that, within 15 years, more than 90 percent of news would be written by computers.[11] This claim might have been more about gaining publicity for his company, Narrative Science, than about making a realistic claim, but this kind of gravitas fits nicely with the world of technology companies, Wired profiles, and TED talks. Whether or not Hammond made the claim seriously, journalists certainly took notice. In the midst of a media blitz, journalists and commentators began taking up the question raised in the Wired profile of Narrative Science: Can machines write better than humans? For journalists, the follow-up question was fairly obvious: Can an algorithm do the job better? Rebecca Greenfield of The Atlantic saw little cause for concern, arguing that Narrative Science's stories offered little in the way of analysis or context.[12] Her primary example was a story generated by one of Hammond's algorithms about the New York Times Company's earnings.[13] This particular story is just one example of the many earnings previews that Narrative Science's algorithms write for Forbes each month, and its first sentences demonstrate that it is a fairly formulaic synthesis of the data:

> Share prices of New York Times Company's (NYT) stock have fallen 23% during the last three months and closed at $6.20 on April 16, 2012. On Thursday, April 19, 2012 New York Times Company (NYT) can help stop the slide when it reports its first quarter results.[14]

The structure of this story is the same as every other earnings preview that Narrative Science generates for Forbes. Each has the same subheadings and generates a formulaic account of the data available. The sentences are grammatical, and the report is readable (even if it is a bit dull). The focus of the story is on the data available leading up to the New York Times Company's report of first quarter results, and the Narrative Science algorithms do not step outside of that data.

Greenfield compared this account to two other stories, one by Joe Pompeo and another by Alexander Abad-Santos. Pompeo's story addressed the New

York Times Company's financials in the context of whether Will Sulzberger (who was serving as interim chief executive officer) would be the next CEO.[15] The CEO search came up during a quarterly earnings conference phone call, and Sulzberger hedged a bit when asked about the search. This became a focal point of Pompeo's story, which addresses the earnings reports after discussing Sulzberger, though Pompeo doesn't explicitly link these two stories together aside from saying that the company's financial reports and its search for a new CEO were both discussed during the conference call. Abad-Santos focused on a downturn in both print and digital advertising revenue and revenue generated from the sale of regional newspapers.[16] While the Narrative Science story is focused on synthesizing a finite dataset into narrative form, Pompeo and Abad-Santos take different approaches to the story. Pompeo focuses on Sulzberger while Abad-Santos delves a bit deeper into the reasons behind falling revenues. One might be tempted to say that the humans have taken what journalists call an "angle" on the story while the Narrative Science algorithm has not. But even this doesn't quite work, given that Narrative Science's software contains "angle" variables that allow the software to choose the best angle on an earnings report or a baseball game's box score. We'll examine examples of these angle variables later in this chapter.

Greenfield argues that the Narrative Science story provides "no real context, or analysis, or prose."[17] While I'm not quite sure of her definition of "prose" (all three stories are examples of prose writing), it is fair to argue that Pompeo and Abad-Santos are presenting context in a way that Narrative Science is not. Or it is perhaps better to say that these two humans are operating with a different dataset when crafting their narratives. All three of these authors have taken a set of data and transformed it into a narrative. The difference is that the Narrative Science algorithm does not move outside of documentation about earnings estimates, so it does not deal with information about advertising revenue or who will eventually step in as CEO. Interestingly, this suggests that the Narrative Science algorithm offers a *narrower* ethical program than both Abad-Santos and Pompeo, confining itself to a finite database. The two humans cast a wider net, welcome more data into their narratives. This chapter is concerned with this relationship between database and narrative, with how each brings its own set of assumptions, and with how we might mediate the two. The narrow ethical program of the Narrative Science robot as compared to these two humans is further evidence that the worldviews of narrative and database do not map neatly onto the categories of "human" and "nonhuman," respectively.

Regardless of its limitations, the algorithmically generated story about the New York Times Company is evidence that Narrative Science has succeeded in taking data and spinning a narrative. In interviews and blog posts, Hammond argues that narratives "provide us with a structured arc for communication that allows us to impart new information in a way that supports our listeners' expectations."[18] Those expectations are set up by the order in which a narrator delivers facts:

> If I tell you that a team has won a game and then go into detail about a particular play, you will assume that the play referenced contributed to that win. If I tell you that a company's earnings are up, and I follow up with information about a change in management, I am implying that this later fact gave rise to the earlier one. And, if I tell you that a sales person has beat his or her target for the year, you expect me need [sic] to focus the rest of my story on why this is the case. It is simply part of our social contract with regard to communication.[19]

A spreadsheet offers no such story. As Hammond explains, it "lacks the narrative form that we need to pull these disparate facts together. Data sets alone lack the connective tissue that we use to build a coherent understanding of what they mean."[20] For Hammond, when it comes to a spreadsheet, "the cognitive burden is placed on the reader, who now must struggle to draw the right conclusions."[21] Narrative Science's algorithms try to lighten that burden by synthesizing data into narrative—that is, they enact an ethical program by determining what information is most important and how it should be delivered to an audience. The robot decides for us, delivering us one path through the data. Such robots now sit alongside human journalists who are attempting to aid in the interpretation of hospitable databases. Our contemporary media environment allows access to a staggering amount of data. Of course, as this book has argued, that welcoming gesture is never purely realized, and no database welcomes all information. The Law of hospitality remains unreachable, since it is visible only at the moment that we sift, sort, and restrict. The hospitable database simultaneously welcomes data and serves as a gatekeeper, deciding what information can pass and how it will be sorted. This sorting represents one more example of the laws of hospitality, which always sit in tension with the Law of hospitality. This problem manifests in the worldviews of database and narrative, both of which require that one decide how to filter and sort, how to order data in particular ways. Each of these worldviews applies certain procedures when enacting its ethical program.

These ethical programs are motivated and rhetorical—they enact ethical arguments, and they address the challenges of the Law of hospitality. While tracking down the motives of any ethical program is complicated, we can examine how the program is enacted and how it generates certain results. By doing so, we can draw some conclusions about the ethics embedded in a particular machine. And just as we can never arrive at a human's true motive or intention, we can never arrive at the "truth" behind a computational machine. For even if we do gain access to a machine's code, it is only one way of making sense of how that machine takes input, processes it, and generates output. The availability of code helps, but we should resist the temptation of positing code as being "closer" to truth than other layers of computational meaning. Still, even if accessing code does not allow us to arrive at the "intention" of a particular computational machine, it can help us link interface to internal process. This is Wardrip-Fruin's project in *Expressive Processing* as he defines three ways of understanding the relationship between user experience and computational operations—the Tale-Spin Effect, the Eliza Effect, and the SimCity Effect. Each of Wardrip-Fruin's effects demonstrate different relationships between process and interface. In fact, in the case of the Narrative Science algorithm I examine in this chapter, we find an instance of Wardrip-Fruin's Tale-Spin Effect, in which a user's surface interaction with a computational machine fails to reveal the complex processes at work. Wardrip-Fruin's analysis of narrative generation machines and games at the level of code and at the level of output presents a way for us to conceptualize the relationships between data, process, and interface.

In the interest of digging into the processes of Narrative Science's robot journalists, we can examine some of the code of a project called Stats Monkey, a project that led to the launch of the company. This analysis will help us understand how a computational machine processes data in order to create narratives. By paying close attention to how data and process work together to generate admittedly simple recap stories for baseball games, we can begin to imagine how Narrative Science's more complex engines work. In addition, this particular system is accompanied by a white paper that explains how it works and what the variables mean. This presents yet another opportunity for making sense of how Stats Monkey generates narratives. Still, the challenge when attempting analysis of proprietary systems is that we will always have limited access to code, and it is worth pausing to consider the implication of these limits for software studies. In some sense, we are *settling* when analyzing this older version of Stats Monkey. We are not gaining access to the proprietary systems that Narrative Science and companies like it are developing each day for the likes of *Forbes* magazine. However, my hope is that a detailed account of this early iteration of the technology can help develop strategies for cultivating a machinic sensibility and for gaining a more nuanced sense of the proprietary systems to which we do not have access. That sensibility aids readers and writers as they approach an array of software situations, some of which offer us access to code and some that do not. Thus, this discussion is in line with other work in software studies that insists that studying software does not always mean studying code. While studying code must be part of the project of software studies, code can never be considered the only artifact of analysis. Otherwise, the field is left with nothing to say about proprietary systems.

As we approach the Stats Monkey software, it is also helpful to understand how this project emerged. Much of the work done by Narrative Science is the result of collaborations between journalists and computer scientists (they employ people from both fields as what they call "meta-writers"), and some of the company's earliest ideas emerged out of a course at Northwestern University that included both programmers and journalists. Steven Levy describes one of the projects from that course:

> In 2009, Hammond and his colleague Larry Birnbaum taught a class at Medill [School of Journalism] that included both programmers and prospective journalists. They encouraged their students to create a system that could transform data into prose stories. One of the students in the class was a stringer for the *Tribune* who covered high school sports; he and two other journalism students were paired with a computer science student. Their prototype software, Stats Monkey, collected box scores and play-by-play data to spit out credible accounts of college baseball games.[22]

The system impressed Stuart Frankel, a former executive at a company called DoubleClick, who eventually founded Narrative Science with Hammond and Birnbaum.

As of this writing, a version of Stats Monkey still lives on the Internet. While the available version of Stats Monkey is dated and somewhat limited (as impressed as Frankel was and as interested as he was in developing the idea, he admitted that the system was very simplistic), it still helps us see the "guts" of this particular narrative generator. Stats Monkey offers a database of games (the database contains games from Major League Baseball's 2009 season) from which a user can "write" a story. The scare quotes here stem from the fact that, regardless of the fact that a user clicks a button that reads "write a story with this data," a user of Stats Monkey is not doing the writing. Further, this version of the software does not dynamically generate stories— each click of the "write a story" button will always generate the same narrative. Still, what's most important to notice here is that this software uses computation to generate a narrative and to enact an ethical program that makes decisions about what data is most important and what should or should not be included.

Luckily, users are not left in the dark when using Stats Monkey. The system presents a look into the data and processes used to generate narratives.

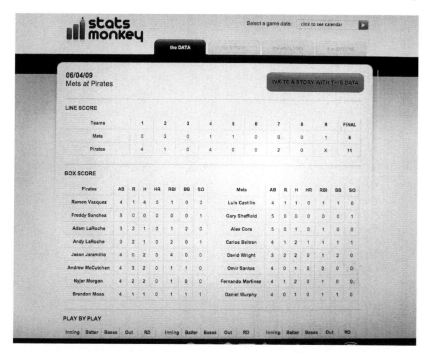

Fig 4. Stats Monkey's "Data" Screen
("Stats Monkey," accessed March 28, 2014, http://jermaine.cs.northwestern.edu/baseball/.)

In order to offer a close reading of this system, I have chosen a June 4, 2009, game between the Pittsburgh Pirates and the New York Mets. This game, like many of a Major League Baseball team's 162 regular season games, was relatively uneventful. Still, as I have already suggested, the promise of baseball when illustrating the relationship between database and narrative is that the sport is obsessed with statistics. Stats Monkey takes advantage of this abundance of data by interpreting it and crafting narratives. The system does not merely read or generate a box score—the traditional record of a baseball game, which includes the batting and pitching stats of each player and the total numbers for each team. Instead, it uses data that tracks important moments in the game, and it even uses "angles" when generating stories. If a journalist looks for an angle during a baseball game—a player who is having a spectacular day at the plate or a pitcher who is recording a large number of strikeouts—so does Stats Monkey. Both human and computational machine use motivated procedures to generate narratives.

Here is the story generated by Stats Monkey for the June 4, 2009 game between the Pirates and the Mets:

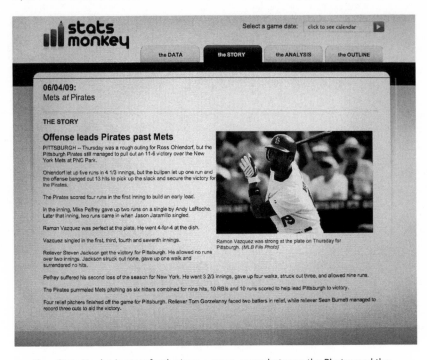

Fig 5. Stats Monkey's story for the June 4, 2009, game between the Pirates and the Mets

("Stats Monkey," accessed March 28, 2014, http://jermaine.cs.northwestern.edu/baseball/.)

This game recap is a fairly dry and straight-ahead recounting of the game's major events, and we might be tempted to immediately compare it to human-generated recaps for the same game. We will look at these human-written stories shortly, but first notice that this story is the result of a fairly complex set of computational procedures. It would be a mistake to think that the story is merely arranging a set of facts. It does in fact read this way, but while it is not especially engaging to read and seems to lack much in the way of transitions between ideas, the narrative presented here is the result of a computational machine making decisions about the data and the story's angle.

In order to get a clearer sense of how Stats Monkey works, we can look at two other views provided by the software. First, we can examine the software's dataset (see figure 6), which presents the user with the information that is typically included in a baseball box score. For instance, we know from this screen that Ramon Vasquez of the Pirates had four hits, one run batted in, and one run, but the format of this screen is different from the typical box score. Most box scores list players in the batting order. In this particular game, Andrew McCutchen batted first for the Pirates, and this would usually mean that

PLAY BY PLAY

Inning	Batter	Bases	Out	RD	Inning	Batter	Bases	Out	RD	Inning	Batter	Bases	Out	RD
1	133321	—	1	0	3	494686	1-	2	2	6	133321	—	1	4
1	112116	—	2	0	3	435408	12-	2	2	6	112116	—	2	4
1	136860	-2-	2	0	3	460059	—	3	2	6	136860	—	3	4
1	122111	—	3	0	3	461235	—	1	2	6	425560	—	1	4
1	457705	1-	0	0	3	452232	—	2	2	6	451188	—	2	4
1	460579	1-3	0	0	3	407496	1-	2	2	6	461235	—	3	4
1	408108	-2-	1	0	3	456027	—	3	2	7	122111	—	1	4
1	425560	1-	1	0	4	133321	—	1	2	7	431151	—	2	4
1	451188	12-	1	2	4	112116	—	2	2	7	502517	1-	2	4
1	461235	123	1	2	4	136860	—	2	1	7	494686	—	3	4
1	452232	12-	1	4	4	122111	—	3	1	7	452232	—	1	4
1	407496	123	1	4	4	457705	1-	0	1	7	407496	1-	1	4
1	456027	—	3	4	4	460579	-2-	1	1	7	400134	—	2	4
2	431151	1-	0	4	4	408108	-3	2	1	7	457705	1-	2	5
2	502517	1-	0	3	4	425560	1-	2	1	7	460579	-3	2	6
2	494686	1-3	0	3	4	451188	12-	2	1	7	408108	—	3	6
2	435408	12-	1	3	4	461235	123	2	2	8	435408	—	1	6
2	460059	1-3	1	3	4	452232	12-	2	4	8	430598	—	2	6
2	133321	-23	2	2	4	407496	12-	2	5	8	133321	—	3	6
2	112116	1-3	2	1	4	456027	—	3	5	8	425560	—	1	6
2	136860	12-	2	1	5	431151	1-	0	5	8	407155	—	2	6
2	122111	—	3	1	5	502517	1-	1	5	8	461235	—	3	6
2	457705	—	1	1	5	494686	-2-	1	4	9	112116	1-	0	6
2	460579	-3	1	1	5	435408	-3	2	4	9	136860	-3	1	6
2	408108	-3	2	1	5	111548	—	3	4	9	122111	-3	2	6
2	425560	-2-	2	2	5	457705	—	2	4	9	431151	-2-	2	5
2	451188	—	3	2	5	460579	—	2	4	9	502517	—	3	5
3	431151	1-	0	2	5	408108	—	3	4					
3	502517	1-	1	2										

Fig 6. Stats Monkey data for the June 4, 2009, game between the Pirates and the Mets
("Stats Monkey," accessed March 28, 2014, http://jermaine.cs.northwestern.edu/baseball/.)

he would be listed first in the box score. Instead, he is listed sixth. Though this may seem like a minor difference, we already have some clues that the system is manipulating the game data toward particular ends. We can gather from the Stats Monkey game recap that Vasquez is listed first because he had four hits, a relatively rare occurrence in a baseball game. The ordering of the players beyond this is not quite clear, but it is most important that even a screen called "the DATA" is already manipulated and is not merely "raw." An ethical program that decides which data is most important has already been enacted.

In addition to this more traditional data, we also get "play-by-play" data that offers a detailed account of individual plays in the game. From this set of data, we get a kind of "machine's-eye-view" of the game's plays (see figure 7).

By examining the play-by-play data of this game at *Yahoo Sports* (like many websites, *Yahoo!* archives box scores, play-by-play, and story recap data for Major League Baseball games), we learn that this data translates as: "Alex Cora popped out to Shortstop. The Mets are losing by zero runs." The "Bases" field tells us if anyone is on base (if someone had been on first base at the time of this play, it would read "1- -"), the "Out" field tells us that there is now one out

Inning	Batter	Bases	Out	RD
1	133321	---	1	0

Fig 7. A single line from the "Play by Play" data
("Stats Monkey," accessed March 28, 2014, http://jermaine.cs.northwestern.edu/baseball/.)

in the inning, and the "RD" or "Runs Down" field indicates how many runs the away team is losing by. The number in the "batter" field is Cora's "Elias ID." Elias Sports Bureau tracks all statistical information for Major League Baseball games. Thus, from the software's perspective, each player is a number, and this means that the data can be manipulated more easily. However, it's worth mentioning that the Elias database is used by a number of websites, including MLB.com and Baseball Prospectus. These sites have URLs for each player, and that URL often includes the player's Elias ID. We might take this opportunity to acknowledge that "the database" in this case is distributed across multiple sites and entities. Even a seemingly finite dataset such as a baseball box score ends up leaking out into other databases, and this is one more reminder of networked hospitality.

The play-by-play data presents an abbreviated, alphanumeric representation of the events of the game. The box score at the top of the screen presents the cumulative stats, but the play-by-play data contextualizes that data by linking it to certain moments in the game. As we will see, Stats Monkey values events differently depending on when they happen in the game.

The third tab on Stats Monkey's web interface is the "analysis" screen (see Figure 8). This screen shows us how Stats Monkey manipulates the data and look for patterns. The "Best Players" portion of the screen tracks two statistics. The first is "Game Score," a number that quantifies an individual batter's performance by awarding points to certain events, such as hits and runs.[23] The second statistic in this section is Win Probability Added (WPA), which "attempts to measure a player's contribution to a win by figuring the factor by which each specific play made by that player has altered the outcome of a game."[24] Baseball is a team game, but it has also historically been concerned with tracking the individual contributions of its players. This can be difficult.[25] Stats such as WPA and Game Score are attempts to separate out an individual player's accomplishments.

The Analysis screen also shows us that Stats Monkey looks for "Key At Bats" and "Tough Spots." Though these fields are empty for this particular game, other games would show us particular moments of import. The

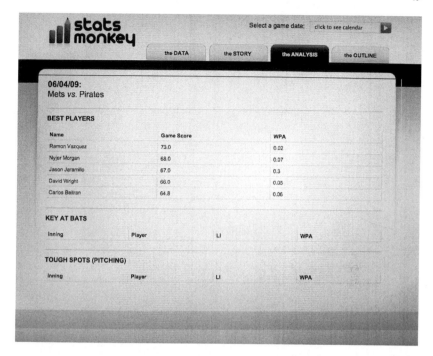

Fig. 8. Stats Monkey's "Analysis" screen
("Stats Monkey," accessed March 28, 2014, http://jermaine.cs.northwestern.edu/baseball/.)

system uses a statistic called "Win Probability" to seek out the most important moments in the game. In a white paper, the designers explain how they use this stat: "Win probability is the historical likelihood of a team winning the game when faced with a certain game state. Tracking this data allows StatsMonkey to find the plays that impacted the outcome of the game the most."[26] This screen also features a "Leverage Index" field, which tracks "the historical ability for win probability to shift on a given play." This index "picks out the plays that had the potential for the greatest impact on the game" and allows Stats Monkey to "search for missed opportunities and crucial moments in the game."[27] The Leverage Index field is evidence that Stats Monkey is looking for what is *not* in the box score data. If a player strikes out when there are three players on base and his team is losing by three runs, Stats Monkey will be particularly interested in this moment in the game. Like the human journalists in the press box, Stats Monkey is attempting to assign significance to events and is working to craft a narrative that does more than just arrange data.

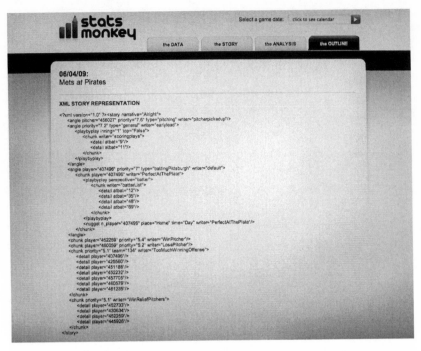

Fig 9. Stats Monkey's "Outline" screen
("Stats Monkey," accessed March 28, 2014, http://jermaine.cs.northwestern.edu/baseball/.)

Finally, we have a screen called "the Outline," which presents us with what is perhaps the most interesting view of Stats Monkey's writing process (see Figure 9). The lead of this story gives us some insight into how the system chooses events and determines the importance of those events:

```
<?xml version="1.0" ?><story narrative="Alright">
    <angle pitcher="456027" priority="7.6" type="pitching"
        writer="pitcherpickedup"/>
    <angle priority="7.2" type="general" writer="earlylead">
        <playbyplay inning="1" top="False">
            <chunk writer="scoringplays">
                <detail atbat="9"/>
                <detail atbat="11"/>
            </chunk>
        </playbyplay>
    </angle>
```

Again, we get a glimpse at how Stats Monkey sees the data. Translated into a human readable narrative, we get this:

> PITTSBURGH—Thursday was a rough outing for Ross Ohlendorf, but the Pittsburgh Pirates still managed to pull out an 11–6 victory over the New York Mets at PNC Park.
>
> Ohlendorf gave up five runs in 4 1/3 innings, but the bullpen gave up one run and the offense banged out 13 hits to pick up the slack and secure the victory for the Pirates.
>
> The Pirates scored four runs in the first inning to build an early lead.
>
> In the inning, Mike Pelfrey gave up two runs on a single by Andy La-Roche. Later that inning, two runs came in when Jason Jaramillo singled.

From the XML code, we can see that the system has chosen two angles: "pitch-erpickedup" and "earlylead." Ross Ohlendorf had an unsuccessful pitching outing, but his offense "picked him up" by scoring a number of runs early in the game. The supporting evidence for these assertions is provided in the next portions of the code (and in the following paragraphs). The system determines that the Pirates' first inning was a significant (or, perhaps, "high leverage") moment in the game, given that they scored four runs. It thus presents the scoring plays that took place in the bottom of the first inning. From these opening lines of prose and code, we can see that the system is generating both angles (the field "writer" presents various angles for the story) and priorities for those angles. A higher "priority" number pushes that portion of the story toward the beginning, and this fits with journalism's "inverted pyramid" approach to writing stories. The most important information is placed at the top, and the least important information appears later in the article. Stats Monkey makes these decisions based on significant moments in the game and on the presence of noteworthy performances by certain players.

So, how does this narrative compare to those written by humans? The human-written stories (though, given that the algorithms of Stats Monkey were written by humans, this label is an imperfect one) of this particular game are quite different when compared to the Stats Monkey version. If the play-by-play, WPA, and Game Score tell us that the game was about the Pirates bailing out Ross Ohlendorf and about Ramon Vazquez's four hits, the beat reporters remind us that every box score sits in relation to some other "big picture" stories (this "big picture" is what the designers of Stats Monkey were trying to capture, according to their white paper). From the perspective of the Pittsburgh Pirates and their fans, this game was as much about a player who was absent as it was about any of the individuals who actually contributed to the win. One day prior, the Pirates traded away their star center fielder, Nate McLouth. The move was unexpected as the Pirates had just signed McLouth to a long-term contract, but the Pirates traded the outfielder for three younger prospects. In a related move, the team promoted their star prospect, Andrew McCutchen, to play center field. McCutchen made his debut on June 4, going 2–4 with a walk and a stolen base. This was pretty much the angle on this game in the Pittsburgh news outlets.[28] In New York, on the other hand, the story of this game was not about McCutchen or Vazquez but rather about how the Mets star outfielder Carlos Beltran was embarrassed to lose two straight games to the hapless Pirates.[29] The *New York Daily News* headline was "Pirates Pound Mike Pelfrey to Sweep 'Embarrassed' Mets." Finally, the *New York Times* angle was about how the team's All-Star shortstop Jose Reyes and relief pitcher J. J. Putz were battling injuries.[30] As with the Pittsburgh media's coverage of the game, the primary angles came from a much broader database of information.

We could, like Greenfield, use these comparisons as an opportunity to determine who or what writes "better" narratives, and one would be hard pressed to find a reader who judged the Stats Monkey narrative as better than the game stories published by the AP, the *Pittsburgh Post-Gazette*, or the *New Daily News*. However, we might also take this opportunity to consider how software like Stats Monkey serves as a reminder of what we share with machines. While humans may not consciously write procedures for generating their narratives, they do in fact operate by way of machine-like procedures. Humans, like Narrative Science's computational machines, organize data into groupings and categories and then apply processes to that data in order to interpret it. Those efforts are motivated. The Pittsburgh beat reporters are motivated to put this game in the context of the McLouth trade and McCutchen's debut, the New York reporters are motivated to discuss the Mets' loss to the hapless Pirates, and Stats Monkey is motivated by a desire to understand the game's most important moments and star players. We can arrive at these motives by thinking machinically, by examining the data, the processes, and the outputs of these authors. What a "close reading" of Stats Monkey provides is an in-depth account of what motivates this particular ethical program: key moments in the game, outstanding efforts by specific players, and (perhaps surprisingly) a contextualized account of certain data points. Stats Monkey's context might not be as broad as a human beat reporter's, but the software does seek to understand, rank, and synthesize information so that human readers can gain insight into a box score. Both beat reporter and robot operate by way of the inverted pyramid, an economy of language, and a desire to transform a series of events into a story.

Stats Monkey is a fairly simple narrative generation system, but it does present us with some valuable insights about how Narrative Science uses computation to transform data into narratives. What do we get when we examine not only the narratives generated by the system (output) but also the innards of that system (data and process)? For one, we should grant that Stats Monkey, even if it is an interesting computational experiment, does not spin particularly interesting narratives. However, the dismissal of this or any other story-generation system because of its boring narratives would miss much of what's happening behind the scenes in the realm of data and process. As Wardrip-Fruin shows with the example of the *Tale-Spin* story-generation system, many computational artifacts require that we examine more than their interface or output. Prior to Wardrip-Fruin's treatment of this system, many humanist accounts of it focused on the nonsensical stories that it generated while most computer scientists tended to treat it as an interesting computational artifact. What we find in his detailed account of the system's expressive processes is that *Tale-Spin* "creates a surface illusion of process simplicity and arbitrary action."[31] Wardrip-Fruin names this the *Tale-Spin* Effect, arguing that the study of processes is crucial for scholars of digital media: "in the world of digital media, and perhaps especially for digital fictions, we have as much to learn by examining the model that drives the figurative planetarium as by looking at a particular image of the stars (or even the animation of their movement)."[32] The argument here is similar to those made by Matthew Kirschenbaum and Nick Montfort about "screen essentialism." Taking up Montfort's arguments that media studies scholars have a "prevailing bias . . . toward display technologies that would have been unknown to most computer users before the mid 1970s," Kirschenbaum argues that "one does not always need to look at screens to study new media, or to learn useful things about the textual practices that accumulate in and around computation."[33] If we focus only on the end result or screen output of something like Stats Monkey, we find little of interest. It is in analyzing its computational processes that we learn how this system is making decisions in the generation of narratives.

My analysis of Stats Monkey provides a kind of behind-the-scenes look at how computational procedures generate narratives and how those procedures are motivated by rhetorical considerations such as audience expectations and genres. An analysis of Stats Monkey serves as a reminder that all processes, computational or otherwise, are motivated and rhetorical and that understanding these sets of rules allows us to oscillate between the worldviews of narrative and database. Instead of choosing between the ethics of narrative, which presents one particular perspective on the available data, and the ethics of database, which offers a flatter world in which multiple pathways can exist simultaneously, we can learn to oscillate between the two. So, while Stats Monkey might not replace the beat writers covering the Pittsburgh Pirates and

New York Mets, it does provide us with some insight into the values of computational thinking. By linking data with process, we learn how computational machines sit in the liminal space between narrative and database. Machinic thinking means we don't have to choose between the worldview of narrative or database. Rather, it allows us to oscillate between the two.

Thinking Like a Machine

Though information overload is not an altogether new phenomenon, one would have to grant that networked life has put this problem at the forefront and that our contemporary environment represents a shift in the relationship between database and narrative. This raises questions about how one deals with an onslaught of data, with how we create and judge the conflicting and competing narratives that cross our screens. This is a question of hospitality, of the intersection between the hospitable database that welcomes more and more information and the attempts to write ethical programs that transform data into narratives. As many have pointed out, this means that attention is a precious commodity. In The Economics of Attention, Richard Lanham explains this in terms of economies of "stuff" and "fluff": "In an economy of stuff, the laws of property govern who owns stuff. In an attention economy, it is the laws of intellectual property that govern who gets attention."[34] For Lanham, the move to an attention economy presents an opportunity for the arts and letters to move to the center, since they study "how attention is allocated."[35] More specifically, Lanham sees rhetoric as a new economics that helps us toggle between the worlds of stuff (physical things) and fluff (what we say about physical things). In another text, The Electronic Word, Lanham describes this movement in terms of looking "at" text (noticing surface and style) and "through" text (reading for meaning). For Lanham, a rhetorical education presents us with the tools to move between looking "at" and "through" texts and, therefore, to shift attitudinal worlds. Lanham calls this movement oscillatio.[36]

How does one respond to the hospitable database? This predicament requires the ability to oscillate between narrative and database, two different worldviews that make different ethical assumptions. In a hospitable network, readers and writers are inundated with information and have a finite amount of time and attention for making sense of that information. Further, they must also confront a growing database of narratives. In short, networked life requires that we effectively move between the worldviews of narrative and database and that we understand how procedures (sometimes computational, sometimes not) operate between these two spheres. In her argument for making "algorithms" the "fourth 'R'" of the educational system, Cathy Davidson suggests that algorithmic thinking "provides an alternative to fact-based mastery and proposes, instead, iterative, process-oriented, constructive, innovative thinking."[37] For Davidson, such thinking is not only about learning to program a computer. In fact, she argues that introducing this type of learning at the K-12 level would be "less about 'learning code' than 'learning to code.'"[38] While it is certainly necessary and beneficial for programming to be introduced into K-12 education, Davidson's larger argument is that algorithmic and computational approaches to all kinds of problems should be the driving force behind such curricular developments. Davidson is a literary scholar interested in the digital humanities, and her call for such an approach shows how fields in the humanities are slowly but surely understanding computer programming as something more than just a specialized technical practice. Davidson's work is very much in line with the goals of many in software studies who aim to demystify programming and provide terms and concepts for nonexperts. While learning to code should never be off the table, other ways of engaging with software can also help the general public understand how programs cut across activities.

Such calls for algorithmic thinking and a broad application of computational thought have also come from within the field of computer science. Of these calls, Jeannette Wing's has been one of the most influential. In her article on how computational thinking might be able to go mainstream, Wing also steps through the basics of computational thinking and how we might begin to incorporate it into the system of education. Wing's oft-cited article returns to the fundamental practice of computer science, the creation of abstractions, in order to argue for a rethinking of the educational system.[39] That rethinking would bring algorithmic and computational thought to K-12 education and to other disciplines. By discussing computing in these broad terms, Wing (like Davidson) is able to show that computational thinking is about much more than programming computers. By understanding algorithmic and computational thought as broad theoretical constructs, we can use the contemporary cultural moment to think differently about all communicative practices.

Wing argues that while approaching the world through the lens of algorithmic thought may mean that we focus on how computers work, those computers need not be made of metal.

> Yes, a computer could be a machine, but more subtly it could be a human. Humans process information: humans compute. In other words, computational thinking does not require a machine. Moreover, when we consider the combination of a human and a machine as a computer, we can exploit the combined processing power of a human with that of a machine. For example, humans are still better than machines at parsing and interpret-

ing images; on the other hand, machines are much better at executing certain kinds of instructions far more quickly than humans and processing datasets far larger than a human can handle.[40]

As Wing suggests, while machines exceed our capabilities in terms of processing large datasets—that is, iterating an algorithm millions of times across a large corpus—they are (currently) less adept at analyzing particular situations. While a computer can synthesize a spreadsheet into a brief story, it may not be as well equipped to explain how that spreadsheet and its accompanying narrative fit with other narratives circulating at the same time or with other trends emerging in disparate databases across a network. If computational machines can help us find patterns across a large corpus, perhaps those same machines can be aided by the human thinker's ability to apply procedures on a smaller scale, locating the importance of certain trends in a broader context of conflicting and competing narratives. Noticing the differences between humans and computational machines does not require that we select one as "better." In fact, such judgments can often serve as a distraction from more productive questions.

These recent arguments for a "4th R" represent attempts to introduce innovations into the educational system, and it is significant that they are *additive* attempts. These thinkers, for better or worse, are not looking to tear down existing pedagogical structures but rather to augment them for the contemporary moment. This is fortuitous for the rhetorician, who operates with a set of tools that is more than 2,000 years old. Those working in digital rhetoric are, like Davidson and Wing, looking to retrofit these tools. Among these rhetoricians, Collin Brooke's work is particularly useful here, offering a way to navigate the waters of narrative and database. In *Lingua Fracta: Towards a Rhetoric of New Media*, Brooke reimagines each of the canons of rhetoric—invention, arrangement, style, memory, and delivery—in light of new media technologies.[41] Brooke's discussion of arrangement is applicable to my own analysis in this chapter since it engages directly with Manovich's narrative/database coupling. Whereas arrangement is typically concerned with how a rhetor orders his or her ideas, Brooke updates this canon by suggesting that a rhetoric of new media moves this canon from arrangement to "patterning."

Brooke, along with others such as Liz Losh and Ian Bogost, takes Manovich to task for his reductive view of rhetoric. Manovich links rhetoric to the printed word, and he argues that print "encoded human knowledge and memory, instructed, inspired, convinced, and seduced their readers to adopt new ideas, new ways of interpreting the world, new ideologies."[42] While he sees the slim possibility of developing a "rhetoric of hypermedia," Manovich sees the prevalence of hyperlinking as evidence that hypermedia serves to "distract the reader from the argument," and he speculates that "hyperlinking exemplifies the continuing decline of the field of rhetoric in the modern era."[43] The ability to access more information in a nearly infinite number of combinations means that the digital text no longer relies on a particular arrangement:

> Rather than seducing the user through a careful arrangement of arguments and examples, points and counterpoints, changing rhythms of presentation (i.e., the rate of data streaming, to use contemporary language), simulated false paths, and dramatically presented conceptual breakthroughs, cultural interfaces, like RAM itself, bombard the user with all the data at once.[44]

Manovich does account for the possibility of a digital rhetoric, but that possibility is offered begrudgingly. Digital rhetoric would "have less to do with arranging information in a particular order and more to do simply with selecting what is included and what is not included in the total corpus presented."[45] Manavich's digital rhetoric is described as having "less to do with ordering of time by a writer or an orator, and more with spatial wandering."[46] Manovich's language here is instructive. He deploys the rhetorical figure of "anaphora" to lend emphasis to this point: if there is a place for a digital rhetoric, it will be a restricted one. This language indicates a general mood of reduction. Rhetoric will change, and its role will become smaller. Rhetoric will have a very specific task—selecting what is included in the database and then allowing an audience to choose its own path through that data.

Losh returns to Manovich's dismissal of rhetoric in *Virtualpolitik*, a text that does important work in bringing together rhetorical studies and new media studies. She insists that Manovich's account is questionable, arguing that his account of hypertext presenting "all the data at once" is inaccurate and that his link between rhetoric and print is "particularly counterfactual in light of the number of professional rhetoricians throughout history who have grounded their field in classical oratory and the norms of social interaction in oral culture."[47] Bogost also revisits this passage in order to argue that Manovich has a "rather curious view of hypertext that seems to equate hypermedia with media gluttony."[48] Bogost argues that hypertext is often used to build arguments and that links can provide "supporting arguments, evidence, or citation, very old and very traditional tools in written rhetoric."[49] He even makes what has become a standard move of software studies by pointing out Manovich's failure to account for the protocols—HTTP, TCP/IP, HTML—that play an integral part in any hypertext and that "make it possible to link and click in the first place."[50] This last critique is especially interesting given that Manovich himself is credited with launching the field of software studies.

These critiques of Manovich's account of rhetoric have offered an important corrective, and they are crucial if rhetoric is to be a part of software studies research. However, it is Brooke's account that I would like to focus on here since it both critiques Manovich and makes a place for rhetoric in the narrative/database coupling. Brooke situates Manovich's account in a long tradition of hypertext scholars who render arrangement "irrelevant" in the wake of hypertext. That is, scholars of hypertext have argued that the reader's ability to rearrange texts—or, at least, to carve a path through the text—means that the rhetor's arrangement of text is not important. This is indeed what Manovich's account seems to do. For Brooke, Manovich makes two moves. He reduces rhetoric to arrangement and then swiftly "extends obsolescence to an entire discipline."[51] As Brooke notes, Manovich's explanation of the modularity of new media—one of Manovich's key terms in *The Language of New Media*—makes "arrangement, and hence rhetoric, unnecessary."[52] For Brooke, Manovich's account is one of many that operates with a "straw version of arrangement" and that presumes "that arrangement must be an all-or-nothing affair: Either a text is painstakingly ordered by its producer and passively consumed, or new media is the 'confused heap' that Quintilian warns of."[53] Brooke's response to this argument is to rework the canon of arrangement in terms of "patterning": "Although databases may contain no predetermined order, they are useful to us to the degree that they provide some sort of order when they are acted on by users."[54] Each user moves through the database creating (or arranging) different patterns. For Brooke, arrangement and rhetoric do not disappear in new media environments; they merely reemerge in new forms.

Brooke's reinvention of arrangement as patterning offers an account of how the digital rhetor moves between narrative and database. But it is more than an analytical tool; it is more concerned with rhetorical production than with interpretation:

> Arrangement, which for a long time has been one of the most visible of canons, must be thought of in terms of *practice* if it is to thrive in the interfaces of new media. Whether a particular textual object evinces signs of arrangement is a question that is left over from print culture; the issue is not whether arrangement predates our textual encounters, but rather what practices we might develop with new media to make sense of them.[55]

Brooke's notion of patterning remakes arrangement without holding on too tightly to the assumptions of print. One could argue that a digital rhetor arranges *both* databases and narratives, but Brooke argues for a different conception of arrangement altogether: "Rather than seeing arrangement as a canon that is divided into categories like narrative and database, it is possible to reconceive it as a practice that mediates those categories."[56] Thus, patterning is about how the rhetor moves between database and narrative. If Lanham presents a framework for a digital rhetoric with his *oscillatio* and the "shifting of attitudinal worlds" then Brooke's patterning presents a specific rhetorical strategy for such oscillations. Patterning allows the rhetor to move between the attitudinal worlds of narrative and database.

Brooke is primarily concerned with rethinking the five canons of rhetoric—invention, arrangement, style, memory, and delivery—to build a digital rhetoric, and he does so by referencing a number of networked computing platforms (from blogs to social bookmarking sites). While he doesn't apply his idea directly to how such platforms work at the level of code and computation, his framework perfectly suits this chapter's dealings with how computational machines navigate the worldviews of narrative and databases. Brooke's concept of patterning describes how software like Stats Monkey navigates the relationship between narrative and database and how it enacts ethical programs to make decisions. The software seeks out patterns, orders data, interprets that data, and builds a narrative from a database. These patterns exclude certain bits of information, making them ethical through and through. Narrative Science's algorithms sit in the liminal space between database and narrative, toggling between stuff and story. This toggling is a useful way of understanding both the generation and interpretation of narratives.[57]

Understanding computational machines as the development of patterns that mediate narrative and database leaves behind the concerns of whether machines or humans are "winning" and prevents us from getting bogged down in choosing between narrative and database once and for all. Given our growing databases, we require ways of moving between the worldviews of database and narrative, and this means setting aside the distractions of determining once and for all how humans are different from or superior to computational machines. What Narrative Science's robot writers provide us with is not a way to draw a line between human and computational machine. There are certainly important distinctions between the two, and the stories cited by Greenfield in her discussion of Narrative Science are a perfect example of this. But each time we attempt to clearly delineate human from computational machine, we find difficulties. In fact, the algorithms that generate Narrative Science's stories are written by what the company calls "meta-writers." These meta-writers are often journalists who understand the generic expectations of news writing. In such a situation, where does human intervention end? Where does computational process begin? Debates about robot writers are almost instantaneously transformed into contests between robots and humans. Which can write better? Which can provide context? Better prose? A more "complete picture"?

But while the debate surrounding Narrative Science and other robot writers can tend to focus on whether and how robots would replace humans, we could take this controversy about robot journalists in another direction. Instead of using Narrative Science's algorithmic stories and big claims about Pulitzer Prizes as an opportunity to defend humanity, we might instead notice that stories are always machinic manipulations of data. To make sense of Narrative Science's robots, we'd need to understand the software at work in the generation of their narratives. We would, in Noah Wardrip-Fruin's words, need to examine their "expressive processes," how they use computation to make meaning and how they express complex design histories.[58] And yet, wouldn't this same approach work for human-authored stories? Couldn't we think of all narratives in terms of the machinic, procedural movement between narrative and database? Instead of waging the humans vs. robots war yet again, couldn't we ask a different set of ethical questions: How does one judge and evaluate the conflicting and competing narratives spun by machines and humans? What ethical programs should citizens and media consumers use to sift through competing and conflicting narratives? How do we make judgments in situations when different authors and organizations carve different paths through the same database? One possibility is to cultivate a machinic sensibility. Such a practice could be useful not only for examining stories written by computational machines. It would be useful as a general tool for making sense of narratives, and it would help us navigate the ethical predicaments that emerge as we attempt to move between the worldviews of narrative and database.

Rhetoric's Machines

While algorithmic and computational thinking are both very much tied to digital computing, these modes of thought have precedents in a longer tradition of scholarship and pedagogy. For instance, the rhetorical tradition offers a set of machines for producing and critiquing arguments. Those machines will always be reworked and revised based upon the rhetorical situation, and any rhetorician worth her salt rejects a purely "textbook" version of rhetoric's algorithms. In particular, most rhetoricians are concerned with an approach that assumes rules can by plugged into any rhetorical situation. For Aristotle, the "handbook writers" of his time did not focus on developing a theory of persuasion but rather focused on "verbal attack and pity and anger and such emotions of the mind" that do "not relate to fact but are appeals to the juryman."[59] These handbook writers were more concerned with manipulation than with a theory of rhetoric, and they attempted to sell a one-size-fits-all approach to persuasion. In a sense, they were teaching a weak form of machinic thinking by suggesting that one acontextual set of rules could be used to generate arguments and manipulate audiences. These same concerns might be brought to the present day as teachers of rhetoric and writing are skeptical of rigid rules of grammar and style. The "rules" of grammar and style are, for most contemporary writing teachers, rhetorical. That is, they are historical constructs that must be fitted to particular situations. Rhetoric is concerned with contingent, fluid situations in which the rhetor must respond to audiences and demands that crop up, and grammar and style are no exception to this more fluid notion of what is proper or decorous.

Still, Aristotle's *Rhetoric* is considered the most influential rhetorical handbook in history. Their long-standing suspicion of handbooks and formulaic approaches to persuasion hasn't stopped rhetoricians from teaching and employing rules. Any number of rhetorical pedagogies might be indicative of a kind of "machinic-ness." Aristotle's text lists 28 *topoi* that lay out procedures for generating arguments. A rhetor may argue "from opposites" or "from analogy or precedent" or from other "places" (the word *topos* can be translated as place).[60] These *topoi* are the algorithms that help a rhetor craft or invent an argument, and they present ways to transform data into narratives (even if Aristotle would never have used these terms). One of Aristotle's examples is the argument "to be temperate is a good thing; for to lack self- control is harmful," but one could use similar data (temperance and self-control) to deploy different *topoi*.[61] For instance, we could argue "from definition" by discussing definitions of temperance and self-control or "from a better plan" by suggesting that sometimes temperance and self-control are a poor fit to the situation at hand. Aristotle does not necessarily provide us with exact procedures by which we might create arguments, and this is likely because he so looked down upon the handbook writers. He was aiming to provide a theory of persuasion rather than a guidebook. However, his text has become a key resource for those of us who study how to analyze and produce arguments, and that is largely because he presents us with ways of generating what rhetoricians such as Erasmus called *copia*, an abundance of ideas and arguments. Rhetoric's algorithms are particularly useful ways of taking the same facts and ideas and generating a number of different arguments.

Elsewhere, I have argued that Erasmus's notion of *copia* offers strong evidence of a machinic tradition within rhetoric, a tradition that helps us conceptualize how to live, think, and write in a world shaped by computation.[62] By rewriting the sentence "Your letter pleased me greatly" nearly two hundred ways, Erasmus develops a machine for generating discourse. But the machines of rhetoric are numerous, and they extend to contemporary rhetorical theory as well. Kenneth Burke's pentad is the machine that is most in line with the discussion of this chapter as it presents a way of processing text and determining what motivates the author of that text. For Burke, a textual corpus presents an opportunity to understand an author's (or a group of authors') motives. Burke's pentad—act, agent, agency, scene, purpose—presents the rhetorical critic with a set of terms by which to analyze texts. When analyzing a text or speech, the critic can seek to understand which of these terms serves as the central focus. Is the text focused on specific actions (acts), who or what is doing the acting (agents), what the actors are using (agency), the context for actions (scene), or the reason those actions are carried out (purpose)? Burke sets up ratios using these terms, and those ratios can reveal the motives at work in the corpus. The pentad seeks to understand and describe the "forms of thought" that motivate "systematically elaborated metaphysical structures, in legal judgments, in poetry and fiction, in political and scientific works, in news and in bits of gossip offered at random."[63] Burke suggests that the pentad would allow the critic to see how a school or "philosophy" works: "Speaking broadly we could designate as 'philosophies' any statements in which these grammatical resources are specifically utilized."[64] If the critic finds that a particular author (or grouping of authors) relies on a scene-act ratio, she can then draw larger conclusions about the workings of that "philosophy" and what motivates it.

This leads Burke to argue that "the different philosophic schools are to be distinguished by the fact that each school features a different one of the five terms, in developing a vocabulary designed to allow this one term full expression (as regards its resources and its temptations) with the other terms being comparatively slighted or being placed in the perspective of the featured term."[65] Thus, the writings of a particular school of philosophy might focus on "scene." That school would not disregard the other four terms, and it would certainly feature "ratios" ("act-scene" or "agent-scene," for instance). However, "scene" would be the guiding term for this particular school. Burke, in fact, does identify a school of thought that focuses on scene: materialism. Alternately, he associates a concern with "agency" with pragmatism.[66] For our purposes, tracing out Burke's exact reasons for assigning such a survey of philosophical schools (he provides a school for each of his five terms) is less important than noticing how Burke uses machinic procedures to sift and sort a database. Burke's analysis moves back and forth between database and narrative, constructing arguments about a textual corpus by way of his pentadic machine.

Using Burke's method we might examine Rebecca Greenfield's account of

Narrative Science's robot journalists with Burke's pentad, noticing that she draws upon each of these terms. She describes what the robots do, providing the New York Times Earnings Report as an example; she discusses the agents involved by focusing on Kristian Hammond and his "robots"; she suggests (though she does not go into detail) that these agents use software to generate stories, which addresses Burke's notion of agency; she describes the shifting terrain of journalism as the business has begun to value the quantity of stories over their quality; and she addresses the purposes of robot journalists, suggesting that they might be most useful as collaborators rather than replacements. It is the latter two pentadic terms that get the most attention in Greenfield's discussion of robot journalists, and this is best exemplified by the two paragraphs that close her discussion:

> Ultimately, whether or not journalists (and the people who rely on them) should fear a machine-powered future of journalism depends on what you think journalism is. There are whole businesses built on the idea of producing massive quantities of news stories, quality controlled by machine-like formulas. Narrative Science may one day put a lot of these journalists out of work. But when most people talk about journalism, they're not thinking about rote earnings reports or baseball game recaps. (Certainly no one goes into journalism out of a passion for such things.) And shrinking one part of an industry is never good for the workforce in the rest of it.
>
> But there is a best-case scenario—for everyone involved—out there. Hammond says that he thinks human-journalists will increasingly use his machine-journalism as a tool. "Maybe at some point, humans and algorithms will collaborate, with each partner playing to its strength. Computers, with their flawless memories and ability to access data, might act as legmen to human writers," writes Levy. In other words, if journalists focused less on trying to do the rote stuff that machines are better at, they might focus on producing more interesting journalism. If the threat of machine journalism ultimately makes human journalists step up their game, we'd welcome those robot overlords.[67]

Greenfield's focus on scene (shifts in the field of journalism) and purpose (using robots to do the grunt work of journalism) is clearly motivated by her desire to protect her livelihood and that of her colleagues. In fact, she deploys the first-person plural throughout the piece: "we're still not convinced it's all that threatening to the future of journalism."[68] This reliance on a scene-purpose ratio provides some insight into what motivates Greenfield's discussion of Narrative Science's robot journalists. We don't necessarily need Burke's pentad to arrive at this insight, but conducting our rhetorical analysis in these terms allows us to approach Greenfield's piece machinically. She is presenting a narrative, a single path through the database, and it is one that focuses on particular data points while neglecting others. For instance, Greenfield shows little interest in examining how Narrative Science's robots work (agency). Greenfield's scene-purpose machine is her way of transforming data (news of Narrative Science's robots and the grandiose claims of Hammond) into narrative. A rhetorical analysis of her piece seeks out these procedures in an attempt to reverse engineer her argument and to understand how Greenfield herself straddles the worldviews of narrative and database.

Burke's pentad is a different type of machine from those of Aristotle and Erasmus. Whereas the latter are concerned with how to generate arguments, Burke's pentad is a tool for interpretation. In fact, when others have attempted to pitch the pentad toward the production of arguments, Burke has been quick to point out that this is quite different from what he has in mind: "My job was not to help a writer decide what he might say to produce a text. It was to help a critic perceive what was going on in a text that was already written."[69] Many would argue that rhetoric is primarily a productive art (that is, it is concerned with how a rhetor designs and produces an argument), but the rhetorician is also concerned with dissecting and analyzing arguments. While the present chapter is mostly concerned with analysis, it is helpful to keep in mind that these two types of activities—production and interpretation—are fairly blurry when it comes to cultivating a machinic approach to database and narrative. Burke's pentad may be primarily concerned with determining the motives of a text or set of texts, but his procedure for doing so is an *authored artifact*. In her dissertation, "Speculative Computing: Instruments for Interpretive Scholarship," Bethany Nowviskie argues that humanists have often failed to see algorithms and heuristics as expressive, crafted artifacts:

> Algorithms—like various hermeneutic methods and historical schools of thought more dear to humanities scholars—can be understood as problem-solving and (with a slight methodological recasting I will suggest in a discussion of the "ludic algorithm") as open, participatory, explorative devices.[70]

Thus, Burke's pentad is a machine, but it is a machine that he has created in order to explore a database of texts. He applies his heuristic to a textual corpus, and he is simultaneously producing and interpreting. Further, Burke's machine is focused on ratios and relationships rather than static categories. That machine is an agile one that computes but does not adhere to rigid, systematic determinations. Burke's pentad is one example of how rhetoric is an art that can help readers and writers work back and forth between data and narrative, understanding and *authoring* the processes that mediate the world-views of narrative and database.

Ethical Programs as Interstitial Machines

Every narrative makes ethical determinations. It sorts data in a particular way, searches for patterns in that data, determines which patterns are most important, and (by necessity) excludes certain other patterns. These determinations are necessary in the worlds of both database and narrative. Databases are the results of ethical determinations as well. Certain categories serve to produce and erase entities and identities.[71] Given these inevitable exclusions, it is crucial to develop methods for oscillating between the worldviews of database and narrative. Here is where rhetoric is best up to the challenge, presenting a set of tools for understanding the relationship between narrative and database. Through its machines, rhetorical theory can help us write the programs that will help us make sense of data. By noticing the machinic roots of rhetorical theory, we begin to see how software studies can have a broad impact on work in many fields, from computer science to political science.

The machines we develop to move between narrative and database need not be written in computer code. The rhetorical tradition, machinic at its core, is evidence of this. Rhetoricians have spent millennia building a vast library of machines that can help us understand the motives at work as data is used to spin narratives. These procedures have not necessarily been put forth as machines, but reframing rhetorical analysis as the process of creating reading and writing machines presents us with a particularly useful approach to our contemporary predicament. Narrative Science's software presents us with an opportunity to think machinically and to watch how software mediates database and narrative. These computational machines serve as reminders that all attempts to oscillate between these two worldviews apply sets of rules and seek out patterns. Thankfully, rhetoric has a long tradition of rule-based thinking that is nimble enough to shift with the situation. Rhetoric's concern with contingency means that it helps us write the laws of hospitality in the face of the Law of hospitality.

Rhetoric does not present us with a magic bullet for uncovering the motives or the assumptions underlying any given attempt to tell the story of a particular dataset. Instead, it offers methods for standing between the worldviews of narrative and database. Whether a narrative is generated by a human or by software, it can be understood in terms of the motivated procedures that highlight certain portions of the database while neglecting others. And even if rhetoric is not the magic bullet, its machines do present us with ways to reverse engineer narratives, looking for the rules that generated it, or to craft new narratives, mining data for different patterns. This is what rhetorical analysis and rhetorical production have always been about: mining arguments for the procedures that generate and motivate them. This is often done in the interest of invention. The rhetor mines existing arguments for content and procedures that she might use in her own arguments. The hope is that a closer look at these procedures provides insight into the motives and assumptions underlying that argument. In its worst form, this approach becomes little more than a way of revealing the secret machinery of an argument. But in its best form, rhetorical analysis presents us with a tool for understanding how arguments are put together and how they work. If rhetorical analysis has always been machinic, then rhetoric becomes an essential tool for understanding and authoring new ethical programs in a world of hospitable databases. As we have seen with Stats Monkey, computational machines are just as motivated as humans, and any authoring effort will make ethical choices about how to sit in between the worldviews of database and narrative. The machines we author to carry out this work are the ethical programs that will help determine how we understand the shifting relationship between narratives and databases.

About, With, In—Hospitality and the Rhetorics of Software

This book began with a discussion of the "swarm" that confronts us in net-worked life. The faceless foes that inundate networks make it difficult to imagine how one can adequately face up to and deal with the other. One of the premises of *Ethical Programs* is that the predicament of hospitality is the primary ethical problem that addresses networked rhetorical situations. That predicament presents itself over and over again, in the form of the *Law* of hospitality, and we continually attempt to answer it by way of the *laws* of hospitality, the contingent responses we author in order to deal with the swarm. The arrival of others scrambles what we might typically conceive of as a rhetorical situation—a clearly understood context in which a rhetor addresses an audience toward some particular end. The problem of defining context is not new, it is not specific to the study of rhetoric, and it is not created by the messy spaces of networked technology. Nonetheless, the hospitable network does raise a number of questions about how one understands and theorizes a rhetorical situation.

For instance, during a February 2007 press conference, President George W. Bush discussed the complexities of knowing one's audience. Bush was answering questions about his proposal for a "troop surge" that would increase the number of U.S. troops in Iraq. Recent debate about the surge had led White House press secretary Tony Snow to ask whether congressional remarks about capping troop levels would make it easier for Iranians or al Qaeda members to make inroads in Iraq. Snow had been criticized for trying to silence debate, since his remarks suggested that any opposition to Bush's plan would embolden the enemy. When asked about Snow's remarks, the president said the following:

> The only thing I can tell you is that when I speak, I'm very conscience [sic] about the audiences that are listening to my words. The first audience, ob-

viously, is the American people. The second audience would be the troops and their families. That's why I appreciate the question about whether or not—about the troop morale, it gave me a chance to talk to the families and how proud we are of them. Third, no question people are watching what happens here in America. The enemy listens to what's happening, the Iraqi people listen to the words, the Iranians.[1]

In a remark that does not directly address whether Snow's remarks were intended to have a chilling effect on the debate, the president gestured toward the complexities of understanding one's audience in a world shaped by information networks. This same set of problems arose during Mitt Romney's infamous remarks at a fundraiser about the 47 percent of Americans that would never support him because they represented a segment of the population "dependent upon government, who believe that they are victims, who believe the government has a responsibility to care for them."[2] When video of these remarks leaked, Romney quickly discovered that the hospitable network means that one's remarks can be distributed in unknown and complex ways. While Bush seemed to be aware of the multiple audiences he was always addressing, Romney appeared to have (at least temporarily) forgotten this fact. Regardless, politics in the hospitable network means that the rhetor has already welcomed multiple audiences to the rhetorical situation, audiences that exceed the intended audience and that arrive with conflicting and competing interests.

These problems of audience are directly tied to the predicament of hospitality, to the problems that emerge when we recognize that networked life is founded on the Law of hospitality. But though Bush seems to have at least a somewhat nuanced understanding of the networked rhetorical situation (even if he is using such an understanding to raise questions about the danger of arguments opposing his policies), he still conceives of that situation as a collection of discrete entities. This approach is understandable as we attempt to address the complexities of contemporary information environments. Networked life invites others, meaning that audiences, texts, and contexts become infinitely more complicated. However, this understanding takes what Jenny Edbauer calls a "conglomeration" approach to understanding rhetorical situations by simply adding more and more entities to such situations. For Edbauer, this approach ignores the ways that components overlap and intersect and how they "bleed into one another." To address this situation, she suggests that we theorize not rhetorical situations but rather *rhetorical ecologies* in the interest of "add[ing] the dimensions of history and movement (back) into our visions/versions of rhetoric's public situations, reclaiming rhetoric from artificially elementary frameworks."[3] Rather than adding elements to our models of rhetorical situations, Edbauer argues for understanding persuasion and communication in terms of overlapping and intersecting ecologies, allowing us to "more fully theorize rhetoric as a public(s) creation."[4] If rhetorical action helps to create and maintain publics, then Edbauer insists that we take up a more complex, ecological approach to understanding the processes by which this happens.

Ethical Programs has taken on the complexities of rhetorical ecologies by focusing on how computational artifacts help to shape and constrain rhetorical action in the network. My focus on software is not meant to suggest that software creates such ecologies or that it is purely determinative of rhetorical action. In addition, a consideration of software is something more than the addition of another discrete rhetorical factor. Instead, the previous chapters have shown that software *bleeds out* into other dimensions of a rhetorical ecology, affecting how rhetors read, write, argue, or persuade. It is nearly impossible to separate software out from our rhetorical ecologies or to consider it separately from other important overlapping components of our rhetorical ecologies. For instance, chapter 2 demonstrated how the Obama campaign's software used procedural rhetoric to funnel volunteers to certain kinds of activities. These procedural arguments were not confined to the software itself but were also locatable in the phone-banking scripts distributed to volunteers. By following the procedural rhetorics of the campaign through software and beyond, tracking them even to the procedures authored by volunteers, that chapter demonstrated how procedures bled out and transformed, entering into overlapping and intersecting rhetorical ecologies. This example shows that any decision to focus *only* on software would limit our ability to understand how protocological power circulated through the campaign.

Software serves as the starting point for each of the rhetorical analyses presented in this book, and this is in part an answer to Ian Bogost's critique of work in digital rhetoric that has failed to address computation. I take up this critique in more detail in the next section, but for now I want to note how *Ethical Programs* continues the approach of much work in software studies, focusing on situated activities in order to ask broader questions about computation and software. The authors of *10 PRINT CHR$(205.5+RND(1)); : GOTO 10*, a text that uses a single line of code in order to explore the history of creative computing, explain that this method is the opposite of much work in the digital humanities. While a great deal of digital humanities scholarship uses computation to address large sets of texts and other media, *10 PRINT* and other work in software studies instead operate "as if under a centrifugal force, spiraling outward from a single line of text to explore seemingly disparate aspects of culture."[5] This focus on the specific serves to guard against bombastic arguments, which often tell us less about how particular technologies operate than they do about the theoretical and political agendas of the arguers. Rather than making large claims about software's role in networked life, the approach enacted in this book insists on sitting with specific rhetorical ecologies and tracing their effects.

Of course, the danger of this type of approach is that the results might not be generalizable and that we learn something about a particular situation or piece of software without learning something broader about computational life. One answer to this critique lies in the use of the term "centrifugal" by the authors of 10 PRINT, which describes how work in software studies can take something as minute as a single line of code as a launching point for discussions about disparate cultural trajectories. However, another way to address this problem of the particular and the generalizable is to embrace the specificity of such approaches and to call for many more of them. Each attempt to describe and analyze specific ecologies involving software may provide only a sliver of understanding, a snapshot of how computational artifacts operate as cultural artifacts. However, in aggregate such studies help us build an archive that can aid scholars across disciplines develop methods and approaches for studying software as a cultural form. Given the relative youth of software studies, we are only at the early stages of developing such an archive, but the willingness of scholars in the field to embrace multiple approaches is already bearing fruit.

If a focused analysis of particular ecologies is one of the central methods of software studies, then rhetorical studies has much to offer such conversations. Software and rhetoric both benefit from an ecological approach in two ways. First, both rhetoric and software help to shape, enable, and constrain what is possible in a given rhetorical ecology. Rhetoric is the study of the available (or, as I argue in chapter 3, *possible*) means of persuasion, the study of what we can do or say in a given space, but it also offers strategies for transforming that possibility space and inventing new arguments and approaches. Similarly, software lays out a possibility space, whether it's a videogame that uses procedures to control certain behaviors or a word processing program that determines what is available to a writer. In the case of both software and rhetoric, an ecology of action is shaped and, in some sense, coded (and recoded). However, both software and rhetorical action are "ecological" in another sense: they are crafted as responses to overlapping (and sometimes conflicting) exigencies. It is now a commonplace in software studies and in new media studies more broadly that computer programming is much more than a specialized technical practice used to create tools. That is, software is not just the background for rhetorical action, the thing we use to get things done. As an authored artifact, software is also the result of rhetorical action; it is the medium for expressing ideas and making arguments. Software is thus woven through rhetorical action. It is the *result* of rhetorical action, since it uses computation as an expressive medium. But, as I have suggested above, software also helps to launch and distribute what we normally think of as rhetorical action: the distribution of arguments across media channels. Thus, software sits chiasmatically between different types of rhetorical action, simultaneously the result of and grounding for our attempts at persuasion and communication. Given that rhetoric and software are tied together in the creation, maintenance, and (sometimes) disruption of our attempts to interact, it becomes clear that rhetoricians and software studies scholars have much on which to collaborate.

Still, the focus on particular ecologies is not a way of ignoring "the swarm" of hospitable networks by focusing on a single entity or object. Carried out in a narrow way, such analysis could be seen as *grounding* rhetorical ecologies in software. But grounding a rhetorical ecology transforms it back into a situation, conceiving of it as something easily bounded and understood. As the previous chapters have demonstrated, software is not determinative of rhetoric and ethics in networked life. Software establishes ethical programs, but such programs are often (though, not always) manipulated and reconfigured by actors in a rhetorical ecology. Beginning from software is not an attempt to simplify complex rhetorical action but is instead an attempt to open up new paths of inquiry, demonstrating that computational artifacts can be the starting point for understanding complex ecologies, even as that analysis sometimes spins out and gives way to centrifugal force. Beginning rhetorical analysis from computational artifacts focuses our attention on an entity that is often seen as part of the background, something that scholarship in software studies has successfully called into question.

What the analyses in this book have offered are demonstrations of how the language and methods of rhetorical studies provide a particularly useful way of drawing our attention to computational artifacts. Software addresses (and helps us to address) the complications of hospitality, which stand as the primary ethical predicament of networked life. The ethical programs enacted by such software—programs that I have described as attempts to author the laws of hospitality—reconfigure our rhetorical ecologies, calling for new persuasive strategies and shaping what can or cannot happen in a given space. However, to this point, the subtitle of this book—"Hospitality and the Rhetorics of Software"—has remained in the background. While I have argued throughout for different understandings of how software intersects with rhetorical theory and practice, I have not yet explicitly defined the *rhetorics* of software that emerge in networked life. In the remainder of this concluding chapter, I remedy this situation, moving from the local approach of earlier chapters to a more global approach that presents some terms and concepts for tracking the rhetorics of software.

The Rhetorics of Software: Procedural Rhetoric and Beyond

In addition to providing a way for rhetoricians to understand the persuasive dimensions of computation, Bogost's *Persuasive Games* also offers a powerful critique of much of the work in digital rhetoric. Citing a number of works in the field, Bogost argues that much of this scholarship ends up "mistaking subordinate properties of the computer for primary ones."[6] That is, digital rhetoricians have tended to focus on the use of computers to write, create images, or distribute arguments rather than on how computation itself can be used to craft arguments:

> In short, digital rhetoric tends to focus on the presentation of traditional materials—especially text and images—without accounting for the computational underpinnings of that presentation. . . . digital rhetoric must address the role of procedurality, the unique representational property of the computer.[7]

For Bogost, a key example of this is Richard Lanham's *Electronic Word*, one of the first texts to explicitly link rhetorical theory to digital technologies and a text that opened the way for a generation of digital rhetoricians. Lanham focuses on how computers can manipulate the appearance of text (something Lanham himself insists is not unique to digital technology) and does not attend to what new rhetorical possibilities emerge in computational environments. When Lanham demonstrates how the manipulations of text on screen allows us toggle between looking "at" text (noticing surface and style) and "through" text (reading for meaning), he is not necessarily telling us much about the rhetorical affordances of the computer itself. Instead, he is linking computational technologies to the rhetorical tradition without considering how such technologies might actually introduce novel rhetorical theories of persuasion, communication, or identification.

Bogost's argument has been a necessary corrective for the field of digital rhetoric, and I myself have found the concept of procedural rhetoric extremely useful in understanding both the rhetorical capacities of software and the rhetorical nature of procedures more generally. As I have argued, procedural rhetoric becomes a useful rhetorical strategy for navigating the complex and contradictory power relations of protocological networks. However, my analysis in this book has aimed to examine the *rhetorics* (plural) of software. From exploits, which expose what's possible in a given space, to *ethos*, which presents the digital rhetor with resources for living and arguing in deep archives, to machinic thinking, which allows for movement between the worldviews of database and narrative, I have argued for a more expansive understanding of the rhetorics of software. Procedural rhetoric offers one inroad for rhetoricians analyzing software, but it is only one of the possible rhetorics of software. In the interest of making explicit this notion of the *rhetorics* of software, I offer here a discussion of these different rhetorics. Given that the hospitality of networked life provokes, shapes, enables, and constrains rhetorical action, I describe these rhetorics in terms of the Law of hospitality and the laws of hospitality. If the hospitable network scrambles our rhetorical situations and forces us to instead attend to rhetorical ecologies, and if software helps to enact the ethical programs that engage the hospitality of networked life, then we require new ways of understanding how software links up with different levels of rhetorical action.

To this end, I offer three rhetorics of software—arguing *about* software, arguing *with* software, and arguing *in* software—as a way of productively reexpanding digital rhetoric beyond procedural rhetoric. These three realms of rhetorical action are not discrete or separable; all the intersecting rhetorics of software participate in complex rhetorical ecologies.

Arguing about Software

This is the rhetorical realm that most would imagine as the rhetorician's primary purview: how we talk about software. While such work offers only one way of understanding the broader cultural implications of software, examining how we talk and argue about software is important. Given that more people are programming (beyond specialized disciplines such as engineering and computer science), these conversations will no doubt become more interdisciplinary and will invite the expert and the novice. The Law of hospitality extends a broad invitation. Who will accept this invitation and what laws will be authored in response? Here, hospitality is playing out in a particularly striking way. Projects such as Code Academy, which found New York City mayor Michael Bloomberg among its pupils in 2012, are now inviting many to learn how to write code.[8] This means that conversations about software design are expanding outward, calling on both experts and novices to analyze, critique, and write software. In addition to this mixing of expert with newcomer, our hospitable networks are also inviting interdisciplinary conversations about code, and software studies presents a key set of methods for enabling these conversations.

However, for arguments about software to happen in a productive way, all parties will require a deeper understanding of computational processes and functions. Recent work in new media studies has pushed beyond the interface, attempting to correct decades of work that treated the screen as another page. This effort is ongoing, and there is more to be done. However, these same efforts can and should be extended to spaces and conversations outside of the academy as well. This means studying (and perhaps even intervening in) arguments about software, examining how such conversations are conducted, noticing where they succeed and fail, and accounting for how power dynamics shape these arguments. The questions one might ask when approaching arguments about software are the following: How do conversations about software happen? Who participates, and who doesn't? How inclusive are these conversations? What power relations shape arguments about software? What commonplaces circulate? Who are the overlapping and intersecting audiences for such arguments?

In previous chapters, we have seen a number of arguments about software. Chapter 3 offers some of the clearest examples of how these conversations happen in networked spaces and how such conversations will always have to respond to the predicament of hospitality. The Twitter onMouseover exploit invited a far-reaching conversation about software, one that drew in journalists, software designers, and everyday users of Twitter. One discursive space—the website Stackoverflow.com—is of particular interest when considering arguments about software. A site that combines the functions of a wiki and a message board, Stackoverflow.com offers novice and expert a space to discuss software, to ask questions, and to enter what we might view as a complex set of master-apprentice relationships. This space may or may not cultivate a nurturing space for budding programmers or curious tinkerers, and that is largely linked to the hospitality described in this book. Networked life means that we bump up against others, whether or not we want to. The results of these collisions may bring happy results or they may alienate newcomers, but a space like Stackoverflow.com at least allows for the possibility that arguments and discussions about software can happen among those from different backgrounds. When the onMouseover exploit occupied Twitter users for part of a day (and when I myself began studying the exploit and its aftermath), this site became a useful resource for those seeking explanations. These arguments and discussions about the exploit were one level of that particular rhetorical ecology, one of the rhetorics of software circulating around this event.

Arguments and discussions about the other exploit examined in chapter 3—the OAuth exploit—took a decidedly different shape. While the onMouseover exploit forced a conversation that mixed expert with novice and programmer with user, the OAuth exploit happened among a relatively small circle of programmers, designers, and executives. While this exploit triggered arguments about software, those arguments circulated quite differently, and the result of this discussion was that the exploit was addressed prior to wreaking havoc on users. Happening behind closed doors before being shared with a broader public, this argument about software revealed a very different rhetorical ecology and involved different kinds of power dynamics, but the results of the OAuth exploit were no less important to users than the results of the onMouseover exploit. In fact, we could argue that the implications of the OAuth exploit were much more far reaching, even if a smaller number of people were involved in how it was addressed. The OAuth exploit had the potential to expose a great number of users to a security vulnerability that would have allowed a third-party application to act on their behalf. While the onMouseover exploit demonstrated a relatively low stakes vulnerability, the hack of OAuth could have caused much more harm. Understanding how conversations emerge and happen in the wake of such exploits is crucial for the digital rhetorician interested in understanding how software is discussed, addressed, and reshaped by rhetorical exchange.

While chapter 3's discussion of exploits offers one of the clearest examples of arguing about software, we saw this same level of rhetorical activity at play in discussions of the MyBO software, as critics analyzed how the campaign used different systems to motivate volunteers and to guide volunteers to certain activities. These conversations happened among people involved in political campaigning, but they also happened among software developers whose primary interests and expertise lie outside the realm of campaigning and volunteer coordination. Once again, this was a wide-ranging discussion involving multiple constituencies and levels of expertise. Discussions among journalists regarding Narrative Science's robot journalists fall into this category as well. Those discussions reflected a great deal of suspicion for many reasons, not the least of which was that journalists felt that their livelihood was being threatened by algorithmic journalists. This was a completely understandable (and in many ways, justified) response, but it is a response that would benefit from a deeper and broader discussion of code and computation. Narrative Science itself is an interesting model for this kind of conversation, given that it employs both programmers and journalists. The company's robot writers are the result of many conversations about software, conversations that inform how the software is written. This movement from arguing about software to the practice of composing the software itself brings us to our next level of rhetorical activity.

Arguing with Software

Arguing about software is never sealed off from how we argue *with* software, how we *use* software, code, and computational procedures to make arguments. If arguing about software becomes more complex because of a hospitable network that both welcomes and shuns participants to a discussion, then arguing with software increases in complexity because of the hospitable network's penchant for simultaneously welcoming and turning away hacks, exploits, and other bits of code. Hospitable networks mean that hacking and exploring the possibilities of computational environments are within the scope of rhetorical action. But the "with" here can also be taken another way. While we can use software as a tool for expression and argumentation (as in when we say we are writing "with" a pencil), we might also see software systems as an interlocutor (as in when we say we are arguing "with" another person). These two uses of "with" are not separate—when I attempt to use computation to build an argument, I work with and struggle against the affordances of a given platform or language. While the end result might be an argument expressed by way of software, I have a number of rhetorical exchanges with the software itself—as I write code, I'm writing for multiple human and machine audiences. Arguing with software is a concept meant to account for this entire complex set of relations.

To again take the Twitter exploits of chapter 3 as an example, both conversations about these exploits *and the exploits themselves* are part of the various, circulating, and overlapping rhetorics of software in this ecology. When Kinugawa and others created exploits that exposed a flaw in Twitter's URL parser, they were using software in the interest of rhetorical action. They were both attempting to persuade Twitter to address a security flaw and helping to reveal the possible means of persuasion in this space. Invited by networked software that continuously negotiates between absolute and measured hospitality, between the Law and the laws, these ethical programs expose what is or is not possible in a given space. But more than just initiating a discussion about software (arguing about), Kinugawa, Holm, and the others who circulated the onMouseover exploit used computation itself to make arguments, and they did so by negotiating with the software itself. They performed an ethical argument by way of computation (software as tool) by interacting with and exploiting gaps in the software itself (software as interlocutor).

The exploit is one particularly powerful way of arguing with software, but it is of course coupled with procedural rhetoric. Here the Obama campaign's use of social networking software to funnel users to particular activities comes to mind. The MyBO software was certainly a tool for more efficiently organizing volunteers, but it was also a collection of procedural arguments made by the campaign about how (or *whether*) volunteers might engage opposing arguments. Given a networked campaign infrastructure that purported to invite volunteers to help craft and shape a message, this use of procedural rhetoric is all the more interesting. For while the campaign argued with software, using procedural rhetoric to help control a protocological network, volunteers also used procedural arguments to write back against the campaign and navigate the complex power dynamics of networked power. The volunteer-authored procedural arguments covered in chapter 2 are not examples of arguing with software (even if they are examples of procedural arguments), but this only further demonstrates that all of these rhetorics of software intersect and overlap with one another. Engaging the procedural arguments expressed, in part, by software, Obama campaign volunteers used a similar strategy by translating those strategies into other media, such as phone-banking scripts.

MediaWiki also offers an example of arguing with software, though in this case the arguments are less overt and not as loaded with a particular political program. By considering each keystroke as crucial to the integrity of the database and by welcoming all of this data into its deep textual archive, MediaWiki engages the predicament of hospitality by attempting to absorb all information and not determining ahead of time what is or is not useful or relevant. When usernames and article titles are considered equal in the eyes of the database, we can begin to see MediaWiki as a piece of software that responds to the Law of hospitality by crafting a set of laws, laws that use software to make arguments about how textual discussions should happen and what information should be tracked. The designers of MediaWiki may or may not have had these particular arguments in mind when building the software, but the arguments are nonetheless there, shaping what can or cannot happen as writers edit and create articles or conduct conversations about policy. Chapter 4 explains how this plays out in the most famous MediaWiki installation in the world—Wikipedia. If MediaWiki is an argument made with software, that argument reveals itself in complex ways as Wikipedians try to argue in this software environment (a level of rhetorical activity taken up in the next section). MediaWiki's hospitable database also means that users must engage in arguments with the software itself, and we see this most clearly as Larry Sanger's Citizendium project attempts to work both with and against the affordances of the software. Having to build a credentialing system on top of a system that is designed to exclude credentials as an elevated form of evidence means that the software becomes a party to rhetorical exchange. Sanger and the designers of Citizendium's MediaWiki installation had to argue and struggle with MediaWiki in order to build the kind of dwelling they envisioned.

The questions a rhetorician might ask when exploring arguing *with* software are myriad: How hackable are computational spaces? What kinds of ethical assumptions and arguments are made by software platforms? Who or what is able to manipulate and exploit such platforms? Who or what stands at the thresholds, determining what can or cannot happen in networked spaces? What are the means of persuasion available to those coding and recoding computational environments? How does software design change if we begin to see software as interlocutor and audience? How do designers engage with the affordances and constraints of a platform or language, and what kinds of "conversations" emerge from such interactions? From APIs to URL parsers, software designers and writers help to construct ethical programs, and it is at these thresholds that we can best notice the complexity of how ethical programs must continually engage the arrival of others. As more and more others arrive, networked spaces will have to account for how bits of code are being used to argue and how software is being used to expand or expose the possible means of persuasion.

Arguing in Software

Software helps to shape, enable, and constrain rhetorical action. Given the ubiquity of software, an increasing number of rhetorical ecologies are happening in software environments, meaning that rhetoricians and scholars of all stripes should be attempting to understanding how persuasive acts emerge in such environments. The Law of hospitality plays a key role here by welcoming data, by storing and tracking nearly any keystroke. What rhetorical strategies are most effective in such spaces? How do humans and computational programs deal with this Law of hospitality? Software addresses this Law with some of its own laws, by building deep archives of information. But these ethical programs in turn shape those of humans, who must now address the complex rhetorical ecologies shaped by these archives. Networked spaces encourage certain kinds of strategies and modes of argument, and I have traced a number of these throughout this book. Each of these rhetorical strategies emerge out of software environments and the computational spaces that accumulate data. As we interact with software and as that software serves to help shape rhetorical interactions, it becomes important to understand what strategies are encouraged and foreclosed by software.

In MediaWiki's deep archive, *ethos* emerges as a crucial rhetorical strategy. The controversy surrounding Essjay shows us that MediaWiki's penchant for textual accumulation makes *ethos* the primary way by which Wikipedians both make and critique arguments. MediaWiki is driven by an ethic of database integrity, and it operates most effectively when all information is archived. Even malicious edits are often retained in the edit history of Wikipedia articles, demonstrating that even seemingly "useless" data is kept and archived. In another example of this somewhat radical hospitality, those Wikipedians who attempt to change usernames and identities are thwarted by an archive that keeps track of username changes. Logs of user activity link old usernames to new ones. MediaWiki's ethical programs are best understood in terms of this guiding ethic—the desire to archive rather than to delete. There are certainly exceptions to this rule, but this generalized ethic of preservation stands as what best defines this software dwelling (its *ethos*). Essjay was arguing in this environment, and he benefited from this archive as he built up credibility as a tenured academic. Anyone curious as to why he was carrying weight in a discussion need only have looked at his user page or his previous edits to learn that he was a theological expert. However, he was undone by this same aspect of Wikipedia's dwelling, and his *ethos* crumbled when it was discovered that his situated *ethos*—the portion of *ethos* that is supposed to precede the rhetor and to be outside of his or her control—was in fact an *invented ethos*. MediaWiki played an important role in both the creation and destruction of Essjay, and that role is best understood in terms of how Wikipedians argue in software, taking advantage of (or suffering at the hands of) the particular affordances of software environments.

The examples from chapter 4 make arguing in software even more complex, since the robot journalists circulating through networked life are operating alongside humans in rhetorical ecologies. The algorithms authored to generate news stories are an example of arguing with software—of crafting computational procedures that make arguments about which information is most important and how a narrative should be structured. However, I have argued that the bots themselves present us with key strategies for operating, persuading, and communicating in software environments. By using procedures to sift and sort data and by transforming data into narratives, these bots remind us that the generation of narrative and argument is always, in some sense, machinic. Rhetoric, as a set of procedures for generating and critiquing arguments, offers a long tradition of understanding how to move between the worldviews of narrative and database (although ancient rhetoricians would of course never have put it in these terms). While arguing in software environments that welcome data and that intensifies a situation of "information overload," users can turn to the "meta-writers" of Narrative Science and to the increasing number of computational machines generating narratives for inspiration. Given that the relationship between narrative and database is increasingly complex, we can turn to machinic thinking as we develop strategies for arguing in software.

The case of procedural rhetoric is also interesting in this regard, since it becomes both a way to argue *with* and *in* software. We can craft computational processes that make arguments, and I have demonstrated the complexity of such actions in the preceding chapters, showing that exploits, procedural arguments, and less explicit arguments in platforms like MediaWiki demonstrate how computational procedures make arguments and engage the Law of hospitality. However, the phone-banking scripts of Obama campaign volunteers show how we can also craft other types of processes that make arguments. The authors of these scripts engaged (or chose not to engage) opposing arguments, and these choices were made by volunteers who accepted the campaign's invitation to participate. Stepping into a software environment (MyBO) that generated lists of possible voters, clicking through those lists, and making phone calls, the actions of these volunteers were shaped in important ways by the campaign's procedural rhetorics. However, the phone-banking scripts were very different kinds of procedures in that volunteers did not execute them in the same way a computational machine executes a procedure. Instead, volunteers rewrote the scripts in the interest of different kinds of procedural arguments. Here procedural rhetoric sits both in the computational environment of the campaign's software and in the volunteers' use of procedures to engage possible voters. Such hinge points between the different rhetorics of software—the different layers of rhetorical activity in networked, computational spaces—present us with rich possibilities for cultivating complex accounts of rhetorical ecologies. Understanding procedurality as a mode of inscription that can be enacted in both computational media and discursively is but one place where we might notice software's promise as a participant in rhetorical ecologies.

Given how much contemporary rhetorical action happens in software environments, the rhetorician of software can begin to ask: What are the affordances of certain software platforms, and how do users take advantage of or fall prey to those affordances? What persuasive strategies are opened up and closed off by certain software environments? How do user activities lead to changes in software platforms, shifting the available means of persuasion? What does the wide-scale adoption of certain software platforms (from Microsoft Office to Facebook) mean for the possibilities of rhetorical action? How do users take up software in unexpected ways, revealing expressive possibilities within an environment in ways that designers never imagined?

The Future of Ethical Programs

My hope is that these intersecting and overlapping rhetorics of software offer a way forward for those of us interested in examining the ethical programs of networked life. Digital rhetoricians can and should be participating in discussions of computation, and they should do so both by bringing rhetorical theory to bear on software and by rethinking rhetorical theory in light of the unique attributes of computational media. However, while my account of the rhetorics of software offers some possible futures for the analysis of networked software, there remains a different (and perhaps more difficult) question about the future of ethical programs.

What is the future of any ethical program? I don't ask this question in order to make predictions or proclamations about how software will be used or rewritten or recoded in the face of the Law of hospitality. I'm asking a different question, one that considers whether the use of software to institute ethical programs opens up the possibility of a future, of an "unprogrammed" encounter with others. We noted briefly, in chapter 1, that there is a general distrust of computation in many discussions of ethics. Computation is seen as something mechanistic and perhaps even inhuman. A computer can enact procedures, can make rules and follow them, and any responsible ethics would have to move beyond such a stable, inflexible program. Given this, can an ethical program have a future? Or does a program decide beforehand what will happen, closing off the possibility of reimagining what is or is not possible? If software enacts a set of rules that defines a possibility space, that determines how others will be dealt with, then does it allow for novel approaches to continuously arriving ethical questions?

While Levinas set the human against the computer, suggesting that enacting a set of rules too cleanly answers the infinite question of ethics because it is "something of which a computer is capable," then Derrida offers a somewhat more hospitable consideration of computational media.[9] This book owes everything to Derrida's work on hospitality in texts such as *Of Hospitality*, *On Cosmopolitanism and Forgiveness*, and *Adieu to Emmanuel Levinas*. However, it is another text, one that takes up the question of "the animal," that is most applicable to the future of ethical programs. In *The Animal That Therefore I Am*, Derrida is concerned with the limits drawn between "so-called human" and "the animal." His analysis of Kant, Heidegger, Levinas, and Jacques Lacan suggests that each of these thinkers can be traced back to a common "father," namely René Descartes. Each of these thinkers, attempting to undo the Cartesian project, finds himself a Cartesian when it comes to the nonhuman animal.

However, what is of most interest given my own analysis of software, rhetoric, and ethics is how Derrida invokes computation in his interrogation of the multiple limits drawn between "human" and "the animal." His treatment of computation allows us to consider how open Derrida's analysis is to the possibility that a machine may have a future—that a mechanism that is programmed to react to situations by way of code will perhaps open the way toward an "authentic" future that has not already been decided. So, for instance, Derrida examines one of the limits between animal and human by taking up Descartes's insistence that the animal cannot "respond." The human can respond to a question while "the animal" can only react, a distinction of which even Descartes seems unsure. Derrida tracks Descartes's treatment of response and reaction through not only the famous *Discourse on Method* but also through Descartes's letters. In one of those letters, Descartes seems to hesitate, to consider whether in fact "the animal" can respond. But before turning to this letter, Derrida quotes from a moment in the *Discourse on Method* in which Descartes presents his own two-step Turing test:

> If there were machines bearing the image of our bodies, and capable of imitating our actions as far as it is morally possible, there would still remain two most certain tests whereby to know that they were not therefore really men. Of these the first is that they could never use words or other signs arranged in such a manner as is competent to us in order to declare our thoughts to others; for we may easily conceive a machine to be so constructed that it emits vocables, and even that it emits some correspondent to the action upon it of external objects which cause a change in its organs; for example, if touched in a particular place it may demand what we wish to say to it; if in another it may cry out that it is hurt, and such like; but not that it should arrange them variously so as appositely to reply to what is said in its presence, as men of the lowest grade of intellect can do. The second test is, that although such machines might execute many things with equal or perhaps greater perfection than any of us, they would, without doubt, fail in certain others from which it could be discovered that they did not act from knowledge, but solely from the disposition of their organs: for while Reason is an universal instrument that is alike available on every occasion, these organs, on the contrary, need a particular arrangement for each particular action; whence it must be morally impossible that there should exist in any machine a diversity of organs sufficient to enable it to act in all the occurrences of life, in the way in which our reason enables us to act.[10]

This quote is fascinating for any number of reasons, not least of which is Descartes seeming interest in interface design—he describes machines and how they might respond to certain inputs. Most importantly, given our present discussion, Descartes believes that human reason can reconfigure its "organs" given a particular rhetorical ecology, situating itself in a way that meets an exigence. That is, a human can respond. A machine (or "the animal," it makes little difference to Descartes) cannot do this—it can only react by way of "the disposition of [its] organs." It can only execute its code. Upon taking us through Descartes's discourse on automata, Derrida turns to a letter in which Descartes rethinks this hard-line stance. Here, Descartes reconsiders his argument that the animal-machine can't respond, arguing instead that the animal-machine, while it might be able to respond to commands, cannot respond "to questions, questioning concerning 'what is asked of them.'"[11] Thus, the animal might be able to respond to its name, but neither animal nor machine could "produce different arrangements of words so as to give an appropriately meaningful answer to whatever is said in its presence, as the dullest of men can do."[12]

This brief detour through Descartes (and Derrida's reading of Descartes) gets us to the moments when Derrida allows for the future of the computer. First, Derrida notes that Descartes probably "could not have imagined in their refinements, capacity, and complexity all the powers of reaction-response that today we can, and tomorrow we should be better and better able to attribute to machines."[13] One can only imagine how Descartes would have responded to Apple's Siri. But more than pointing out technological advances that Descartes could not have foreseen, Derrida signals that machines, like "the animal," are forcing a wholesale reconsideration of what we think we know about the human. In particular, they are forcing us to rethink what we mean by the supposed human realm of the authentic question—a question that is not programmed or robotic and that is not simply answered by way of a program. What are we asking about when we consider the distinction between "human" responses and "machine" reactions?

> The question of the response is thus that of the question, of the response as response to a question that, at one and the same time, would remain unprogrammable and leave to the other alone the freedom to respond, presuming that were possible (a techno-historical field with a bright future, even though the programmation of question and response seems to foreclose the future).[14]

This remark about a "bright" future is, of course, not a celebration. It is instead an acknowledgment of two contradictory ideas: (1) that our only chance at a "bright future" is to pursue the unprogrammable question, the authentic encounter that does not decide the answer ahead of time; (2) that there is no encounter with an other, no ethics, without a program. The Law of hospitality is what allows for the possibility of a future, one that does not decide in advance who can arrive, but the laws authored in response to that Law will unavoidably miss the mark. The laws, as ethical programs, find themselves in this impossible space, attempting to answer an impossible demand.

Derrida's passage about programming and "bright futures" points to the possibility of a program—ethical or otherwise, computational or otherwise— that does not necessarily decide in advance the entire range of possibilities. This is a program that does not know exactly where it is going. To put it in the terms laid out in this book, it would be an ethical program that is a provisional response to the Law of hospitality. Such a program would, to some extent, define what is possible, and we might find it difficult to locate a radical "future" in computational machines that execute code. But the Law of hospitality makes it difficult for any ethical program, even one carried out by a computational machine, to remain in place forever. The future of ethical programs requires a continuous vigilance in this regard, a vigilance that insists upon constant reexamination of the laws. For networked life in a computational world, this means attempting to understand how our programs are written, how they lay out what can or cannot happen in a given space. At any given moment, an ethical program might be futureless—it will have already decided what will happen. But the reprogrammability of computational machines allows for the possibility of ethical programs that are open to possibility.

The overlapping and intersecting rhetorics of software traced in this conclusion aim to understand and *to write* the futures of ethical programs, to understand computation not as a foreclosed space of rules that will always offer a rigid program of action but rather to understand software as enacting contingent responses to the Law of hospitality and to understand our interactions with software as similarly contingent. The laws, even those enacted by computational machines, will always be haunted by the Law. This possibility is our only justification for the hope that any ethical program—computational or otherwise—has a future.

Notes

Introduction

1. Wendy Hui Kyong Chun, *Control and Freedom: Power and Paranoia in the Age of Fiber Optics* (MIT Press, 2006), 3.

2. Ibid.

3. Jared Newman, "Microsoft Changes Its Mind on Xbox One's Used Games and Always-Online Policies," *Time*, June 19, 2013, http://techland.time.com/2013/06/19/microsoft-changes-its-mind-on-xbox-ones-used-games-and-always-online-policies/.

4. Ian Steadman, "XBox One's Always-on Camera Shows the Subtle Ways We Accept Being Watched," *New Statesman*, November 20, 2013, http://www.newstatesman.com/future-proof/2013/11/xbox-ones-always-camera-shows-subtle-ways-we-accept-being-watched.

5. "Sneakernet," *Wikipedia, the Free Encyclopedia*, July 22, 2014, http://en.wikipedia.org/w/index.php?title=Sneakernet&oldid=617601318.

6. Emmanuel Levinas, "Substitution," in *Emmanuel Levinas: Basic Philosophical Writings*, ed. Adriaan T. Peperzak, Simon Critchley, and Robert Bernasconi (Indiana University Press, 2008), 81.

7. Avital Ronell, *The Telephone Book: Technology, Schizophrenia, Electric Speech* (University of Nebraska Press, 1989), 2.

8. Levinas, "Substitution," 88.

9. Carl Schmitt, *The Concept of the Political: Expanded Edition* (University of Chicago Press, 2008), 27.

10. As many have noted, Schmitt's friend-enemy distinction (and the ease with which one makes this decision) is particularly stomach turning given his affiliations with the Nazi Party. It is nearly impossible to consider the different approaches of Levinas and Schmitt without recognizing that Schmitt was a Nazi and that Levinas was a prisoner of war in a German camp. Levinas and other Jewish soldiers were separated from their fellow soldiers in the camp.

11. Alexander R. Galloway and Eugene Thacker, *The Exploit: A Theory of Networks* (University of Minnesota Press, 2007), 66.

12. Francisco Varela, *Ethical Know-How: Action, Wisdom, and Cognition* (Stanford University Press, 1999), 10.

13. Ibid., 18.

14. Lev Manovich, *Software Takes Command* (Continuum Publishing, 2013), 42.

15. "PSA: If You Get the 'Looks Like You're Either a Brand New User or Your Posts Have Not Been Doing Well Recently. You May Have to Wait a Bit to Post Again.' Message, Solution Inside. • /r/help," *Reddit*, December 6, 2012, accessed September 16, 2014, http://www.reddit.com/r/help/comments/14erjc/psa_if_you_get_the_looks_like_youre_either_a/.

16. Information Sciences Institute University of Southern California, "RFC 761—DoD Standard Transmission Control Protocol," January 1980, http://tools.ietf.org/html/rfc761.

17. Eric Allman, "The Robustness Principle Reconsidered," *Communications of the ACM* 54, no. 8 (August 1, 2011): 40, doi:10.1145/1978542.1978557.

18. Ibid.

19. Ibid.

20. Ibid.

21. Alexander R. Galloway, *Protocol: How Control Exists after Decentralization* (MIT Press, 2006), xv.

22. Ibid., 167.

23. Kris Hammond, "Just to Clarify: Why We Like Stories: The Power of Narratives over Numbers," *Just to Clarify*, June 21, 2012, http://khammond.blogspot.com/2012/06/why-we-like-stories-power-of-narratives.html.

24. Ian Bogost, *Persuasive Games: The Expressive Power of Videogames* (MIT Press, 2010), 25.

25. Annette Vee, "Text, Speech, Machine: Metaphors for Computer Code in the Law," *Computational Culture* 2 (September 2012), http://computationalculture.net/article/text-speech-machine-metaphors-for-computer-code-in-the-law.

26. Kevin Brock, "Engaging the Action-Oriented Nature of Computation: Towards a Rhetorical Code Studies" (North Carolina State University, 2013), 8–9, http://repository.lib.ncsu.edu/ir/handle/1840.16/8460.

27. David Rieder, "Snowballs and Other Numerate Acts of Textuality," *Computers and Composition Online*, n.d., 2010, accessed September 19, 2013.

28. Ian Bogost, *Persuasive Games: The Expressive Power of Videogames* (MIT Press, 2007), 3.

29. Collin Gifford Brooke, *Lingua Fracta: Toward a Rhetoric of New Media* (Hampton Press, 2009), 22.

Chapter 1

1. Andrew Osborn, "Suicide Bomber Killed 'Early' by Text Message," *Times* (London), January 27, 2011, National edition.

2. "Global Jihad—Zeinat Suyunova," accessed June 18, 2014, http://www.globaljihad.net/view_page.asp?id=2023.

3. Osborn, "Suicide Bomber Killed 'Early' by Text Message."

4. Jacques Derrida and Anne Dufourmantelle, *Of Hospitality* (Stanford University Press, 2000), 77.

5. Ibid., 79.

6. Ibid.

7. Aristotle, *On Rhetoric: A Theory of Civic Discourse*, trans. George A. Kennedy, 2nd ed. (Oxford University Press, 2006), 1355b; Ivor Armstrong Richards, *The Philosophy of Rhetoric* (Oxford University Press, 1936), 3.

8. Diane Davis, *Inessential Solidarity: Rhetoric and Foreigner Relations* (University of Pittsburgh Press, 2010), 9.

9. Ibid., 3.

10. Matthew Fuller, *Media Ecologies: Materialist Energies in Art and Technoculture* (Leonardo Book Series) (MIT Press, 2007), 43.

11. Ibid., 49.

12. Jon Anderson et al., eds., "Exploring the Potential for More Strategic Civil Society Use of Mobile Phones," in *Reformatting Politics: Information Technology and Global Civil Society* (Routledge, 2006), 113–14.

13. "Stateless Protocol," *Wikipedia, the Free Encyclopedia*, May 10, 2014, http://en .wikipedia.org/w/index.php?title=Stateless_protocol&oldid=602733620, emphasis in original.

14. "Telcos Start Using Spam Filters to Block SMS Scams," *Australian*, July 2, 2013, accessed September 17, 2014, http://www.theaustralian.com.au/technology/telcos-start-using-spam-filters-to-block-sms-scams/story-fn4iyzsr-1226672759422.

15. Derrida and Dufourmantelle, *Of Hospitality*, 47.

16. Ibid., 91.

17. Ibid., 125.

18. Ibid., 51.

19. Ibid., 61.

20. Ibid., 65.

21. John Trimbur, "Composition and the Circulation of Writing," *College Composition and Communication* 52, no. 2 (December 2000): 210.

22. Ibid., 190.

23. Rebecca Dingo, *Networking Arguments: Rhetoric, Transnational Feminism, and Public Policy Writing* (University of Pittsburgh Press, 2012), 7–8.

24. Jeff Rice, *Digital Detroit: Rhetoric and Space in the Age of the Network* (Southern Illinois University Press, 2012), 36; Dingo, *Networking Arguments*, 19.

25. James Porter, *Rhetorical Ethics and Internetworked Writing* (Praeger, 1998), 69.

26. Ibid., xiii.

27. Ibid., 3.

28. Ibid., xiii.

29. Ibid., xii.

30. Ibid., xi–xii.

31. While Porter refers to the hacker in this story as a student, I found no evidence that the person was in fact a student.

32. Porter, *Rhetorical Ethics and Internetworked Writing*, 154.

33. Rice, *Digital Detroit*, 38.

34. Virilio quoted in ibid., 195.

35. Ibid., 196.

36. Ibid., 199.

37. Ibid., 206.

38. Ibid., 217.

39. Quintilian, *Institutio Oratoria, Books I–III*, trans. H. E. Butler, accessed September 27, 2014, http://archive.org/stream/institutiooratorooquin/institutiooratorooquin_djvu.txt.

40. Michael J. Hyde, "Rhetorically, We Dwell," in *The Ethos of Rhetoric*, ed. Michael J. Hyde (University of South Carolina Press, 2004), xiii.

41. Calvin O. Schrag, *The Ethos of Rhetoric*, ed. Michael J. Hyde (University of South Carolina Press, 2004), xviii.

42. Ibid., xviii.

43. Rob Kitchin and Martin Dodge, *Code/Space: Software and Everyday Life* (MIT Press, 2014), 6.

44. Ibid., 219.

45. Carolyn R. Miller, "Expertise and Agency: Transformations of Ethos in Human-Computer Interaction," in *The Ethos of Rhetoric*, ed. Michael J. Hyde and Calvin O. Schrag (University of South Carolina Press, 2004), 198.

46. Simon Critchley and Richard Kearney, preface to *On Cosmopolitanism and Forgiveness* (Routledge, 2001), xii.

47. Emmanuel Levinas, "Peace and Proximity," in *Emmanuel Levinas: Basic Philosophical Writings*, ed. Adriaan T. Peperzak, Simon Critchley, and Robert Bernasconi (Indiana University Press, 2008), 169.

48. Mathew Ingram, "Twitter CFO Says a Facebook-Style Filtered Feed Is Coming, Whether You Like It or Not," September 4, 2014, http://gigaom.com/2014/09/04/twitter-cfo-says-a-facebook-style-filtered-feed-is-coming-whether-you-like-it-or-not/.

Chapter 2

1. Sean Gallagher, "Inside Team Romney's Whale of an IT Meltdown," *Ars Technica*, accessed February 18, 2014, http://arstechnica.com/information-technology/2012/11/inside-team-romneys-whale-of-an-it-meltdown/.

2. Janet H. Murray, *Hamlet on the Holodeck: The Future of Narrative in Cyberspace* (MIT Press, 1998), 73.

3. Ibid., 74, 79.

4. Ibid., 83.

5. Ibid., 152.

6. Bogost, *Persuasive Games*, 2010, 3.

7. Ibid., 113.

8. Ibid., 114.

9. Ibid., 28.

10. Ibid., 46.

11. Ibid., 7.

12. Jennifer Stromer-Galley and Kirsten A. Foot, "Citizen Perceptions of Online Interactivity and Implications for Political Campaign Communication," *Journal of Computer-Mediated Communication* 8, no. 1 (2002).

13. Ibid.

14. Ibid.

15. Ibid.

16. Kirsten A. Foot and Steven M. Schneider, *Web Campaigning* (MIT Press, 2006), 22.

17. Ibid., 17.

18. Ibid., 207.

19. Gary W. Selnow, *Electronic Whistle-Stops: The Impact of the Internet on American Politics* (Praeger Publishers, 1998).

20. Ibid., xxi.

21. Bruce Gronbeck, "The Web, Campaign 07–08, and Engaged Citizens: Political, Social, and Moral Consequences," in *The 2008 Presidential Campaign: A Communication Perspective*, ed. Robert E. Denton Jr. (Rowman & Littlefield, 2009), 238.

22. Ibid., 230.

23. Selnow, *Electronic Whistle-Stops*, 133.

24. Ibid., 99.

25. Ibid., 135.

26. Chris Swain, *The Redistricting Game* (USC Game Innovation Lab, 2007), http://re-districtinggame.org/.

27. Bogost, *Persuasive Games*, 2010, 135.

28. Ibid., 136.

29. Ibid., 137.

30. Ibid., 139.

31. Ibid.

32. Galloway, *Protocol*, 7.

33. Ibid.

34. Ibid., 8.

35. Ibid., 9.

36. Many speculated that this was how the Egyptian government turned off the Internet during protests of January 2011. However, a piece in *Gizmodo* suggests that turning off DNS would have been an imperfect solution, since protesters could have used overseas DNS servers. Instead, the Egyptian government withdrew Border Gateway Protocol routes, "the places where networks connect and announce which IP addresses they are responsible for." Kyle Vanhemert, "How Egypt Turned Off the Internet," *Gizmodo*, January 28, 2011, accessed February 18, 2014, http://gizmodo.com/5746121/how-egypt-turned-off-the-internet.

37. Wendy Hui Kyong Chun, *Control and Freedom: Power and Paranoia in the Age of Fiber Optics* (MIT Press, 2008), 15.

38. Ibid., 28.

39. Annette Vee, "Proceduracy: Computer Code Writing in the Continuum of Literacy" (University of Wisconsin at Madison, 2010).

40. After the 2008 presidential election, the MyBO website shifted its focus from electing Obama to more general community organizing. The site's URL has remained the same (my.barackobama.com), but the site's name and goal have shifted. It now operates as the home base for Organizing For America.

41. "Announcing the MyBO Activity Tracker," August 7, 2008, http://www.facebook.com/note.php?note_id=26133366652.

42. Chris Hughes, "Introducing Points," *Chris Hughes' Blog*, August 27, 2007, https://my.barackobama.com/page/community/post/chrishughesatthecampaign/CJ7C.

43. Ian Bogost, "'Gamification Is Bullshit,'" *Atlantic*, August 9, 2011, http://www.theatlantic.com/technology/archive/2011/08/gamification-is-bullshit/243338/.

44. Sebastian Deterding, Dan Dixon, Rilla Khaled, and Lennart Nacke. "From game design elements to gamefulness: defining 'gamification'" in *Proceedings of the 15th International Academic MindTrek Conference: Envisioning Future Media Environments*, 13.

45. Jane McGonigal, *We Don't Need No Stinkin' Badges: How to Re-Invent Reality without Gamification*, Game Developers Conference 2011 (San Francisco, CA, 2011), http://www.gdcvault.com/play/1014576/We-Don-t-Need-No.

46. Gene Koo, "My.BarackObama.com—2008 Game of the Year," *Anderkoo*, November 16, 2008, http://blogs.law.harvard.edu/anderkoo/2008/11/mybarackobamacom-2008-game-of-the-year/.

47. Ibid.

48. Brendan Howley, "Yes She Did," *Marketing Magazine*, April 8, 2009, http://www.marketingmag.ca/news/marketer-news/yes-she-did-8005.

49. Koo, "My.BarackObama.com—2008 Game of the Year."

50. Martin Fowler, "Software and Obama's Victory," July 30, 2009, http://martin-fowler.com/articles/obamaSoftware.html.

51. Ibid.

52. Ibid.

53. "United For Change Host Guide," *My.barackobama.com*, n.d., accessed February 18, 2014, https://my.barackobama.com/page/content/uniteguide/.

54. Ibid.

55. For one example of a phone-banking script, see http://www.scribd.com/doc/6372442/Obama-Phone-Bank-Script. Volunteers used different scripts at different moments in the campaign, depending on circumstance. One of the challenges of conducting research for this was locating some of the artifacts used during the campaign. The MyBO website has changed significantly since 2008, and recovering the look and feel of the site is next to impossible. The Internet Archive provides some help in this regard, but it is not designed to archive dynamically generated web pages or forms. Remnants exist, but the archive is far from extensive. This should remind us of Matthew Kirschenbaum's arguments in *Mechanisms: New Media and the Forensic Imagination*. Our archiving practices have yet to fully grasp that new media is anything but ephemeral. Our tendency to think of electronic texts as fleeting and fluid often means that we do not adequately archive digital objects in their iterations: "in the realm of archives and curatorial practice, it will be important to insist that digital objects are no more homogenous or self-identical than other artifacts, and that the relationships between individual digital objects (and versions of those objects) should be preserved along with the actual works themselves." Matthew G. Kirschenbaum, *Mechanisms: New Media and the Forensic Imagination* (MIT Press, 2012), 22.

56. Elise, "Daily Kos: How to (Ba)Rock a Phone Bank," *Daily Kos*, January 10, 2008, http://www.dailykos.com/story/2008/01/10/434667/-How-to-Ba-Rock-a-Phone-Bank.

57. Too often, we associate computation with predictability and rigidity. By this way of thinking, computers "merely" execute code; a piece of software merely "runs." Humans are complex; machines are simple. However, Wendy Chun reminds us that computation mediates, even if our focus on source code as a "text" to be read often allows us to forget about that process of mediation. She argues that fetishizing source code leads to "the erasure of the vicissitudes of execution." Source code has always required the processes of execution (interpreting, compiling, and so on), meaning that it is mediated and not merely passed along in perfect form from one step to the next. This was true when the term "computer" referred to a woman doing calculations, and it is no less true for digital computers that process and execute code. Wendy Hui Kyong Chun, *Programmed Visions*, 53.

58. While I was unable to confirm this, my assumption is that Renata's last name is not actually Hussein. During the campaign, Obama's middle name became a point of controversy. Some saw it as evidence that he was a "secret Muslim." A number of supporters changed their middle name (legally or informally) to "Hussein" as a show of support. The URL for her blog post contains the character string "renatagolden," which is most likely her actual name.

59. Renata Hussein, "Obama for America," *Obama for America*, January 24, 2008, http://www.barackobama.com/headers-footers/tools-header/.

60. Fowler, "Software and Obama's Victory."

61. "Organizing for America–Speakout," *Organizing for America*, n.d., accessed July 6, 2010, http://my.barackobama.com/page/speakout.

62. This may say a great deal about popular assumptions regarding writing and speech instruction. While phone-banking scripts provided a high level of detail and instruction, these two words—"be concise"—are all that is offered to the author of a letter to the editor. What does this say about the Obama campaign's assumptions with regard to the teaching of effective writing? What does the lack of a detailed procedural argument (the only real instructions encourage authors to include personal stories) for writing a letter to the editor say about contemporary assumptions regarding rhetorically effective writing?

63. Ed O'Keefe, "Obama's Evolving Position on Talking to Iran," *ABC News Blogs*, June 4, 2008, http://abcnews.go.com/blogs/politics/2008/06/obamas-evolving/.

64. Michael James, "Obama Proposes 'Team of Rivals' Cabinet," *ABC News Blogs*, May 2008, accessed March 17, 2014, http://abcnews.go.com/blogs/politics/2008/05/obama-proposes/.

Chapter 3

1. "Exploit (Computer Security)," *Wikipedia*, n.d., accessed July 19, 2011, http://en.wikipedia.org/wiki/Exploit_%28computer_security%29.

2. Wayne C. Booth, *The Rhetoric of RHETORIC: The Quest for Effective Communication* (Wiley-Blackwell, 2004), 11.

3. Galloway, *Protocol*, 147.

4. Many previous treatments of digital rhetoric and ethics have focused more on what should happen rather than on what can happen, and this is largely due to rhetoric's ties to the discursive. Rhetoric is seen as method for discussing ethical problems and thus has typically remained in the realm of what ought to happen rather than the realm of what can or cannot happen. Jim Porter's "rhetorical ethics," which is taken up in chapter 1, is indicative of this approach: "What I am referring to as a rhetorical ethics addresses the should of writing activities: What should a writer do? To answer this question, the writer must explore several lines of inquiry: What ethical constraints (i.e., understandings between reader and writer) are operating in any given writing situation? How does the writing help constitute or shape those conventions? By what inquiry procedure can the writer determine what those conventions might be?" Porter, *Rhetorical Ethics and Internetworked Writing*, 69.

5. Galloway and Thacker, *The Exploit*, 81.

6. Ibid.

7. Ibid., 81–82.

8. Aristotle, *On Rhetoric*, 2006, 1355b.

9. Translator's footnote, ibid., 37.

10. Ibid., 1356b.

11. Ibid., 1357a.

12. My aim is to find a home for rhetoric in theorizations of the exploit, and finding a home for rhetoric has always been tricky. Rhetoricians have often sought out a safe place, at least since the Sophists plied their trade by traveling from town to town, teaching what many thought to be mere pandering. This desire for relevance beyond lying, pandering, or "flowery language" is present even in the field's difficult disciplin-

ary identity. Situated in English and Communication departments and sometimes even as stand-alone departments, rhetoric is dispersed across the academy. What's more, it is constantly shape-shifting, becoming larger and smaller, depending on the theorist. In 2006, the Rhetoric Society of America met under the theme of "Sizing Up Rhetoric," a theme that Josh Gunn playfully critiqued in a paper called "Size Matters" that tracked the "apocalyptic tone" of such discussions. See Joshua Gunn, "Size Matters: Polytoning Rhetoric's Perverse Apocalypse," *Rhetoric Society Quarterly* 38, no. 1 (2008): 82–108.

13. Gaonkar has actually been one of the most influential critics of "big rhetoric," arguing that the field's move beyond theorizations of rhetoric as a productive, oratorical art have stretched things too thin. My focus will be not on Gaonkar's arguments against an expanded understanding of rhetoric but instead on his account of how rhetoricians after Aristotle have aligned themselves with the probable and contingent. This argument will help us see the significance of understanding rhetoric as being aligned with all of the *possible* means of persuasion.

14. Dilip Parmeshwar Gaonkar, "Contingency and Probability," in *A Companion to Rhetoric and Rhetorical Criticism*, ed. Walter Jost and Wendy Olmsted (Blackwell Publishing, 2004), 5.

15. Ibid., 8.

16. Ibid., 7.

17. Ibid., 16.

18. Nancy S. Struever, *Rhetoric, Modality, Modernity* (University of Chicago Press, 2009), 7, emphasis added.

19. Ibid., 2.

20. Galloway and Thacker, *Exploit*, 82.

21. Ibid., 83.

22. Christina Warren, "New Facebook Clickjacking Attack Uses Justin Bieber as Bait [WARNING]," *Mashable*, June 2, 2010, http://mashable.com/2010/06/02/facebook-clickjack-justin-bieber/.

23. Thus, when someone types the character string http://twitter.com/@james brownjr they will arrive at my profile. Since the "@" character has become such an iconic one (even other social networking platforms such as Facebook and Google+ allow users to tag others using @), it is understandable that the Twitter parser would want to allow users to include the symbol in URLs (rather than banning it altogether).

24. "Today's XSS On on Mouseover Exploit on Twitter.com," accessed February 19, 2014, http://stackoverflow.com/questions/3762746/todays-xss-ononMouseover-exploit-on-twitter-com/3762899#3762899.

25. McKenna's contribution was actually an edit of Michael Foukarakis's post explaining the exploit. Stackoverflow.com has a wiki-like structure that allows users to edit posts and to track those edits. In his remarks on his edit, McKenna notes that he has "added detail about the regex [which] will probably make it a easier for some to understand." Brian Mckenna, "Revisions," September 22, 2010, http://stackoverflow.com/posts/3762899/revisions.

26. "Today's XSS onMouseover Exploit on Twitter.com."

27. Charles Arthur, "The Twitter Hack: How It Started and How It Worked," *Guardian Technology Blog*, September 21, 2010, http://www.guardian.co.uk/technology/blog/2010/sep/21/twitter-hack-explained-xss-javascript.

28. @boblord, "All about the 'onMouseover' Incident," *Twitter Blog*, September 21, 2010, http://blog.twitter.com/2010/09/all-about-ononMouseover-incident.html.

29. Ryan Tate, "How Twitter Hatched a Virus That Reached the White House," *Gawker*, September 21, 2010, http://gawker.com/5644077/how-twitter-hatched-a-virus-that-reached-the-white-house.

30. Noah Wardrip-Fruin, *Expressive Processing: Digital Fictions, Computer Games, and Software Studies* (MIT Press, 2009), 258.

31. Ibid.

32. Ibid., 259.

33. Arthur, "The Twitter Hack: How It Started and How It Worked."

34. Ibid.

35. Jonathan Fildes, "Twitter Scrambles to Block Worms," September 21, 2010, http://www.bbc.co.uk/news/technology-11382469.

36. Stan Schroeder, "17-Year-Old Australian Boy, Japanese Developer Take Blame for Twitter Meltdown," *Mashable*, September 22, 2010, http://mashable.com/2010/09/22/twitter-meltdown-17-year-old/.

37. Larry Seltzer, "Cross-Site Scripting Attack Hits Twitter," *PCMag Security Watch*, September 21, 2010, http://blogs.pcmag.com/securitywatch/2010/09/cross-site_scripting_attack_hi.php.

38. Kevin Purdy, "Mouse-Over Exploit Hits Twitter.com," *Lifehacker*, September 21, 2010, http://lifehacker.com/5643778/mouse+over-exploit-hits-twittercom-stick-to-third+party-clients-for-now.

39. Tim Carmody, "onMouseover Exploit Spreads Porn on Twitter," *Gadget Lab*, September 21, 2010, http://www.wired.com/gadgetlab/2010/09/twitter-com-onMouseover-exploit-or-why-browsers-are-for-porn/.

40. Tate, "How Twitter Hatched a Virus That Reached the White House."

41. Eran Hammar-Lahav, "The OAuth 1.0 Guide—History" (*Hueniverse*, July 15, 2011), http://hueniverse.com/oauth/guide/history/.

42. Eran Hammar-Lahav, "The OAuth 1.0 Guide—Terminology" (*Hueniverse*, December 26, 2009), http://hueniverse.com/oauth/guide/terminology/.

43. All of this is complicated when we begin to question who *owns* the resources. In the OAuth protocol's terminology, the owner of data is the user. That is, a Twitter user owns their tweets and a Flickr user owns their images. But this isn't necessarily the most accurate way of understanding the property relationship at work. Reading through the Terms of Service of services such as Twitter and Facebook will immediately reveal that one is never the sole proprietor of the images or text that one uploads to such services. While this is to be expected when dealing with for-profit corporations, many users fail to grasp the complexity of this relationship. Once I upload an image to Facebook, I relinquish certain rights, and I lose some control of that image.

44. Hammar-Lahav, "OAuth 1.0 Guide—Terminology."

45. Eran Hammar-Lahav, "OAuth 2.0 (without Signatures) Is Bad for the Web," *Hueniverse*, September 15, 2010, http://hueniverse.com/2010/09/oauth-2-0-without-signatures-is-bad-for-the-web/.

46. Ibid.

47. Eran Hammar-Lahav, "WRAP, and the Demise of the OAuth Community," *Hueniverse*, November 23, 2009, http://hueniverse.com/2009/11/wrap-and-the-demise-of-the-oauth-community/.

48. Ibid.

49. Ben Adida, "It's a WRAP," *Benlog*, December 22, 2009, http://benlog.com/articles/2009/12/22/its-a-wrap/.

50. Ibid.

51. Scott Loganbill, "OAuth Security Exploit Tests Limits of Open Web Standards," *Webmonkey*, April 24, 2009, http://www.webmonkey.com/2009/04/oauth_security_exploit _tests_limits_of_open_web_standards/.

52. Marshall Kirkpatrick, "How the OAuth Security Battle Was Won, Open Web Style," *Read Write Web*, April 25, 2009, http://www.readwriteweb.com/archives/how_ the_oauth_security_battle_was_won_open_web_sty.php.

53. Loganbill, "OAuth Security Exploit Tests Limits of Open Web Standards."

54. Kirkpatrick, "How the OAuth Security Battle Was Won, Open Web Style."

55. McCarthy quoted in ibid.

56. "Acknowledgement of the OAuth Security Issue," *OAuth Blog*, April 22, 2009, http://blog.oauth.net/2009/04/22/acknowledgement-of-the-oauth-security-issue/.

57. David Recordon, Dick Hardt, and Eran Hammar-Lahav, "The OAuth 2.0 Authorization Protocol," July 8, 2011, 44–45, http://tools.ietf.org/html/draft-ietf-oauth-v2–18.

58. Loganbill, "OAuth Security Exploit Tests Limits of Open Web Standards."

59. Cynthia Haynes, "Afterword: <meta> Casuitic Code," in *From A to <A> : Keywords of Markup*, ed. Bradley Dilger and Jeff Rice (University of Minnesota Press, 2010), 232.

60. Ibid., 230.

61. Ibid., 232.

62. Levinas, "Substitution," 169.

Chapter 4

1. Wikipedia has a number of user access levels, including steward, bureaucrat, and administrator (sometimes called "sysop"). Stewards wield the most power and are able to add or remove privileges of other users, delete edits, and determine a user's IP address with a function called "checkuser." Bureaucrats fall next on the pecking order. Some bureaucrats can use the "checkuser" function—Essjay had this type of access— but, by and large, bureaucrats are able to perform functions such as promoting other users or renaming accounts. Administrators have a number of privileges, including the ability to lock pages that are prone to vandalism and to block certain users. Finally, anyone who contributes to Wikipedia is referred to as an editor.

2. Stacy Schiff, "Know It All," *New Yorker*, July 31, 2006, http://www.newyorker. com/archive/2006/07/31/060731fa_fact.

3. Alan Liu, *The Laws of Cool: Knowledge Work and the Culture of Information* (University of Chicago Press, 2004), 71–72.

4. Ibid., 61.

5. Liu, *Laws of Cool*, 70.

6. Ibid., 69.

7. Liu, *Laws of Cool*, 21.

8. Noam Cohen, "Wikipedia May Restrict Public's Ability to Change Entries," blog, *New York Times: Bits*, January 23, 2009, http://bits.blogs.nytimes.com/2009/01/23/ wikipedia-may-restrict-publics-ability-to-change-entries/.

9. "Extension: FlaggedRevs," *Mediawiki.org*, accessed February 24, 2014, http:// www.mediawiki.org/wiki/Extension:FlaggedRevs.

10. Larry Sanger, "The New Politics of Knowledge," accessed February 24, 2014, http://www.larrysanger.org/newpoliticsofknowledge.html.

11. Andrew Orlowski, "There's No Wikipedia Entry for 'Moral Responsibility,'"

Register, December 12, 2005, http://www.theregister.co.uk/2005/12/12/wikipedia_no_responsibility/.

12. The MediaWiki search function would not take this capitalization difference into account, but the article title with both words capitalized would not link to the same article as "hello world" or "Hello world."

13. Daniel J. Barrett, *MediaWiki (Wikipedia and Beyond)* (O'Reilly Media, 2008), 77.

14. Brion Vibber, "[Mediawiki-L] How to Allow All-Lower-Case Usernames," September 26, 2005, http://lists.wikimedia.org/pipermail/mediawiki-l/2005-September/007241.html.

15. GhostInTheMachine, "User:GhostInTheMachine/Lowercase Usernames," April 27, 2009, http://www.mediawiki.org/wiki/User:GhostInTheMachine/Lowercase_Usernames.

16. The archive impulse runs deep in MediaWiki, and this is very much tied to an abundance of server space. Wikipedia is largely composed of text files, though it does contain images as well. But even in a large project like Wikipedia, there is no concern about storage space. While only the biggest geeks might be interested in their very own version of the Wikipedia database, the larger point is that MediaWiki software is designed with little regard for storage constraints. Hard drive space is cheap, and MediaWiki seems to take this into account.

17. Rob Church, "[Wikitech-L] Removing Spammer Accounts," June 2, 2007, http://markmail.org/message/hmcfxsodfoqnlo76.

18. "Extension talk:User Merge and Delete," accessed February 24, 2014, http://www.mediawiki.org/wiki/Extension_talk:User_Merge_and_Delete.

19. Ibid.

20. "Wikipedia:Username Policy," accessed February 24, 2014, http://en.wikipedia.org/wiki/Wikipedia:Username_policy.

21. "User talk:Essjay," February 2, 2007, http://en.wikipedia.org/w/index.php?title=User_talk:Essjay&oldid=105049125#Profiles_don.27t_mesh.

22. Things get muddled when we attempt to draw a line between "Essjay" and "Ryan Jordan." I will use the name "Jordan" to refer to the Wikia employee and "Essjay" to refer to the Wikipedian. This allows me to manage complexity, but it also serves to smooth over a productive question: Where does Jordan end? Where does Essjay begin?

23. "User talk:Essjay."

24. Fuller, *Media Ecologies*, 148.

25. "User talk:Essjay."

26. "Wikipedia:Username Policy."

27. "Wikipedia:Changing Username," accessed February 24, 2014, http://en.wikipedia.org/wiki/Wikipedia:Changing_username.

28. "User talk:Essjay."

29. Ibid.

30. Schiff, "Know It All."

31. Ian King, "A Wiki Web They've Woven," March 2, 2007, http://liveweb.archive.org/http://vancouver.24hrs.ca/Columnists/KingsCorner/.

32. "User:Essjay/RFC," March 4, 2007, http://en.wikipedia.org/w/index.php?title=User:Essjay/RFC&oldid=466593807.

33. "Wikipedia:Requests for Comment/Essjay/Straw Poll," March 2, 2007, accessed February 24, 2014, http://en.wikipedia.org/wiki/Wikipedia:Requests_for_comment/Essjay/Straw_Poll#No.

34. Schiff, "Know It All."

35. Andrew Lih, "Essjay's Third Transgression | Andrew Lih," March 3, 2007, accessed March 28, 2014, http://www.andrewlih.com/blog/2007/03/03/essjays-third-transgression/.

36. Noam Cohen, "Wikipedia Ire Turns against Ex-Editor," *New York Times*, March 6, 2007, http://www.nytimes.com/2007/03/06/technology/06iht-wiki.4817747.html?_r=0.

37. Martyn Williams, "Wikipedia Founder Addresses User Credentials," *PC World*, January 15, 2008, http://www.pcworld.com/article/id,129702-c,webservices/article.html.

38. Andrew Keen, "Laughter and Forgetting on Wikipedia," *The Great Seduction*, March 7, 2007, accessed July 19, 2011, http://www.zdnet.com/blog/keen/laughter-and-forgetting-on-wikipedia/108.

39. Ibid.

40. A full engagement with this text and its many flawed arguments is outside the scope of this book, and I can only hope that some of my arguments here act as answers to Keen's flimsy claims. Others have found Keen's text wanting as well. Lawrence Lessig points out that Keen's text "purports to be a book attacking the sloppiness, error and ignorance of the Internet" and is simultaneously "shot through with sloppiness, error and ignorance. It tells us that without institutions, and standards to signal what we can trust (like the institution (Doubleday) that decided to print his book), we won't know what's true and what's false. But the book itself is riddled with falsity—from simple errors of fact, to gross misreadings of arguments, to the most basic errors of economics." Lawrence Lessig, "Keen's 'The Cult of the Amateur': BRILLIANT," *Lessig.org*, May 31, 2007, http://www.lessig.org/2007/05/keens-the-cult-of-the-amateur/.

41. "Essjay Controversy," *Wikipedia*, March 2, 2007, http://en.wikipedia.org/w/index.php?title=Essjay_controversy&oldid=111967702.

42. Noam Cohen, "A Contributor to Wikipedia Has His Fictional Side," *New York Times*, March 5, 2007, sec. Technology, http://www.nytimes.com/2007/03/05/technology/05wikipedia.html.

43. Jimbo Wales, "User:Jimbo Wales/Credential Verification," June 21, 2010, http://en.wikipedia.org/wiki/User:Jimbo_Wales/Credential_Verification.

44. Misza13, "User:Misza13/Nobody Cares about Your Credentials," March 22, 2007, http://en.wikipedia.org/wiki/User:Misza13/Nobody_cares_about_your_credentials.

45. Ibid.

46. While he is not a formally trained philosopher, cofounder Jimmy Wales also had philosophical roots. He administered an Objectivist philosophy mailing list for many years, and he named his daughter Kira, after a character in Ayn Rand's novel *We the Living*. Alan Deutschman, "Why Is This Man Smiling?," *Fast Company*, April 1, 2007, http://www.fastcompany.com/59260/why-man-smiling.

47. Joseph Reagle, "TIMELINESWikipedia," *Interactions* 16, no. 3 (May 2009): 42, doi:10.1145/1516016.1516026.

48. Peter Saint-Andre, "Tools-L Structure and Simplicity," accessed February 24, 2014, http://web.archive.org/web/20030520143850/www.nupedia.com/pipermail/tools-l/2000-April/000023.html.

49. Jimmy Wales, "Tools-L Tools Used?," June 8, 2000, http://web.archive.org/web/20030520143259/www.nupedia.com/pipermail/tools-l/2000-June/000059.html.

50. Saint-Andre, "Tools-L Structure and Simplicity."

51. Larry Sanger, "The Early History of Nupedia and Wikipedia: A Memoir," in *Open Sources 2.0: The Continuing Evolution*, ed. Chris DiBona, Danese Cooper, and Mark Stone (O'Reilly, 2006), 315.

52. Larry Sanger, "[Nupedia-L] Wikipedia Is Up!," January 17, 2001, http://web.archive.org/web/20010506042824/www.nupedia.com/pipermail/nupedia-l/2001-January/000684.html.

53. Sanger, "Early History of Nupedia and Wikipedia: A Memoir," 2006, 317.

54. Ibid., 311.

55. Larry Sanger, "Why Wikipedia Must Jettison Its Anti-Elitism," *Kuro5hin*, December 31, 2004, http://www.kuro5hin.org/story/2004/12/30/142458/25.

56. Sanger, "The Early History of Nupedia and Wikipedia: A Memoir," in *Open Sources 2.0: The Continuing Evolution*, ed. Chris DiBona, Danese Cooper, and Mark Stone (Nabu Press, 2010), 326.

57. "Special: Request Account," *Citizendium*, accessed February 24, 2014, http:// en.citizendium.org/wiki/Special:RequestAccount.

58. Ibid.

59. That Sanger would institute such a policy is not surprising, especially given his discussion of the problem of "meta-justification" in his dissertation. Sanger's question in that project is "[v]ery roughly, how are standards of justification themselves ultimately justified?" His solution to this problem is telling: "The core intuition behind my solution is this: it is silly to ask that we use reason to support the claims of reason's reliability, or to think that anything important is established thereby . . . . we can take reason's reliability for granted, and there is nothing whatever wrong with such a move." Citizendium is based on this ethic in that it sets aside a certain number of questions, namely questions about who has the authority to drive discussion. Those with the proper credentials are not asked to justify their justifications. Larry Sanger, "Epistemic Circularity: An Essay on the Problem of Meta-Justification" (PhD diss., Ohio State University, 2000), http://enlightenment.supersaturated.com/essays/text/ larrysanger/diss/preamble.html.

60. For instance, John Siegenthaler, former assistant to Robert Kennedy, was falsely implicated in Kennedy's assassination by a Wikipedia vandal.

61. "CZ: MediaWiki Customizations," accessed February 24, 2014, http:// en.citizendium.org/wiki/CZ:MediaWiki_customizations.

62. "CZ: How to Convert Wikipedia Articles to Citizendium Articles," accessed February 24, 2014, http://en.citizendium.org/wiki/CZ:How_to_convert_Wikipedia_articles _to_Citizendium_articles.

63. "CZ: The Author Role," accessed July 19, 2011, http://en.citizendium.org/wiki/ CZ:The_Author_Role.

64. "CZ: Fundamentals," accessed February 24, 2014, http://en.citizendium.org/ wiki/CZ:Fundamentals.

65. "Sex," *Wikipedia, the Free Encyclopedia*, September 28, 2014, http://en.wikipedia. org/w/index.php?title=Sex&oldid=163778039.

66. A tool called Wikiscanner developed by Virgil Griffith traces individual Wikipedia edits to particular IP addresses. The tool has exposed Wikipedians at Fox News, the Vatican, Wal-Mart, and other powerful institutions. This should give us pause when claiming that Wikipedia is run by "amateurs." No, these edits were not the work of professional encyclopedists, but they were most likely written by professionals in other fields, such as public relations.

67. Larry Sanger, "Jimmy Wales' Latest Response on the Essjay Situation," *Citizendium Blog*, March 3, 2007, http://blog.citizendium.org/?p=135.

68. Larry Sanger, "Wikipedia Firmly Supports Your Right to Identity Fraud," *Citizendium Blog*, March 1, 2007, http://blog.citizendium.org/?p=133.

69. Nicholas Carr, "Essjay Disrobed," *Rough Type*, February 27, 2007, http://www.roughtype.com/archives/2007/02/never_trust_an.php.

70. Marshall Poe, "The Hive," *Atlantic*, September 2006, http://www.theatlantic.com/magazine/archive/2006/09/the-hive/5118/.

Chapter 5

1. A team constructed entirely of the league's worst players is expected to win roughly 48 of 162 games. In order to calculate a player's value, WAR estimates how many wins should be added to that total of 48 due to a single player's contributions, and it does so by accounting for offensive and defensive statistics.

2. Two different websites calculate WAR slightly differently, and both are reputable. The website Baseball Reference calculated Trout's WAR to be 10.7 and Cabrera's to be 6.9. Another site, Fangraphs, calculated Trout's as 10.0 and Cabrera's as 7.1.

3. "BBWAA.com: Official Site of the Baseball Writers' Assn. of America.," accessed June 9, 2014, http://bbwaa.com/voting-faq/.

4. Craig Calcaterra, "Mike Trout vs. Miguel Cabrera a Proxy Battle in a Larger Cold War," November 15, 2013, http://hardballtalk.nbcsports.com/2013/11/15/mike-trout-vs-miguel-cabrera-a-proxy-battle-in-a-larger-cold-war/.

5. Michael Lewis, *Moneyball: The Art of Winning an Unfair Game* (W. W. Norton, 2004), 33.

6. Lev Manovich, *The Language of New Media* (MIT Press, 2002), 225.

7. Lev Manovich, Interview with Lev Manovich, interview by Inna Razumova, April 8, 2003, http://switch.sjsu.edu/web/v5n3/J-1.html.

8. N. Katherine Hayles, *How We Think: Digital Media and Contemporary Technogenesis* (University of Chicago Press, 2012), 182.

9. Ibid., 183.

10. Hayles herself would never cleanly separate the human from the nonhuman. Throughout her work on electronic literature, cognition, and cybernetics, Hayles argues that machine and human collaborate with and intermediate one another. In *Electronic Literature: New Horizons for the Literary*, Hayles offers the concept of intermediation as a way of understanding how works of electronic literature "achieve their effects and how these effects imply the existence of entangled dynamic heterarchies binding together humans and intelligent machines." N. Katherine Hayles, *Electronic Literature: New Horizons for the Literary* (University of Notre Dame Press, 2008), 59. Throughout her research, Hayles presents human and machine as parts of complex cognitive systems that work together to make meanings. So, while Hayles's discussion of narrative and database seems to grant that humans sit more comfortably than computers in a world of narratives, she would no doubt refuse to separate human and machine in any final way.

11. Steven Levy, "Can an Algorithm Write a Better News Story Than a Human Reporter?," *WIRED*, April 24, 2012, http://www.wired.com/gadgetlab/2012/04/can-an-algorithm-write-a-better-news-story-than-a-human-reporter/all/1.

12. Rebecca Greenfield, "Robot Journalism Still Doesn't Sound So Scary," *At-*

lantic Wire, April 25, 2012, http://www.theatlanticwire.com/technology/2012/04/robot-journalism-still-doesnt-sound-scary/51557/.

13. Narrative Science, "Forbes Earnings Preview: New York Times Company—Forbes," *Forbes*, accessed July 3, 2012, http://www.forbes.com/sites/narrativescience/2012/04/17/forbes-earnings-preview-new-york-times-company-3/.

14. Ibid.

15. Joe Pompeo, "Will Sulzberger Be the Next Times Company C.E.O.? He Doesn't Quite Say 'No.'" | *Capital New York*, April 19, 2012 accessed July 3, 2012, http://www.capitalnewyork.com/article/media/2012/04/5735533/will-sulzberger-be-next-times-company-ceo-he-doesnt-quite-say-no.

16. Alexander Abad-Santos, "New York Times' Earnings Show Advertising Still Down," *Atlantic Wire*, April 19, 2012, http://www.theatlanticwire.com/business/2012/04/new-york-times-earnings-show-advertising-still-down/51333/.

17. Greenfield, "Robot Journalism Still Doesn't Sound So Scary."

18. Hammond, "Just to Clarify."

19. Ibid.

20. Ibid.

21. Ibid.

22. Levy, "Can an Algorithm Write a Better News Story Than a Human Reporter?"

23. There are at least two versions of this statistic, one developed by the renowned baseball statistician Bill James, and another developed by Sean Forman, a former mathematics and computer science professor who now runs the website Baseball-Reference.com. See "Play Index Glossary," *Baseball-Reference.com*, accessed February 25, 2014, http://www.baseball-reference.com/about/pi_glossary.shtml.

24. Wikipedia contributors, "Win Probability Added," *Wikipedia, the Free Encyclopedia* (Wikimedia Foundation, July 5, 2012), http://en.wikipedia.org/w/index.php?title=Win_probability_added&oldid=480726751.

25. For instance, one popular baseball statistic is "runs batted in" (RBI). Each time a batter's hit results in another player crossing home plate, that batter earns an RBI. While the RBI stat tells us something about a player's performance, it is also a statistic that is dependent upon the actions of other players. A good player on a bad team might have few RBIs because that player's teammates rarely get on base.

26. Nicholas Allen et al., "StatsMonkey: A Data-Driven Sports Narrative Writer," in *AAAI Fall Symposium 2010*, Association for the Advancement of Artificial Intelligence (AAAI) Conference, Arlington, Virginia, November 11–13, 2010.

27. Ibid.

28. Chuck Finder, "McCutchen 'Excited' about Pirates Debut Today," *Pittsburgh Post-Gazette*, June 4, 2009, http://www.post-gazette.com/stories/sports/pirates/mccutchen-excited-about-pirates-debut-today-344470/.

29. Adam Rubin, "Pirates Pound Mike Pelfrey to Sweep 'Embarrassed' Mets," *New York Daily News*, June 4, 2009, http://www.nydailynews.com/sports/baseball/mets/pirates-pound-mike-pelfrey-sweep-embarrassed-mets-article-1.372731.

30. Ben Shpigel, "Game Is Lost; Reyes and Putz Could Be Next," *New York Times*, June 4, 2009, sec. Sports/Baseball, http://www.nytimes.com/2009/06/05/sports/baseball/05mets.html.

31. Wardrip-Fruin, *Expressive Processing*, 2009, 122.

32. Ibid., 157.

33. Kirschenbaum, *Mechanisms*, 31.

34. Richard A Lanham, *The Economics of Attention: Style and Substance in the Age of Information* (University of Chicago Press, 2006), xii.

35. Ibid.

36. Richard A. Lanham, *The Electronic Word: Democracy, Technology, and the Arts* (University of Chicago Press, 1995), 5.

37. Cathy Davidson, "Why We Need a 4th R: Reading, wRiting, aRithmetic, algoRithms," *DMLCentral*, January 25, 2012, http://dmlcentral.net/blog/cathy-davidson/why-we-need-4th-r-reading-writing-arithmetic-algorithms.

38. Ibid.

39. Jeannette M. Wing, "Computational Thinking," *Communications of the ACM* 49, no. 3 (2006): 33–35.

40. Jeannette M. Wing, "Computational Thinking and Thinking about Computing," *Philosophical Transactions. Series A, Mathematical, Physical, and Engineering Sciences* 366, no. 1881 (October 28, 2008): 3717–25, doi:10.1098/rsta.2008.0118.

41. Brooke, *Lingua Fracta*.

42. Manovich, *Language of New Media*, 76–77.

43. Ibid., 77.

44. Ibid., 77–78.

45. Ibid., 78.

46. Ibid.

47. *Virtualpolitik: An Electronic History of Government Media-Making in a Time of War, Scandal, Disaster, Miscommunication, and Mistakes* (MIT Press, 2009), 85–86.

48. Bogost, *Persuasive Games*, 2010, 26.

49. Ibid., 27.

50. Ibid.

51. Brooke, *Lingua Fracta*, 77.

52. Ibid., 91.

53. Ibid.

54. Ibid., 101.

55. Ibid., 92.

56. Ibid., 112.

57. Stephen Ramsay has shown that we (humans and computational machines alike) are all reading machines and all "critical reading practices already contain elements of the algorithmic." For Ramsay, every reading of a text deforms that text, and it does so by way of a set of procedures that seeks out patterns. In fact, Ramsay shows us that algorithmic criticism blurs the lines between reading and writing, since every reading requires that we *author* an algorithm and then test it out across a given textual corpus. And just as literary theory presents algorithms for deforming texts and asking new questions, rhetorical theory's procedures manipulate a dataset in the interest of understanding what motivates it. See Stephen Ramsay, *Reading Machines: Toward an Algorithmic Criticism* (University of Illinois Press, 2011), 16.

58. Wardrip-Fruin, *Expressive Processing*, 4.

59. Aristotle, *On Rhetoric*, I.1.4.

60. Ibid., 1397a–1397b.

61. Ibid., 1397a.

62. James J. Brown Jr., "The Machine That Therefore I Am," *Philosophy & Rhetoric* 47, no. 4 (2014): 493–513.

63. Kenneth Burke, *A Grammar of Motives*, reprint (University of California Press, 1969), xv.

64. Ibid., xvi.

65. Ibid., 127.

66. Ibid., 128.

67. Greenfield, "Robot Journalism Still Doesn't Sound So Scary."

68. Ibid.

69. Kenneth Burke, "Questions and Answers about the Pentad," *College Composition and Communication* 29, no. 4 (1978): 332.

70. Bethany Nowviskie, "Speculative Computing: Instruments for Interpretive Scholarship" (PhD diss., University of Virginia, 2004), 32–33, http://www2.iath.virginia.edu/bpn2f/diss/dissertation.pdf.

71. This process of rhetorical production and erasure in databases is most clearly articulated in Bowker and Star's *Sorting Things Out*, which presents a devastating account of, among other things, the sorting mechanisms of apartheid. Geoffrey C. Bowker and Susan Leigh Star, *Sorting Things Out: Classification and Its Consequences* (MIT Press, 2000).

Conclusion

1. "President Bush Holds a News Conference," *Washington Post*, February 14, 2007, sec. Politics, http://www.washingtonpost.com/wp-dyn/content/article/2007/02/14/AR2007021400775.html.

2. Lucy Madison, "Fact-Checking Romney's '47 Percent' Comment," *CBS News*, September 25, 2012, http://www.cbsnews.com/8301-503544_162-57515033-503544/fact-checking-romneys-47-percent-comment/.

3. "Unframing Models of Public Distribution: From Rhetorical Situation to Rhetorical Ecologies," *Rhetoric Society Quarterly* 35, no. 4 (2005): 9.

4. Ibid.

5. Nick Montfort et al., *10 PRINT CHR$(205.5+RND(1)); : GOTO 10* (MIT Press, 2012), 4.

6. Bogost, *Persuasive Games*, 2010, 25.

7. Ibid., 28.

8. Sarah Kessler, "NYC Mayor Bloomberg Vows to Learn Code in 2012," *Mashable*, January 5, 2012, http://mashable.com/2012/01/05/bloomberg-codecademy/.

9. Levinas, *Emmanuel Levinas*, 169.

10. Rene Descartes, *Discourse on Method*, ed. Charles W. Eliot, vol. 34, pt. 1, Harvard Classics (P.F. Collier & Son, 1914), http://www.bartleby.com/34/1/5.html.

11. Jacques Derrida, *The Animal That Therefore I Am* (Fordham University Press, 2008), 84.

12. Ibid., 84.

13. Ibid.

14. Ibid., 84, emphasis added.

Bibliography

@boblord. "All about the 'onMouseOver' Incident." Twitter Blog, September 21, 2010. http://blog.twitter.com/2010/09/all-about-onmouseover-incident.html.

Abad-Santos, Alexander. "New York Times' Earnings Show Advertising Still Down." *Atlantic Wire*, April 19, 2012. http://www.theatlanticwire.com/business/2012/04/new-york-times-earnings-show-advertising-still-down/51333/.

"Acknowledgement of the OAuth Security Issue." *OAuth Blog*, April 22, 2009. http://blog.oauth.net/2009/04/22/acknowledgement-of-the-oauth-security-issue/.

Adida, Ben. "It's a WRAP." *Benlog*, December 22, 2009. http://benlog.com/articles/2009/12/22/its-a-wrap/.

Allen, Nicholas, John Templon, Patrick McNally, Larry Birnbaum, and Kristian Hammond. "StatsMonkey: A Data-Driven Sports Narrative Writer." In *AAAI Famll Symposium 2010*. Association for the Advancement of Artificial Intelligence (AAAI), Arling, Virginia, November 11–13, 2010.

Allman, Eric. "The Robustness Principle Reconsidered." *Communications of the ACM* 54, no. 8 (August 1, 2011): 40. doi:10.1145/1978542.1978557.

Anderson, Jon, Jodi Dean, Geert Lovink, and Okoth Fred Mudhai, eds. "Exploring the Potential for More Strategic Civil Society Use of Mobile Phones." In *Reformatting Politics: Information Technology and Global Civil Society*. Routledge, 2006.

"Announcing the MyBO Activity Tracker." August 7, 2008. http://www.facebook.com/note.php?note_id=26133366652.

Aristotle. *On Rhetoric: A Theory of Civic Discourse*. Translated by George A. Kennedy. 2nd ed. Oxford University Press, 2006.

Arthur, Charles. "The Twitter Hack: How It Started and How It Worked." *Guardian Technology Blog*, September 21, 2010. http://www.guardian.co.uk/technology/blog/2010/sep/21/twitter-hack-explained-xss-javascript.

Barrett, Daniel J. *Mediawiki (Wikipedia and Beyond)*. O'Reilly Media, 2008.

"BBWAA.com: Official Site of the Baseball Writers' Assn. of America." Accessed June 9, 2014. http://bbwaa.com/voting-faq/.

Bogost, Ian. "'Gamification Is Bullshit.'" *Atlantic*, August 9, 2011. http://www.theatlantic.com/technology/archive/2011/08/gamification-is-bullshit/243338/.

Bogost, Ian. *How To Do Things with Videogames*. University of Minnesota Press, 2011.

Bogost, Ian. *Persuasive Games: The Expressive Power of Videogames*. The MIT Press, 2007.

Booth, Wayne C. *The Rhetoric of RHETORIC: The Quest for Effective Communication*. Wiley-Blackwell, 2004.

Bowker, Geoffrey C., and Susan Leigh Star. *Sorting Things Out: Classification and Its Consequences*. MIT Press, 2000.

Brock, Kevin. "Engaging the Action-Oriented Nature of Computation: Towards a Rhetorical Code Studies." North Carolina State University, 2013. http://repository.lib. ncsu.edu/ir/handle/1840.16/8460.

Brooke, Collin Gifford. *Lingua Fracta: Toward a Rhetoric of New Media.* Hampton Press, 2009.

Brown, James J., Jr. "The Machine That Therefore I Am." *Philosophy & Rhetoric* 47, no. 4 (2014): 493–513.

Burke, Kenneth. "Questions and Answers about the Pentad." *College Composition and Communication* 29, no. 4 (1978): 330–35.

Burke, Kenneth. *A Grammar of Motives.* Reprint. University of California Press, 1969.

Calcaterra, Craig. "Mike Trout vs. Miguel Cabrera a Proxy Battle in a Larger Cold War." November 15, 2013. http://hardballtalk.nbcsports.com/2013/11/15/mike-trout-vs-miguel-cabrera-a-proxy-battle-in-a-larger-cold-war/.

Carmody, Tim. "Mouseover Exploit Spreads Porn on Twitter." *Gadget Lab,* September 21, 2010. http://www.wired.com/gadgetlab/2010/09/twitter-com-mouseover-exploit-or-why-browsers-are-for-porn/.

Carr, Nicholas. "Essjay Disrobed." *Rough Type,* February 27, 2007. http://www.rough-type.com/archives/2007/02/never_trust_an.php.

Chun, Wendy Hui Kyong. *Control and Freedom: Power and Paranoia in the Age of Fiber Optics.* MIT Press, 2006.

Chun, Wendy Hui Kyong. *Programmed Visions: Software and Memory.* MIT Press, 2011.

Church, Rob. "[Wikitech-L] Removing Spammer Accounts." June 2, 2007. http://markmail.org/message/hmcfxsodfoqnlo76.

Cohen, Noam. "A Contributor to Wikipedia Has His Fictional Side." *New York Times,* March 5, 2007, sec. Technology. http://www.nytimes.com/2007/03/05/technology/05wikipedia.html.

Cohen, Noam. "Wikipedia Ire Turns against Ex-Editor." *New York Times,* March 6, 2007. http://www.nytimes.com/2007/03/06/technology/06iht-wiki.4817747.html?_r=0.

Cohen, Noam. "Wikipedia May Restrict Public's Ability to Change Entries." Blog, *New York Times: Bits,* January 23, 2009. http://bits.blogs.nytimes.com/2009/01/23/wikipedia-may-restrict-publics-ability-to-change-entries/.

Critchley, Simon, and Richard Kearney. "Preface." In *On Cosmopolitanism and Forgiveness.* Routledge, 2001.

"CZ: The Author Role." N.d. Accessed July 19, 2011. http://en.citizendium.org/wiki/CZ:The_Author_Role.

"CZ: Fundamentals." N.d. Accessed February 24, 2014. http://en.citizendium.org/wiki/CZ:Fundamentals.

"CZ: How to Convert Wikipedia Articles to Citizendium Articles." N.d. Accessed February 24, 2014. http://en.citizendium.org/wiki/CZ:How_to_convert_Wikipedia_articles_to_Citizendium_articles.

"CZ: MediaWiki Customizations." N.d. Accessed February 24, 2014. http://en.citizendium.org/wiki/CZ:MediaWiki_customizations.

Davidson, Cathy. "Why We Need a 4th R: Reading, wRiting, aRithmetic, algo-Rithms." *DMLCentral,* January 25, 2012. http://dmlcentral.net/blog/cathy-davidson/why-we-need-4th-r-reading-writing-arithmetic-algorithms.

Davis, Diane. *Inessential Solidarity: Rhetoric and Foreigner Relations.* University of Pittsburgh Press, 2010.

Derrida, Jacques. *The Animal That Therefore I Am.* Fordham University Press, 2008.

Derrida, Jacques, and Anne Dufourmantelle. *Of Hospitality*. Stanford University Press, 2000.

Descartes, Rene. *Discourse on Method*. Edited by Charles W. Eliot. Vol. 34, pt. 1. Harvard Classics. P.F. Collier & Son, 1914. http://www.bartleby.com/34/1/5.html.

Deterding, Sebastian, Dan Dixon, Rilla Khaled, and Lennart Nacke. "From game design elements to gamefulness: defining 'gamification'" in *Proceedings of the 15th International Academic MindTrek Conference: Envisioning Future Media Environments*. (New York: ACM, 2011), 9–15.

Deutschman, Alan. "Why Is This Man Smiling?" *Fast Company*, April 1, 2007. http://www.fastcompany.com/59260/why-man-smiling.

Dingo, Rebecca. *Networking Arguments: Rhetoric, Transnational Feminism, and Public Policy Writing*. University of Pittsburgh Press, 2012.

Edbauer, J. "Unframing Models of Public Distribution: From Rhetorical Situation to Rhetorical Ecologies." *Rhetoric Society Quarterly* 35, no. 4 (2005): 5–24.

Elise. "Daily Kos: How to (Ba)Rock a Phone Bank." *Daily Kos*, January 10, 2008. http://www.dailykos.com/story/2008/01/10/434667/-How-to-Ba-Rock-a-Phone-Bank.

"Essjay Controversy." *Wikipedia*, March 2, 2007. http://en.wikipedia.org/w/index.php?title=Essjay_controversy&oldid=111967702.

"Exploit (Computer Security)." *Wikipedia*. N.d. Accessed July 19, 2011. http://en.wikipedia.org/wiki/Exploit_%28computer_security%29.

"Extension: FlaggedRevs." *Mediawiki.org*. Accessed February 24, 2014. http://www.mediawiki.org/wiki/Extension:FlaggedRevs.

"Extension talk:User Merge and Delete." N.d. Accessed February 24, 2014. http://www.mediawiki.org/wiki/Extension_talk:User_Merge_and_Delete.

Fildes, Jonathan. "Twitter Scrambles to Block Worms." September 21, 2010. http://www.bbc.co.uk/news/technology-11382469.

Finder, Chuck. "McCutchen 'Excited' about Pirates Debut Today." *Pittsburgh Post-Gazette*, June 4, 2009. http://www.post-gazette.com/stories/sports/pirates/mccutchen-excited-about-pirates-debut-today-344470/.

Foot, Kirsten A., and Steven M. Schneider. *Web Campaigning*. MIT Press, 2006.

Fowler, Martin. "Software and Obama's Victory." July 30, 2009. http://martinfowler.com/articles/obamaSoftware.html.

Fuller, Matthew. *Media Ecologies: Materialist Energies in Art and Technoculture*. Leonardo Book Series. MIT Press, 2007.

Gallagher, Sean. "Inside Team Romney's Whale of an IT Meltdown." *Ars Technica*. November 9, 2012.Accessed February 18, 2014. http://arstechnica.com/information-technology/2012/11/inside-team-romneys-whale-of-an-it-meltdown/.

Galloway, Alexander R. *Protocol: How Control Exists after Decentralization*. MIT Press, 2006.

Galloway, Alexander R., and Eugene Thacker. *The Exploit: A Theory of Networks*. University of Minnesota Press, 2007.

Gaonkar, Dilip Parmeshwar. "Contingency and Probability." In *A Companion to Rhetoric and Rhetorical Criticism*, edited by Walter Jost and Wendy Olmsted, 6–21. Blackwell Publishing, 2004.

GhostInTheMachine. "User:GhostInTheMachine/Lowercase Usernames," April 27, 2009. http://www.mediawiki.org/wiki/User:GhostInTheMachine/Lowercase_Usernames.

"Global Jihad—Zeinat Suyunova." Accessed June 18, 2014. http://www.globaljihad. net/view_page.asp?id=2023.

Greenfield, Rebecca. "RobotJournalism Still Doesn't Sound So Scary." *AtlanticWire*, April 25, 2012. http://www.theatlanticwire.com/technology/2012/04/robot-journalism-still-doesnt-sound-scary/51557/.

Gronbeck, Bruce. "The Web, Campaign 07–08, and Engaged Citizens: Political, Social, and Moral Consequences." In *The 2008 Presidential Campaign: A Communication Perspective*, edited by Robert E. Denton Jr., 228–43. Rowman & Littlefield, 2009.

Gunn, Joshua. "Size Matters: Polytoning Rhetoric's Perverse Apocalypse." *Rhetoric Society Quarterly* 38, no. 1 (2008): 82–108.

Hammar-Lahav, Eran. "The Oauth 1.0 Guide—History." *Hueniverse*, July 15, 2011. http://hueniverse.com/oauth/guide/history/.

Hammar-Lahav, Eran. "The Oauth 1.0 Guide—Terminology." *Hueniverse*, December 26, 2009. http://hueniverse.com/oauth/guide/terminology/.

Hammar-Lahav, Eran. "OAuth 2.0 (without Signatures) Is Bad for the Web." *Hueniverse*, September 15, 2010. http://hueniverse.com/2010/09/oauth-2-0-without-signatures-is-bad-for-the-web/.

Hammar-Lahav, Eran. "WRAP, and the Demise of the OAuth Community." *Hueniverse*, November 23, 2009. http://hueniverse.com/2009/11/wrap-and-the-demise-of-the-oauth-community/.

Hammond, Kris. "Just to Clarify: Why We Like Stories: The Power Of Narratives over Numbers." *Just to Clarify*, June 21, 2012. http://khammond.blogspot.com/2012/06/why-we-like-stories-power-of-narratives.html.

Hayles, N. Katherine. *Electronic Literature: New Horizons for the Literary*. University of Notre Dame Press, 2008.

Hayles, N. Katherine. *How We Think: Digital Media and Contemporary Technogenesis*. University of Chicago Press, 2012.

Haynes, Cynthia. "Afterword: <meta> Casuistic Code." In *From A to <A> : Keywords of Markup*, edited by Bradley Dilger and Jeff Rice, 228–34. University of Minnesota Press, 2010.

Howley, Brendan. "Yes She Did." *Marketing Magazine*, April 8, 2009. http://www.marketingmag.ca/news/marketer-news/yes-she-did-8005.

Hughes, Chris. "Introducing Points." *Chris Hughes' Blog*, August 27, 2007. https://my.barackobama.com/page/community/post/chrishughesatthecampaign/CJ7C.

Hussein, Renata. "Obama for America." *Obama for America*, January 24, 2008. http://www.barackobama.com/headers-footers/tools-header/.

Hyde, Michael J. "Rhetorically, We Dwell." In *The Ethos of Rhetoric*, edited by Michael J. Hyde, 197–218. University of South Carolina Press, 2004.

Information Sciences Institute, University of Southern California. "RFC 761—DoD Standard Transmission Control Protocol." January 1980. http://tools.ietf.org/html/rfc761.

Ingram, Mathew. "Twitter CFO Says a Facebook-Style Filtered Feed Is Coming, Whether You like It or Not." September 4, 2014. http://gigaom.com/2014/09/04/twitter-cfo-says-a-facebook-style-filtered-feed-is-coming-whether-you-like-it-or-not/.

James, Michael. "Obama Proposes 'Team of Rivals' Cabinet." *ABC News Blogs*. March 22, 2008. Accessed March 17, 2014. http://abcnews.go.com/blogs/politics/2008/05/obama-proposes/.

Keen, Andrew. "Laughter and Forgetting on Wikipedia." *The Great Seduction.* March 7, 2007. N.d. Accessed July 19, 2011. http://www.zdnet.com/blog/keen/laughter-and-forgetting-on-wikipedia/108.

Kessler, Sarah. "NYC Mayor Bloomberg Vows to Learn Code in 2012." *Mashable,* January 5, 2012. http://mashable.com/2012/01/05/bloomberg-codecademy/.

King, Ian. "A Wiki Web They've Woven." March 2, 2007 http://liveweb.archive.org/http://vancouver.24hrs.ca/Columnists/KingsCorner/.

Kirkpatrick, Marshall. "How the OAuth Security Battle Was Won, Open Web Style." *Read Write Web,* April 25, 2009. http://www.readwriteweb.com/archives/how_the_oauth_security_battle_was_won_open_web_sty.php.

Kirschenbaum, Matthew G. *Mechanisms: New Media and the Forensic Imagination.* MIT Press, 2012.

Kitchin, Rob, and Martin Dodge. *Code/Space: Software and Everyday Life.* MIT Press, 2014.

Koo, Gene. "My.BarackObama.com—2008 Game of the Year." *Anderkoo,* November 16, 2008. http://blogs.law.harvard.edu/anderkoo/2008/11/mybarackobamacom-2008-game-of-the-year/.

Lanham, Richard A. *The Economics of Attention: Style and Substance in the Age of Information.* University of Chicago Press, 2006.

Lanham, Richard A. *The Electronic Word: Democracy, Technology, and the Arts.* University of Chicago Press, 1995.

Lessig, Lawrence. "Keen's 'The Cult of the Amateur': BRILLIANT." *Lessig.org,* May 31, 2007. http://www.lessig.org/2007/05/keens-the-cult-of-the-amateur/.

Levinas, Emmanuel. *Emmanuel Levinas: Basic Philosophical Writings.* Edited by Adriaan T. Peperzak, Simon Critchley, and Robert Bernasconi. Indiana University Press, 2008.

Levinas, Emmanuel. "Substitution." In *Emmanuel Levinas: Basic Philosophical Writings,* edited by Adriaan T. Peperzak, Simon Critchley, and Robert Bernasconi, 79–96. Indiana University Press, 2008.

Levy, Steven. "Can an Algorithm Write a Better News Story Than a Human Reporter?" *WIRED,* April 24, 2012. http://www.wired.com/gadgetlab/2012/04/can-an-algorithm-write-a-better-news-story-than-a-human-reporter/all/1.

Lewis, Michael. *Moneyball: The Art of Winning an Unfair Game.* W. W. Norton, 2004.

Lih, Andrew. "Essjay's Third Transgression | Andrew Lih." March 3, 2007. Accessed March 28, 2014. http://www.andrewlih.com/blog/2007/03/03/essjays-third-transgression/.

Liu, Alan. *The Laws of Cool: Knowledge Work and the Culture of Information.* University of Chicago Press, 2004.

Loganbill, Scott. "OAuth Security Exploit Tests Limits of Open Web Standards." *Webmonkey,* April 24, 2009. http://www.webmonkey.com/2009/04/oauth_security_exploit_tests_limits_of_open_web_standards/.

Losh, Elizabeth. *Virtualpolitik: An Electronic History of Government Media-Making in a Time of War, Scandal, Disaster, Miscommunication, and Mistakes.* MIT Press, 2009.

Madison, Lucy. "Fact-Checking Romney's '47 Percent' Comment." *CBS News,* September 25, 2012. http://www.cbsnews.com/8301-503544_162-57515033-503544/fact-checking-romneys-47-percent-comment/.

Manovich, Lev. "Interview with Lev Manovich. " Interview by Inna Razumova, April 8, 2003. http://switch.sjsu.edu/web/v5n3/J-1.html.

Manovich, Lev. *The Language of New Media.* MIT Press, 2002.

Manovich, Lev. *Software Takes Command.* Continuum Publishing, 2013.

McGonigal, Jane. *We Don't Need No Stinkin' Badges: How to Re-Invent Reality without Gamification*. Game Developers Conference 2011. San Francisco, CA, 2011. http://www.gdcvault.com/play/1014576/We-Don-t-Need-No.

Mckenna, Brian. "Revisions." September 22, 2010. http://stackoverflow.com/posts/3762899/revisions.

Miller, Carolyn R. "Expertise and Agency: Transformations of Ethos in Human-Computer Interaction." In *The Ethos of Rhetoric*, edited by Michael J. Hyde and Calvin O. Schrag, 197–218. University of South Carolina Press, 2004.

Misza13. "User:Misza13/Nobody Cares about Your Credentials." March 22, 2007. http://en.wikipedia.org/wiki/User:Misza13/Nobody_cares_about_your_credentials.

Montfort, Nick, Patsy Baudoin, John Bell, Ian Bogost, Jeremy Douglass, Mark C. Marino, Michael Mateas, Casey Reas, Mark Sample, and Noah Vawter. 10 PRINT CHR$(205.5+RND(1)); : GOTO 10. MIT Press, 2012.

Murray, Janet H. *Hamlet on the Holodeck: The Future of Narrative in Cyberspace*. MIT Press, 1998.

Narrative Science. "Forbes Earnings Preview: New York Times Company—Forbes." *Forbes*. Accessed July 3, 2012. http://www.forbes.com/sites/narrativescience/2012/04/17/forbes-earnings-preview-new-york-times-company-3/.

Newman, Jared. "Microsoft Changes Its Mind on Xbox One's Used Games and Always-Online Policies." *Time*, June 19, 2013. http://techland.time.com/2013/06/19/microsoft-changes-its-mind-on-xbox-ones-used-games-and-always-online-policies/.

Nowviskie, Bethany. "Speculative Computing: Instruments for Interpretive Scholarship." PhD diss., University of Virginia, 2004. http://www2.iath.virginia.edu/bpn2f/diss/dissertation.pdf.

O'Keefe, Ed. "Obama's Evolving Position on Talking to Iran." *ABC News Blogs*, June 4, 2008. http://abcnews.go.com/blogs/politics/2008/06/obamas-evolving/.

"Organizing for America–Speakout." *Organizing for America*. N.d. Accessed July 6, 2010. http://my.barackobama.com/page/speakout.

Orlowski, Andrew. "There's No Wikipedia Entry for 'Moral Responsibility.'" *Register*, December 12, 2005. http://www.theregister.co.uk/2005/12/12/wikipedia_no_responsibility/.

Osborn, Andrew. "Suicide Bomber Killed 'Early' by Text Message." *Times* (London), January 27, 2011, National edition.

"Play Index Glossary." *Baseball-Reference.com*. Accessed February 25, 2014. http://www.baseball-reference.com/about/pi_glossary.shtml.

Poe, Marshall. "The Hive." *Atlantic*, September 2006. http://www.theatlantic.com/magazine/archive/2006/09/the-hive/5118/.

Pompeo, Joe. "Will Sulzberger Be the Next Times Company C.E.O.? He Doesn't Quite Say 'No.'" *Capital New York*. April 19, 2012. Accessed July 3, 2012. http://www.capitalnewyork.com/article/media/2012/04/5735533/will-sulzberger-be-next-times-company-ceo-he-doesnt-quite-say-no.

Porter, James. *Rhetorical Ethics and Internetworked Writing*. Praeger, 1998.

"President Bush Holds a News Conference." *Washington Post*, February 14, 2007, sec. Politics. http://www.washingtonpost.com/wp-dyn/content/article/2007/02/14/AR2007021400775.html.

"PSA: If You Get the 'Looks Like You're Either a Brand New User or Your Posts Have Not Been Doing Well Recently. You May Have to Wait a Bit to Post Again.' Message, Solution Inside. • /r/help." *Reddit*, December 6, 2012. Accessed September 16, 2014. http://www.reddit.com/r/help/comments/14erjc/psa_if_you_get_the_looks_like_youre_either_a/.

Purdy, Kevin. "Mouse-Over Exploit Hits Twitter.com." *Lifehacker*, September 21, 2010. http://lifehacker.com/5643778/mouse+over-exploit-hits-twittercom-stick-to-third+party-clients-for-now.

Quintilian. *Institutio Oratoria, Books I–III*. Translated by H. E. Butler. Accessed September 27, 2014. http://archive.org/stream/institutiooratorooquin/institutiooratorooquin_djvu.txt.

Ramsay, Stephen. *Reading Machines: Toward an Algorithmic Criticism*. University of Illinois Press, 2011.

Reagle, Joseph. "TIMELINESWikipedia." *Interactions* 16, no. 3 (May 2009): 42. doi:10.1145/1516016.1516026.

Recordon, David, Dick Hardt, and Eran Hammar-Lahav. "The OAuth 2.0 Authorization Protocol." July 8, 2011. http://tools.ietf.org/html/draft-ietf-oauth-v2–18.

Rice, Jeff. *Digital Detroit: Rhetoric and Space in the Age of the Network*. Southern Illinois University Press, 2012.

Richards, Ivor Armstrong. *The Philosophy of Rhetoric*. Oxford University Press, 1936.

Rieder, David. "Snowballs and Other Numerate Acts of Textuality." *Computers and Composition Online*, n.d., 2010. Accessed September 19, 2013.

Ronell, Avital. *The Telephone Book: Technology, Schizophrenia, Electric Speech*. University of Nebraska Press, 1989.

Rubin, Adam. "Pirates Pound Mike Pelfrey to Sweep 'Embarrassed' Mets." *New York Daily News*, June 4, 2009. http://www.nydailynews.com/sports/baseball/mets/pirates-pound-mike-pelfrey-sweep-embarrassed-mets-article-1.372731.

Saint-Andre, Peter. "Tools-L Structure and Simplicity." April 10, 2000. Accessed February 24, 2014. http://web.archive.org/web/20030520143850/www.nupedia.com/pipermail/tools-l/2000-April/000023.html.

samzenpus. "Spam Text Prematurely Blows Up Suicide Bomber—Slashdot." January 28, 2011. Accessed March 17, 2014. http://beta.slashdot.org/story/146936.

Sanger, Larry. "The Early History of Nupedia and Wikipedia: A Memoir." In *Open Sources 2.0: The Continuing Evolution*, edited by Chris DiBona, Danese Cooper, and Mark Stone. O'Reilly, 2006.

Sanger, Larry. "Epistemic Circularity: An Essay on the Problem of Meta-Justification." PhD diss., Ohio State University, 2000. http://enlightenment.supersaturated.com/essays/text/larrysanger/diss/preamble.html.

Sanger, Larry. "Jimmy Wales' Latest Response on the Essjay Situation." *Citizendium Blog*, March 3, 2007. http://blog.citizendium.org/?p=135.

Sanger, Larry. "The New Politics of Knowledge." N.d. Accessed February 24, 2014. http://www.larrysanger.org/newpoliticsofknowledge.html.

Sanger, Larry. "[Nupedia-L] Wikipedia Is Up!," January 17, 2001. http://web.archive.org/web/20010506042824/www.nupedia.com/pipermail/nupedia-l/2001-January/000684.html.

Sanger, Larry. "Why Wikipedia Must Jettison Its Anti-Elitism." *Kuro5hin*, December 31, 2004. http://www.kuro5hin.org/story/2004/12/30/142458/25.

Sanger, Larry. "Wikipedia Firmly Supports Your Right to Identity Fraud." *Citizendium Blog*, March 1, 2007. http://blog.citizendium.org/?p=133.

Schiff, Stacy. "Know It All." *New Yorker*, July 31, 2006. http://www.newyorker.com/archive/2006/07/31/060731fa_fact.

Schmitt, Carl. *The Concept of the Political: Expanded Edition*. University of Chicago Press, 2008.

Schrag, Calvin O. *The Ethos of Rhetoric*. Edited by Michael J. Hyde. University of South Carolina Press, 2004.

Schroeder, Stan. "17-Year-Old Australian Boy, Japanese Developer Take Blame for Twitter Meltdown." *Mashable*, September 22, 2010. http://mashable.com/2010/09/22/twitter-meltdown-17-year-old/.

Selnow, Gary W. *Electronic Whistle-Stops: The Impact of the Internet on American Politics.* Praeger Publishers, 1998.

Seltzer, Larry. "Cross-Site Scripting Attack Hits Twitter." *PCMag Security Watch*, September 21, 2010. http://blogs.pcmag.com/securitywatch/2010/09/cross-site_scripting_attack_hi.php.

"Sex." *Wikipedia, the Free Encyclopedia.* Accessed September 28, 2014. http://en.wikipedia.org/w/index.php?title=Sex&oldid=163778039.

Shpigel, Ben. "Game Is Lost; Reyes and Putz Could Be Next." *New York Times*, June 4, 2009, sec. Sports/Baseball. http://www.nytimes.com/2009/06/05/sports/baseball/05mets.html.

"Sneakernet." *Wikipedia, the Free Encyclopedia*, July 22, 2014. http://en.wikipedia.org/w/index.php?title=Sneakernet&oldid=617601318.

"Special: Request Account." *Citizendium.* N.d. Accessed February 24, 2014. http://en.citizendium.org/wiki/Special:RequestAccount.

Spinuzzi, Clay. "This Spam Problem Is Really Getting out of Hand. http://goo.gl/Dic3n." Microblog. @spinuzzi, Fri, 28 Jan 2011. 16:16:00 GMT. https://twitter.com/spinuzzi/status/31022730555949057.

"Stateless Protocol." *Wikipedia, the Free Encyclopedia*, May 10, 2014. http://en.wikipedia.org/w/index.php?title=Stateless_protocol&oldid=602733620.

"Stats Monkey." Accessed March 28, 2014. http://jermaine.cs.northwestern.edu/baseball/.

Steadman, Ian. "XBox One's Always-on Camera Shows the Subtle Ways We Accept Being Watched." *New Statesman*, November 20, 2013. http://www.newstatesman.com/future-proof/2013/11/xbox-ones-always-camera-shows-subtle-ways-we-accept-being-watched.

Stromer-Galley, Jennifer, and Kirsten A. Foot. "Citizen Perceptions of Online Interactivity and Implications for Political Campaign Communication." *Journal of Computer-Mediated Communication* 8, no. 1 (2002).

Struever, Nancy S. *Rhetoric, Modality, Modernity.* University of Chicago Press, 2009.

Swain, Chris. *The Redistricting Game.* USC Game Innovation Lab, 2007. http://redistrictinggame.org/.

Tate, Ryan. "How Twitter Hatched a Virus That Reached the White House." *Gawker*, September 21, 2010. http://gawker.com/5644077/how-twitter-hatched-a-virus-that-reached-the-white-house.

"Telcos Start Using Spam Filters to Block SMS Scams." *Australian*, July 2, 2013. Accessed September 17, 2014. http://www.theaustralian.com.au/technology/telcos-start-using-spam-filters-to-block-sms-scams/story-fn4iyzsr-1226672759422.

"Today's XSS Onmouseover Exploit on Twitter.com." N.d. Accessed February 19, 2014. http://stackoverflow.com/questions/3762746/todays-xss-onmouseover-exploit-on-twitter-com/3762899#3762899.

Trimbur, John. "Composition and the Circulation of Writing." *College Composition and Communication* 52, no. 2 (December 2000): 188–219.

"United For Change Host Guide." *My.barackobama.com.* N.d. Accessed February 18, 2014. https://my.barackobama.com/page/content/uniteguide/.

"User: Essjay/RFC," March 4, 2007. http://en.wikipedia.org/w/index.php?title=User: Essjay/RFC&oldid=466593807.

"User talk:Essjay," February 2, 2007. http://en.wikipedia.org/w/index.php?title= User_talk:Essjay&oldid=105049125#Profiles_don.27t_mesh...

Vanhemert, Kyle. "How Egypt Turned Off the Internet." *Gizmodo*, January 28, 2011. Accessed February 18, 2014. http://gizmodo.com/5746121/ how-egypt-turned-off-the-internet.

Varela, Francisco. *Ethical Know-How: Action, Wisdom, and Cognition*. Stanford University Press, 1999.

Vee, Annette. "Proceduracy: Computer Code Writing in the Continuum of Literacy." University of Wisconsin at Madison, 2010.

Vee, Annette. "Text, Speech, Machine: Metaphors for Computer Code in the Law." *Computational Culture* 2 (September 2012). http://computationalculture.net/article/ text-speech-machine-metaphors-for-computer-code-in-the-law.

Vibber, Brion. "[Mediawiki-L] How to Allow All-Lower-Case Usernames." September 26, 2005. http://lists.wikimedia.org/pipermail/mediawiki-l/2005-September/007241.html.

Wales, Jimbo. "User: Jimbo Wales/Credential Verification." June 21, 2010. http:// en.wikipedia.org/wiki/User:Jimbo_Wales/Credential_Verification.

Wales, Jimmy. "Tools-L Tools Used?" June 8, 2000. http://web.archive.org/web/ 20030520143259/www.nupedia.com/pipermail/tools-l/2000-June/000059.html.

Wardrip-Fruin, Noah. *Expressive Processing: Digital Fictions, Computer Games, and Software Studies*. MIT Press, 2009.

Warren, Christina. "New Facebook Clickjacking Attack Uses Justin Bieber as Bait [WARNING]." *Mashable*, June 2, 2010. http://mashable.com/2010/06/02/ facebook-clickjack-justin-bieber/.

"Wikipedia:Changing Username." Accessed February 24, 2014. http://en.wikipedia. org/wiki/Wikipedia:Changing_username.

Wikipedia Contributors. "Win Probability Added." *Wikipedia, the Free Encyclopedia*. Wikimedia Foundation, July 5, 2012. http://en.wikipedia.org/w/index. php?title=Win_probability_added&oldid=480726751.

"Wikipedia: Requests for Comment/Essjay/Straw Poll," March 2, 2007. Accessed February 24, 2014. http://en.wikipedia.org/wiki/Wikipedia:Requests_for_comment/ Essjay/Straw_Poll#No.

"Wikipedia:Username Policy." Accessed February 24, 2014. http://en.wikipedia.org/ wiki/Wikipedia:Username_policy.

Williams, Martyn. "Wikipedia Founder Addresses User Credentials." *PC World*, January 15, 2008. http://www.pcworld.com/article/id,129702-c,webservices/article.html.

Wing, Jeannette M. "Computational Thinking." *Communications of the ACM* 49, no. 3 (2006): 33–35.

Wing, Jeannette M. "Computational Thinking and Thinking about Computing." *Philosophical Transactions. Series A, Mathematical, Physical, and Engineering Sciences* 366, no. 1881 (October 28, 2008): 3717–25. doi:10.1098/rsta.2008.0118.

Index